THE FAITHFULNESS
OF THE RISEN CHRIST

THE FAITHFULNESS
OF THE RISEN CHRIST
Pistis and the Exalted Lord
in the Pauline Letters

DAVID J. DOWNS
BENJAMIN J. LAPPENGA

BAYLOR UNIVERSITY PRESS

© 2019 by Baylor University Press
Waco, Texas 76798

All Rights Reserved. No part of this publication may be reproduced, stored in a retrieval system, or transmitted, in any form or by any means, electronic, mechanical, photocopying, recording, or otherwise, without the prior permission in writing of Baylor University Press.

Cover Design by Savanah N. Landerholm
Cover Image by Cumhur Tanrıver. Photograph of TP100.3, a graffito on the basilica in the Agora of Smyrna. Izmir, Turkey.
Book Design by Baylor University Press
Typesetting by Scribe Inc.

The Library of Congress has cataloged this book under
ISBN 978-1-4813-1090-1.

Printed in the United States of America on acid-free paper with a minimum of thirty percent recycled content.

CONTENTS

ACKNOWLEDGMENTS

We have many people to thank for their help in writing this book. Numerous friends and colleagues graciously shared their own materials with us, read portions of our manuscript, or offered sage advice about (and sometimes sharp criticism of) our ideas, including Matthew Bates, Max Botner, Roy Ciampa, David Creech, Rich Erickson, Paul Foster, John Frederick, Beverly Roberts Gaventa, Tommy Givens, Joel Green, Joshua Jipp, David Moffitt, Love Sechrest, Marianne Meye Thompson, Carl Toney, David Westfall, and Steve Young. We are also thankful to Larry McCutcheon for his help in preparing the bibliography and indexes and Raddhitya Badudu for his research assistance. Generous support for writing portions of chapter 7 and the conclusion was offered through a research fellowship at Biola University's Center for Christian Thought, an ideal location for scholarly exchange. Finally, we are grateful to Carey Newman and his outstanding team at Baylor University Press for believing in this project and for their faithful care in producing the volume.

INTRODUCTION
"He Remains Faithful"

There is a slightly humorous scene in book 2 of Milton's *Paradise Lost* that describes various actions undertaken by fallen angels following their expulsion from heaven. After breaking into groups in order to pursue a range of interests, some exiled angels engage in sporting activities, others ready themselves with war exercises, and still others sing of their heroic deeds. A fourth group of would-be theologians "Apart sat on a hill retired, / In thoughts more elevate, and reasoned high / Of providence, foreknowledge, will and fate, / Fixed fate, free will, foreknowledge absolute, / And found no end, in wandering mazes lost" (2.558–561). Had Milton lived in the twenty-first century, he may well have added to this list of seemingly intractable theological topics an additional line: "They argued about πίστις Χριστοῦ in Paul's letters, and yet from that labyrinth never did emerge."

Or perhaps the image of angels practicing for battle provides a more fitting metaphor for the πίστις Χριστοῦ debate. The primary camps are well known. On the one side, proponents of the objective genitive emphasize that for Paul human faith is placed *in Christ*, with Christ as the object of such faith. On the other side, advocates of the subjective genitive contend that the πίστις Χριστοῦ construction refers to the faithfulness *of Christ* himself, with Christ's faithfulness chiefly demonstrated in his willingness to suffer and die for the sake of humanity. Others, sometimes called representatives of a "third view," have argued that the genitive Χριστοῦ is in some sense adjectival or

1

qualitative, denoting a faith that is "Christic."[1] The main lines of interpretation have been drawn and the key Pauline texts have already been dissected (i.e., Gal 2:16, 20; 3:22, 26; Rom 3:22, 26; Phil 3:9; cf. Eph 3:12; 2 Tim 3:15).[2] Yet no clear resolution appears in sight, even while the vigor and persistence with which contemporary interpreters have engaged the conversation testify to the importance of the issue for Pauline soteriology.[3]

It may appear unlikely that any novel perspective has the potential to reshape the current impasse. This book, however, attempts to advance a thesis that has been absent in the recent conversation. If there is one point upon which almost all participants in the debate agree, it is that if Paul did employ the construction πίστις Χριστοῦ to refer to an action or attribute of Jesus Christ himself, then Christ's πίστις is demonstrated in his suffering and death on the cross. Among proponents of the subjective genitive, the connection between Jesus' πίστις and the crucifixion is so axiomatic that it is rarely defended, and alternative possibilities are almost never considered. A statement on the matter from Richard Hays, whose monograph *The Faith of Jesus*

[1] So Otto Schmitz, *Die Christus-Gemeinschaft des Paulus im Lichte seines Genetivigebrauchs*, NTF 1/2 (Gütersloh: Bertelsmann, 1924); Arland Hultgren, "The *Pistis Christou* Formulation in Paul," *NovT* 22 (1980): 248–63. Recently, Preston M. Sprinkle has catalogued and argued for a "third view" that understands the phrase as an integrated descriptor of an objective reality outside an individual's response to God; see his article "Πίστις Χριστοῦ as an Eschatological Event," in *The Faith of Jesus Christ: Exegetical, Biblical, and Theological Studies*, ed. Michael F. Bird and Preston M. Sprinkle (Carlisle, U.K.: Paternoster; Peabody, Mass.: Hendrickson, 2009), 164–84; cf. Benjamin Schliesser, "'Christ-Faith' as an Eschatological Event (Galatians 3.23-26): A 'Third View' on Πίστις Χριστοῦ," *JSNT* 38 (2016): 1–24; Shuji Ota, "The Holistic *Pistis* and Abraham's Faith (Galatians 3)," *HJAS* 57 (2016): 1–12.

[2] The construction appears in slightly different forms in the undisputed Pauline epistles: ἐκ πίστεως Ἰησοῦ Χριστοῦ (Gal 3:22); διὰ πίστεως Ἰησοῦ Χριστοῦ (Gal 2:16; Rom 3:22); διὰ τῆς πίστεως ἐν Χριστῷ Ἰησοῦ (Gal 3:26 in P⁴⁶); ἐκ πίστεως Ἰησοῦ (Rom 3:26); ἐκ πίστεως Χριστοῦ (Gal 2:16); διὰ πίστεως Χριστοῦ (Phil 3:9); cf. διὰ τῆς πίστεως αὐτοῦ in Eph 3:12.

[3] See, for example, R. Michael Allen, *The Christ's Faith: A Dogmatic Account*, T&T Clark Studies in Systematic Theology (Edinburgh: T&T Clark, 2009); David L. Stubbs, "The Shape of Soteriology and the *Pistis Christou* Debate," *SJT* 61 (2008): 137–57; Douglas Harink, *Paul among the Postliberals: Pauline Theology beyond Christendom and Modernity* (Grand Rapids: Brazos, 2003), 25–65.

Christ is rightly credited with reinvigorating the case for the subjective genitive, is illustrative: "It should be said clearly that for Paul, πίστις Χριστοῦ refers to Jesus' obedience to death on the cross: in other words, the meaning of the phrase is focused on the kerygma's narration of his self-giving death, not on the whole ministry of Jesus of Nazareth. This narrower punctiliar sense—focused on the cross—is the only meaning supported by Paul's usage."[4] Hays' assertion helpfully captures the fact that, for almost all recent advocates of the view that the phrase πίστις Χριστοῦ in Paul's letters expresses something about Jesus' own πίστις, this πίστις—whether translated "faith," "faithfulness," "fidelity," or "trust"—is understood to be demonstrated principally, if not exclusively, in the passion of Jesus.

The central claim of this book, however, is that when Paul writes of Christ's πίστις he is referring also to the faithfulness of the risen and exalted Christ. It is not that the death of Jesus is unimportant for Paul or that the crucifixion is unrelated to Paul's understanding of Christ's πίστις. But limiting Christ's πίστις to the faithful death of the human Jesus upon the cross fails to capture the significance for Paul's theology of the resurrection of the living Christ and ignores the emphasis in the Pauline epistles on the exalted Christ's continuing faithfulness to those united to him by πίστις. Indeed, to the extent that the phrase πίστις Χριστοῦ functions as a *"concentric* expression"—one closely linked to Paul's participationist soteriology—that denotes both the πίστις of Christ and the πίστις of believers, such an expression cannot merely describe the πίστις of the human Jesus, for believers share in and benefit from the πίστις of the risen and exalted Christ.[5] Our argument, in short, is that the Pauline expression πίστις Χριστοῦ and related variants refer primarily to the faithfulness of the risen Christ Jesus who will remain faithful to those who, in their own faith, are justified through union with Christ, raised and exalted.[6]

[4] Richard B. Hays, *The Faith of Jesus Christ: The Narrative Substructure of Galatians 3:1–4:11*, 2nd ed. (Grand Rapids: Eerdmans, 2002), 297n58.

[5] The phrase "concentric expression" is taken from the classic essay by Morna Hooker, "ΠΙΣΤΙΣ ΧΡΙΣΤΟΥ," *NTS* 35 (1989): 321–42.

[6] In this study, we generally distinguish Christ's resurrection from his heavenly exaltation and enthronement because we believe this distinction is represented in the Pauline letters (Rom 8:34; Eph 1:20; 2:6; Phil 2:9-11; Col 3:1; cf. Acts 2:32-33; 1 Pet

THE FAITHFULNESS OF THE RISEN AND
EXALTED CHRIST IN 2 TIMOTHY 2:8-13

A passage from 2 Timothy offers a clear summary of how we see the phrase πίστις Χριστοῦ functioning in the undisputed Pauline letters. Therefore, this text, though neglected in recent discussions of πίστις Χριστοῦ because it comes from an epistle whose authorship is disputed, introduces a helpful alternative framework through which we will analyze the πίστις Χριστοῦ construction and related motifs in Romans, 1–2 Corinthians, Galatians, Philippians, and Ephesians. We begin with a consideration of the faithfulness of Christ in 2 Timothy not because we assume, or aim to make a case for, the authenticity of this letter. Instead, we start with 2 Timothy because sometimes considering neglected evidence can produce a fresh approach to an old problem.[7]

In 2 Tim 2:8-13, Paul challenges Timothy, his beloved child in Christ, by offering a theological rationale for the apostle's own endurance in the face of hardship, including his present imprisonment.[8] Paul's warrant is rooted in the exemplary narrative of Jesus Christ's own faithfulness:

> Remember Jesus Christ, raised from the dead, from the seed of David—that is my gospel, in which sphere I am suffering hardship even to the point of being chained like a criminal. But the word of

---

3:18-22); see the discussion in M. Jeff Brannon, *The Heavenlies in Ephesians: A Lexical, Exegetical, and Conceptual Anaysis*, LNTS 447 (Edinburgh: T&T Clark, 2011), 120–22; cf. Alan F. Segal, "Heavenly Ascent in Hellenistic Judaism, Early Christianity, and Their Environment," *ANRW* 23.2:1333–94. Also, we do not conflate ascension and exaltation/enthronement. While it may be true that Christ's heavenly session assumes his ascension into heaven, Paul nowhere narrates an account of Christ's ascension (but cf. 1 Tim 3:16; Eph 4:8-10).

[7] In point of fact, the process of writing an essay on the faithfulness of Jesus Christ in 2 Timothy did generate the idea to reconsider the πίστις Χριστοῦ construction in the undisputed Pauline epistles; see David J. Downs, "Faith(fulness) in Christ Jesus in 2 Timothy 3:15," *JBL* 131 (2012): 143–60. Material in this section on 2 Tim 2:8-13 (and a few lines from the opening of this chapter) draws upon that earlier essay.

[8] For reasons that will become clear, we identify the author of 2 Timothy as Paul because Paul is presented as the author of the letter, whether or not he is the real author.

God is not chained. Therefore, I endure everything for the sake of elect, so that they too might obtain the salvation that is in Christ Jesus, with eternal glory. The word is faithful! For if we have died together, then we will also live together. If we endure, we will also reign together. If we deny him, he will deny us. If we are faithless, he remains faithful—for he cannot deny himself.[9]

Two aspects of Paul's exhortation to Timothy in this section prove fundamental for the analysis of the theme of Christ's πίστις in the ensuing chapters of this book. First, Paul's appeal in 2:8-13 is grounded in his concept of participation in Christ. Paul's own status as a prisoner for Christ involves a kind of *imitatio Christi*, a mimesis that also stands as a challenge to Timothy, especially as Timothy appears to be tempted to be shamed by Paul's gospel (1:6-10).[10] Paul suffers so that the elect "may also obtain the salvation that is in Christ Jesus, with eternal glory (2:10)." In this context the poetic material in 2:11-13 spells out the nature of the salvation that is "in Christ" by strongly emphasizing the partnership that believers share in the death, resurrection, and heavenly rule of Jesus: "if we have died together, then we will also live together; if we endure, we will also reign together" (2:11-12). This short statement articulates a concept of participatory salvation that highlights the sharing of believers in the narrative of Christ's death, resurrection, and heavenly exaltation.[11] Endurance in the present—an implicit challenge to Timothy as he wavers in his commitment to the

---

[9] Unless otherwise noted, all translations in this book are our own. It is possible, as many commentators have suggested, that 2 Tim 2:11b-13 represents a pre-Pauline fragment adapted to the present context (see the discussion in Hanna Stettler, *Die Christologie der Pastoralbriefe*, WUNT 2/182 [Tübingen: Mohr Siebeck, 1998], 181–95). A reasonable claim can be made, however, that these verses do not reflect the citation of pre-Pauline material (so William D. Mounce, *Pastoral Epistles*, WBC 46 [Nashville: Thomas Nelson, 2000], 501). Either way, the issue is not particularly pertinent to the present argument, since whatever the origin of the affirmations in 2:11b-13, this material is seamlessly incorporated into the present context.

[10] Luke Timothy Johnson, *The First and Second Letters to Timothy: A New Translation with Introduction and Commentary*, AB 35A (New York: Doubleday, 2001), 375.

[11] A parallel from the undisputed Pauline letters is found in Rom 6:1-11, especially 2:8: "If we have died with Christ, we have faith that we will also live with him" (εἰ δὲ ἀπεθάνομεν σὺν Χριστῷ, πιστεύομεν ὅτι καὶ συζήσομεν αὐτῷ). On the narrative dynamics of Paul's participationist soteriology, see Constantine R. Campbell, *Paul*

gospel (1:6-8)—will result in reigning with Christ in the future (2:12a), but denial of Christ will result in his denial of "us" (cf. Matt 10:33; Luke 12:9). Yet, in spite of any human faithlessness, Christ remains πιστός, for he cannot deny himself (2 Tim 2:13). Thus, salvation (σωτηρία) is something that believers experience through their participation in Christ and through Christ's faithfulness to them.

This leads to a second noteworthy theme in 2:8-13, namely, Paul's rather pronounced stress on the faithfulness of Christ. Although there is no sense in which the phrase πιστὸς ὁ λόγος in 2:11a should be interpreted christologically, the poetic section is bracketed with references to "faithful" (πιστός) things in 2:11 and 13.[12] In 2:13, however, the motif of faithfulness is explicitly christological, as the adjective πιστός is used of Christ, in contrast to the potential faithlessness of human beings: "If we are faithless, he remains faithful—for he cannot deny himself." According to 2:11-13, then, the risen and exalted Christ is faithful even when human beings are not.

The affirmation of Christ's faithfulness in 2 Timothy has played too little a role in discussions about the πίστις Χριστοῦ construction in the Pauline corpus, largely because 2 Timothy itself is marginalized in Pauline scholarship. In a fitting commentary on this state of affairs, James Dunn has stated in a letter to Richard Hays in the latter's Festschrift, "What I don't find is that Paul made a point of stressing Jesus' 'faithfulness' as such, apart from the disputed πίστις Χριστοῦ phrases. Were it as important as you imply, I would have expected to see the theme signaled in discussions where it could be referred to simply as 'his πίστις,' or in contrast with human (or Israel's) ἀπιστία."[13] Yet

---

and Union with Christ: An Exegetical and Theological Study (Grand Rapids: Zondervan, 2015), esp. 349–52.

[12] The appearance of the construction πιστὸς ὁ λόγος in 1 Tim 1:15; 3:1; 4:9; and Titus 3:8 is one of the many interesting points of contact between 2 Timothy, 1 Timothy, and Titus; see Stettler, Die Christologie der Pastoralbriefe, 181–83.

[13] James D. G. Dunn, "ΕΚ ΠΙΣΤΕΩΣ: A Key to the Meaning of ΠΙΣΤΙΣ ΧΡΙΣΤΟΥ," in The Word Leaps the Gap: Essays on Scripture and Theology in Honor of Richard B. Hays, ed. J. Ross Wagner, A. Katherine Grieb, and C. Kavin Rowe (Grand Rapids: Eerdmans, 2008), 351–66 (355). Similarly, in responding to claims that Phil 3:9 refers to the faithfulness of Christ, Richard Bell writes, "It is difficult to find other texts in Paul which refer specifically to Christ's faithfulness" ("Faith in Christ: Some Exegetical

2 Tim 2:13 develops exactly the notion that Dunn fails to find expressed explicitly in the undisputed Pauline epistles. The connection between salvation and Christ's faithfulness in 2 Tim 2:13 articulates in clear terms the very concept that advocates of the subjective genitive claim to find embedded in the phrase πίστις Χριστοῦ in the undisputed letters: Χριστός is πιστός, and Christ's faithfulness stands in contrast (at least potentially) with human ἀπιστία.

Yet 2 Tim 2:13 also adds a significant piece to the puzzle—or, as we will argue, unpacks what is implicit in the πίστις Χριστοῦ constructions in the undisputed Pauline letters. The entire section in 2:8–13 is framed with reference to the resurrection and kingly rule of the Messiah: "Remember Jesus Christ, raised from the dead, from the seed of David" (2:8). Interestingly, Jesus' resurrection is placed *before* the reference to his lineage from David, and the perfect participle ἐγη-γερμένον highlights the fact "that he has been raised and therefore is now alive and exalted."[14] The opening charge of this section, therefore, emphasizes the importance of the resurrection for Paul's gospel in this context, while also alluding to the heavenly enthronement and rule of Israel's king. In fact, according to 2:8, the message of the resurrected Davidic Messiah is a fitting summary of Paul's gospel (cf. Rom 1:1-4).[15]

---

and Theological Reflections on Philippians 3:9 and Ephesians 3:12," in *The Faith of Jesus Christ: Exegetical, Biblical, and Theological Studies*, ed. Michael F. Bird and Preston M. Sprinkle [Carlisle, U.K.: Paternoster; Peabody, Mass.: Hendrickson: 2009], 111–25 [116]). Puzzling is Moisés Silva's statement that a subjective interpretation of the genitive Χριστοῦ in Phil 3:9 "faces the insuperable linguistic objection that Paul never speaks unambiguously of Jesus as faithful (e.g., *Iēsous pistos estin*) or believing (*episteusen Iēsous*), while he certainly speaks of individuals as believing in Christ" (*Philippians*, BECNT [Grand Rapids: Baker Academic, 2005], 161).

[14] I. Howard Marshall, *The Pastoral Epistles*, ICC (Edinburgh: T&T Clark, 1999), 734.

[15] On Rom 1:1-4, see Matthew W. Bates, *The Hermeneutics of the Apostolic Proclamation: The Center of Paul's Method of Scriptural Interpretation* (Waco, Tex: Baylor University Press, 2012), 80–99, and our discussion in chapter 6. In an illuminating chapter entitled "King and Kingdom: Sharing in the Rule of Christ the King," Joshua Jipp discusses "the royal and messianic roots of Paul's participationist soteriology" (*Christ Is King: Paul's Royal Ideology* [Minneapolis: Fortress, 2015], 141). That Jipp cites 2 Tim 2:8, 11-12a in an epigraph at the beginning of the chapter and yet nowhere discusses this important material from 2 Timothy in the body of the chapter perfectly captures the relative neglect of 2 Timothy in recent Pauline scholarship. Jipp appears to recognize

With this accent on Christ's resurrection and kingly reign at the beginning of the passage, it is worth noting that the "salvation that is in Christ" comes "with eternal glory" (2 Tim 2:10), something that belongs to God but in which believers share through their participation in Christ. Moreover, with the reference to dying and living with Christ in 2:11b as the introductory note to the material that follows, the emphasis within this poetic section is on the continuing faithfulness of the resurrected and exalted Christ in the present and in the future. The fact of Jesus' resurrection does not by any means remove those in Christ from suffering in the present world, as is testified by both Paul's chains (1:8, 12, 16) and the prospect of the apostle's imminent death (4:6-8). Indeed, as important as the stress on Jesus' resurrection is at the beginning of this section, it is immediately qualified with a reference to Christ's identity as the seed of David (2:8b).[16] It is not the perspective of Paul, but of the false teachers whom he opposes, that the resurrection of believers has already taken place (2:18). Paul's call to Timothy is a summons to embody the narrative of the cross, not to pursue power and earthly pleasure.

Yet it is the resurrection and enthronement of Jesus that provides the interpretive lens though which the suffering of Paul and other believers is understood. With the compact phrase εἰ γὰρ συναπεθά-νομεν, καὶ συζήσομεν ("for if we have died together, then we will also live together") in 2:11, Paul draws upon the narrative of believers' participation in the death and resurrection of Jesus. Moreover, believers who endure will also share in the rule of Christ: "If we endure, we will also reign together" (2:12; cf. Eph 2:6). Implicit in this affirmation of believers' co-rule with Christ is the notion of Christ's heavenly enthronement.

---

that 2 Tim 2:8-13 succinctly articulates the very connection between Jesus' kingly identity and representative role, on one hand, and believers' union with him, on the other, which Jipp believes "provides the logic for Paul's participatory discourse" (*Christ Is King*, 209); but see now Michael David Marossy, "The Rule of the Resurrected Messiah: Kingship Discourse in 2 Timothy 2:8-13," *CBQ*, forthcoming.

[16] As Luke Timothy Johnson points out, "The rapid turn to Jesus' human origins, and the immediate connection to Paul's imprisonment . . . point Timothy to the reality that the delegate's present call—as is Paul's own—is to share the human suffering of Jesus that preceded his resurrection" (*Timothy*, 380).

The "salvation that is in Christ Jesus" of which Paul will speak in 2 Tim 3:15 is only possible through the faithfulness of the risen and ascended Christ. As Paul says at the culmination of 2:8-13: "If we are faithless, he remains faithful—for he cannot deny himself" (2:13). This is a rather remarkable conclusion, one that has led many commentators to miss the continued emphasis on participatory soteriology. Yet it stands as a fitting punctuation to the notion that salvation comes through participation "in Christ." In the explanatory clause, Paul proclaims that Christ will remain πιστός in the face of human ἀπιστία because for the faithful one to do otherwise would be for him to deny himself. Paul here suggests that Christ and those "in Christ" share such a deep union that Christ's denial of his people would, in fact, be a denial of himself. Yet such a denial is inconceivable for Paul. Believers like Paul and Timothy are called and enabled to be faithful to the gospel because the risen and exalted Christ is faithful toward them. To the extent that those in Christ *have died* and *will live* and *reign* with him, the risen and exalted Christ will remain faithful to them, for his faithfulness to those who participate in his own cruciform, resurrected, and kingly existence is actually faithfulness to himself.

Thus, 2 Tim 2:8-13 should be seen as an important contribution to the theme of Christ's faithfulness in the Pauline tradition. To return to an earlier exchange between Hays and Dunn, Dunn asks the pointed question:

> What does "the faith of Christ" mean? To what does it refer? The answer is hardly clear. The ministry of Jesus as a whole? The death of Christ in particular? The continuing ministry of the exalted Christ in heaven? Neither the first nor the last of these is a prominent theme in Paul. . . . And if the reference is to the exalted Christ, then we would expect Paul to speak of Christ directly, rather than of his faith.[17]

---

[17] Dunn, "Once More, ΠΙΣΤΙΣ ΧΡΙΣΤΟΥ," in Hays, *The Faith of Jesus Christ*, 259–60. Dunn does acknowledge that "Paul has a concept of the death of Christ as in some sense an ongoing event," indicating that, while Dunn himself argues strongly that the noun Χριστοῦ in the phrase πίστις Χριστοῦ be taken as an objective genitive, the most likely reference for a subjective genitive would be to the death of Jesus.

The author of 2 Timothy answers Dunn's question with a clarity not immediately found in the compact πίστις Χριστοῦ construction in the undisputed Pauline epistles. According to 2:8-13, the faithful Christ is the risen and exalted Christ who will remain true to those "in Christ." This coheres with Paul's earlier confession, likely with reference to Christ, that he knows the one in whom he has trusted and that he is confident in the ability of that one to guard Paul's deposit until the day of eschatological judgment (1:12).[18] Again in 4:18 Paul expresses assurance in "the Lord's" ability to rescue him from present struggles and to save him "for his heavenly kingdom." Here it is perhaps helpful to speak of a narrative substructure upon which the theologizing of 2 Timothy is built. The distinctive contribution of 2:8-13, however, is, with particular clarity, to extend that narrative beyond the cross, through the resurrection, to the risen and exalted Christ "who brought life and immortality to light through the gospel" (1:10). To speak of the faithfulness of Christ in 2 Timothy, then, is primarily to speak of the fidelity of the risen and enthroned Lord, who will ensure the eschatological salvation of those who are "in Christ."[19] Yet 2 Timothy is hardly alone amidst Pauline and other early Christian literature to stress the faithfulness of the risen and ascended Christ. It is the burden of this book to demonstrate that the "continuing ministry of the exalted Christ in heaven" is indeed a prominent theme in Paul, one captured succinctly in the phrase πίστις Χριστοῦ and its variants.

---

[18] Although the antecedent of the relative pronoun ᾧ in 1:12 could be either God (2:9a) or Christ Jesus (2:9b-10), Christ is more likely given the proximity of the reference to Christ Jesus in the sentence (cf. 4:18 for the notion of ὁ κύριος as eschatological deliverer). Yet perhaps we should not draw too sharp a distinction between these two options. As Marshall writes, "Maybe we should not attempt to make a choice, since it seems often that God the Father and Christ were so closely conjoined in Christian thought that the writers themselves were not consciously referring to one rather than the other" (*Pastoral Epistles*, 710).

[19] Shuji Ota contends that references to the πίστις of Christ in the undisputed Pauline epistles allude to Christ's fidelity to human beings and not to God, a position actually quite close to that reflected in 2 Tim 2:8-13. Ota writes, "the genitive case in the πίστις Χριστοῦ formulation refers to *Christ's faithfulness to humanity*, i.e., in the sense of Christ being steadfast, truthful, and trustworthy as God's Christ" ("Absolute Use of ΠΙΣΤΙΣ and ΠΙΣΤΙΣ ΧΡΙΣΤΟΥ in Paul," *AJBI* 23 [1997]: 64–82 [80]).

THE FAITHFULNESS OF THE RISEN CHRIST
IN MODERN SCHOLARSHIP

It is not necessary to rehash the entire πίστις Χριστοῦ debate in the twentieth and early twenty-first centuries in order to assert the relative novelty of the claim that the expression πίστις Χριστοῦ in the Pauline epistles refers to the faithfulness of the risen and exalted Christ.[20] It is not an overstatement to say that all recent interpreters who favor a subjective interpretation of the genitive Χριστοῦ understand Christ's faithfulness to be demonstrated in his earthly ministry and, particularly, his death. Earlier we cited Richard Hays' unambiguous statement that "for Paul, πίστις Χριστοῦ refers to Jesus' obedience to death on the cross."[21] A representative sampling of recent influential voices confirms the standard link between Christ's faithfulness and the cross:

> **J. Louis Martyn**: "It follows that *pistis Christou* is an expression by which Paul speaks of *Christ's atoning faithfulness, as, on the cross, he died faithfully* for human beings while looking faithfully to God."[22]

> **N. T. Wright, summing up the logic of Rom 3:21-31**: "*The Messiah, the faithful Israelite, has been faithful to death, and through him the faithful justice of the covenant God is now displayed for all, Jew and gentile alike.*"[23]

---

[20] The same could be said of nineteenth-century scholarship on the matter, much of which has recently been recovered in a helpful article by Benjamin Schliesser, "'Exegetical Amnesia' and ΠΙΣΤΙΣ ΧΡΙΣΤΟΥ: The 'Faith *of* Christ' in Nineteenth-Century Pauline Scholarship," *JTS* 66 (2015): 61–89.

[21] Hays, *Faith of Jesus Christ*, 297n58. To be clear, this statement comes in an appendix printed in the second edition of Hays' book. Hays' position is consistent throughout the first edition of his revised dissertation, however. He states, for example, "[The] phrase πίστις Χριστοῦ may be understood as a reference to the faithfulness of 'the one man Jesus Christ' whose act of obedient self-giving love on the cross became the means by which 'the promise' of God was fulfilled" (161).

[22] J. Louis Martyn, *Galatians: A New Translation with Introduction and Commentary*, AB 33A (New York: Doubleday, 1997), 271, emphasis added.

[23] N. T. Wright, *Paul and the Faithfulness of God*, 2 vols. (Minneapolis: Fortress, 2013), 841, emphasis original.

Richard Longenecker: "The expression πίστις Χριστοῦ . . . has reference to the 'obedience' and/or 'faithfulness' of Jesus *in his earthly ministry and death*."[24]

Douglas A. Campbell, arguing in favor of a "christological interpretation" of Rom 1:17 and 3:22: "[The phrase πίστις Χριστοῦ] makes a plausible equation between the story of Jesus' martyrdom and the quality of fidelity; and *it is functionally equivalent to Paul's references to Christ's passion elsewhere with respect to ὑπακου- words*, some of which even arguably overlap with πιστ- words in Paul directly."[25]

Martinus de Boer: "The primary *referential meaning* of *pistis* in Galatians, therefore, is (apart from 5:22) always to the faith of Christ himself: *his faithful death on the cross*, not human faith in Christ, which is but a secondary, subordinate implication of the phrase [*pistis Christou*]."[26]

---

[24] Richard N. Longenecker, *Introducing Romans: Critical Issues in Paul's Most Famous Letter* (Grand Rapids: Eerdmans, 2011), 323–24, emphasis added. Longenecker's discussion of the phrase πίστις Χριστοῦ in his introductory monograph on Romans is instructive in that Longenecker initially observes that "Paul's 'high' christology allows him to make an easy association of (1) the titles 'Son' and 'Son of God' as rightfully applied to Jesus, Israel's Messiah and humanity's Lord, (2) his and the early church's references to Christ's 'obedience', and (3) his references to Christ's 'faithfulness'—all of which speak in a functional manner of Jesus' fulfillment of the will of God in effecting human redemption through his earthly ministry, sacrificial death, and physical resurrection" (*Introducing Romans*, 322–23). In this statement, Longenecker at least includes resurrection as one component of Christ's "faithfulness." Yet Longenecker then immediately elucidates this statement with a qualification that elides reference to the resurrection: "In effect, what seems most likely is that Paul used πίστις Χριστοῦ (and its cognate forms) to signal the extremely important historical basis for the Christian gospel—that is, to highlight the fact that the objective basis for the Christian proclamation of 'good news' in this time of the eschatological 'now' is the perfect response of obedience and faithfulness that Jesus, the Son, offered to God, the Father, *both actively in his life and passively in his death*" (323, emphasis added). Longenecker then concludes his discussion by stating his belief that "the expression πίστις Χριστοῦ . . . has reference to the 'obedience' and/or 'faithfulness' of Jesus *in his earthly ministry and death*" (*Introducing Romans*, 323–24, emphasis added).

[25] Douglas A. Campbell, *Deliverance of God: An Apocalyptic Rereading of Justification in Paul* (Grand Rapids: Eerdmans, 2009), 612, emphasis added.

[26] Martinus C. de Boer, *Galatians: A Commentary*, NTL (Louisville: Westminster John Knox, 2011), 192, emphasis added.

In spite of the consistent assumption in recent scholarship that the πίστις Χριστοῦ construction in the (undisputed) Pauline epistles refers to the faithful death of Christ, there is something of a minority report that does not limit Christ's πίστις to the passion. Already by the early part of the twentieth century, Adolf Deissmann had argued that faith for Paul "is something which is effected in the vital union with the spiritual Christ."[27] With respect to the expression πίστις Χριστοῦ in Paul's letters, Deissmann suggested that neither an objective genitive nor a subjective genitive is an appropriate classification. Instead, Deissmann proposed the category of "'mystic genitive,'" because it expresses the mystic fellowship" between the spiritual Christ and those joined to him by faith.[28] Perhaps because of Deissmann's introduction of a special category of genitive, or perhaps because of concerns about Deissmann's romantic attempt to locate Paul's theology in the context of Paul's personal experience of mystical union with Christ, his suggestion that πίστις Χριστοῦ in Paul denotes union with God through the "living and present spiritual Christ" has not been widely received.[29]

[27] Adolf Deissmann, *St. Paul: A Study in Social and Religious History*, trans. Lionel R. M. Strachan (London: Hodder and Stoughton, 1926), 140; translation of *Paulus: eine kultur- und religionsgeschichtliche Skizze: mit je einer Tafel in Lichtdruck und Autotypie sowie einer Karte: die Welt des Apostels Paulus* (Tübingen: J. C. B. Mohr, 1911).

[28] Deissmann, *St. Paul*, 140. In the German edition, Deissmann renders this construction "Christusglauben": "Der 'Glaube Christi Jesu' ist der 'Glaube in Christus' . . . Neben dem 'Christusglauben' stehen bei Paulus die 'Christusliebe,' die 'Christusoffnung,' der 'Christusfriede'" (*Paulus*, 94).

[29] Deissmann, *St. Paul*, 124; cf. the comments about Deissmann in Hays, *Faith of Jesus Christ*, 3–4, 144. An additional factor in the lack of attention to Deissmann's important early contribution to the πίστις Χριστοῦ debate is Deissmann's own hesitancy to define Paul's conception of the "spiritual Christ." Deissmann writes, "But there is no binding definition; we have the greatest possible latitude if we should wish to transplant the apostle's ideas concerning Christ into our own religious thought. To Paul the Spirit, God, the living Christ is a reality, the reality of all realities; therefore there was no need for him to puzzle over definitions. . . . Religious definitions are always attempts to save something" (129). For this reason, Deissmann suggests that Paul's language of being-in-Christ and of Christusglauben must rest "in the atmosphere and language of Eastern and Western mysticism" (130).

Another neglected perspective is offered in Pierre Vallotton's occasionally cited but rarely engaged monograph, *Le Christ et la foi*.[30] In this wide-ranging study, Vallotton considers the πίστις Χριστοῦ construction in Paul's letters in light of the concept of "faith" in its larger canonical and historical context. Vallotton discusses not merely Christ's faith but also God's faithfulness toward—and indeed God's *faith in*—humanity. Faith as the pursuit and assured expectation of goodness and justice is characteristic of God's faith, of Christ's faith, and of human faith.[31] According to Vallotton, Jesus' own πίστις is directed toward God and is manifested in the Son's obedience to the will of the Father, including the Christ's suffering and death on the cross.[32] Vallotton stresses, however, that the faith of Christ for Paul also includes the faith of the resurrected Christ. Key for Vallotton is his interpretation of the phrase ἐν πίστει ζῶ τῇ τοῦ υἱοῦ τοῦ θεοῦ ("I live by the faith[fulness] of the Son of God") in Gal 2:20, a locution that Vallotton understands with reference to the faith of the risen and exalted Christ:

> When the author of the Epistle to the Hebrews calls Jesus Christ ὁ τῆς πίστεως ἀρχηγός καὶ τελειωτής, he not only recalls the Lord's death, but he also evokes his ascension in glory. When Paul says that he now lives by the faith of the Son of God, this not only means that he lives by the benefit of the cross but also that the apostle takes into account the intercession of Christ, ascended and glorious.[33]

---

[30] Pierre Vallotton, *Le Christ et la foi: Etude de théologie biblique*, Nouvelle série théologique 10 (Geneva, Switz.: Labor et Fides, 1960). Hooker ("ΠΙΣΤΙΣ ΧΡΙΣΤΟΥ," 321) also pointed out in 1989 that Vallotton's book had been "strangely ignored." Vallotton is nowhere mentioned in the most recent collection of essays on the πίστις Χριστοῦ debate (i.e., Bird and Sprinkle's *The Faith of Jesus Christ*), for example, and even we were unaware of his monograph when we initially formulated the idea for this project. One small indication of the neglect of Vallotton's book is that the copy of *Le Christ et la foi* in Fuller Theological Seminary's library remained with pages uncut until we checked it out in April of 2016, some fifty-six years after its publication!

[31] Vallotton, *Le Christ*, 98.

[32] Vallotton, *Le Christ*, 121–28.

[33] Vallotton, *Le Christ*, 128.

As Vallotton's reading of Gal 2:20 in light of Heb 12:2 suggests, his analysis of Christ's faith is as theological as it is exegetical, a point made with critical disdain in several of the English-language reviews of *Le Christ et la foi* and likely a factor in the neglect of Vallotton's thesis.[34] Not only did Vallotton's work suffer from its publication in French just before the πίστις Χριστοῦ debate heated up in English, but the monograph's subtitle (*Etude de théologie biblique*) and its methodological approach likely marked it as a dated representative of the "biblical theology movement." The monograph, however, contains a number of helpful observations about the importance of the πίστις of the risen Christ in Paul's letters, and we will have a number of occasions to highlight Vallotton's insights in our exegesis of particular texts.

METHODOLOGICAL APPROACH

Others have occasionally gestured toward the notion—first suggested by Deissmann and then clearly argued by Vallotton—that the πίστις Χριστοῦ construction in Paul's letters might refer to the faithfulness of the risen and exalted Christ.[35] Yet no one, so far as we are aware,

---

[34] See the reviews by C. F. D. Moule, *SJT* 14 (1961): 419–22 and Paul E. Davies, *JBL* 80 (1961): 194. That Vallotton does not appear to have published any significant books or articles aside from *Le Christ et la foi* may also explain the neglect of his monograph among English-speaking scholars.

[35] Drawing on Teresa Morgan's work (*Roman Faith and Christian Faith: Pistis and Fides in the Early Roman Empire and Early Churches* [Oxford: Oxford University Press, 2015]), Peter Oakes has recently suggested that πίστις in Galatians reflects dimensions of Christ's present relationship to humanity: "Common Greek usage and the parallel to ἐν Χριστῷ ought to push us towards seeing πίστις, in 2.16 and elsewhere in Galatians, as probably being an expression of current trust, loyalty and/or reliability, all of these being towards another being or beings. If it is Christ's faithfulness to God or to people, it is probably primarily current faithfulness. If it is people's trust in and/or loyalty to Christ, it is primarily expression of a relationship to the current Christ rather than trust in a past event" ("*Pistis* as Relational Way of Life in Galatians," *JSNT* 40 [2018]: 255–75 [269]). Oakes' essay is limited to Galatians, however, and it does not explore Christ's "current faithfulness" in relation to Paul's understanding of Christ's resurrection or heavenly session. Others who have come close to connecting Christ's πίστις with the living Christ include Ota, "The Holistic *Pistis* and Abraham's Faith (Galatians 3)" and, with her emphasis on πίστις and participation, Morna Hooker, "Another Look at πίστις Χριστοῦ," *SJT* 69 (2016). Interestingly,

has argued the case in a thorough exegetical study that attempts to demonstrate the importance of Paul's language of πίστις for Paul's understanding of resurrection, for Paul's view of Christ's heavenly enthronement, and for Paul's participationist soteriology.[36] In framing this project with an initial glance at 2 Tim 2:8-13 as a key text, we acknowledge that our approach cuts against the grain of mainstream Pauline scholarship.[37] With a few notable exceptions, the πίστις Χριστοῦ debate has taken place almost entirely on the playing field of

---

Karl F. Ulrichs contends that the subjective genitive position suffers from a "christological deficit" (eines christologischen Defizits) in that, according to proponents of the subjective view, Christ is the one who brings faith but Christ's πίστις becomes unnecessary once humans have believed (*Christusglaube: Studien zum Syntagma pistis Christou und zum paulischen Verständnis von Glaube und Rechtfertigung* [Tübingen: Mohr Siebeck, 2007], 250). If Christ's πίστις continues through the resurrection and exaltation, however, the objection is mitigated.

[36] On the ascension in Pauline theology, see Peter Orr, *Christ Absent and Present: A Study in Pauline Christology*, WUNT 2/354 (Tübingen: Mohr Siebeck, 2014); cf. Douglas Farrow, *Ascension and Ecclesia: On the Significance of the Doctrine of the Ascension for Ecclesiology and Christian Cosmology* (Grand Rapids: Eerdmans, 1999); Gerrit Scott Dawson, *Jesus Ascended: The Meaning of Christ's Continuing Incarnation* (Edinburgh: T&T Clark, 2004); and Douglas Farrow, *Ascension Theology* (Edinburgh: T&T Clark, 2011).

[37] Yet several recent studies have offered critical analysis of the ideological and political contexts in which the seven-letter corpus of the so-called "authentic" Pauline epistles emerged. The time is ripe for a fresh analysis of the scholarly consensus regarding the "real" Paul of the seven letters. Although such a critical reexamination is not the aim of the present project, our framework and our literary approach are influenced by those who have disputed the certainty with which contemporary scholars, from all sorts of confessional and nonconfessional contexts, assert and assume a particular orthodoxy regarding the authorship of the Pauline epistles. See, for example, Cynthia Briggs Kittredge, "Rethinking Authorship in the Letters of Paul: Elisabeth Schüssler Fiorenza's Model of Pauline Theology," in *Walk in the Ways of Wisdom: Essays in Honor of Elisabeth Schüssler Fiorenza*, ed. Shelly Matthews, Cynthia Briggs Kittredge, and Melanie Johnson-Debaufre (Harrisburg, Pa.: Continuum, 2003), 318–33; Benjamin L. White, *Remembering Paul: Ancient and Modern Contests over the Image of the Apostle* (Oxford: Oxford University Press, 2014); Douglas A. Campbell, *Framing Paul: An Epistolary Biography* (Grand Rapids: Eerdmans, 2014); Alexander N. Kirk, *The Departure of an Apostle: Paul's Death Anticipated and Remembered*, WUNT 2/406 (Tübingen: Mohr Siebeck, 2015); and T. J. Lang, "Spectres of the Real Paul and the Prospect of Pauline Scholarship," *Marginalia*, https://marginalia.lareviewofbooks.org/spectres-of-the-real-paul-and-the-prospect-of-pauline-scholarship-by-t-j-lang/.

the undisputed Pauline epistles.[38] It is our contention, however, that the possibility of developing a fresh perspective on this stalemated issue is greatly strengthened by placing the question in an alternative framework.

In order to develop the argument that the πίστις Χριστοῦ construction in the undisputed Pauline letters should be interpreted as a reference to the faithfulness of the risen Christ, therefore, we will proceed in a nontraditional fashion. Rather than beginning with the classic and much-discussed texts from the Pauline Hauptbriefe (i.e., Gal 2:16; Rom 3:22, 26), we will work backwards toward those passages from sources that have been somewhat marginalized in the discussion. Our detailed examination of the theme of the faithfulness of the risen and ascended Christ in Pauline literature, therefore, will begin with Philippians. Only then will we turn to the Hauptbriefe, though even there we will first examine a neglected text from the Corinthian correspondence (i.e., 2 Cor 4:7-15) before finally considering the key texts from Galatians and Romans. As this book opens with an examination of a passage from a Pauline letter whose authorship is disputed, the closing frame for our project will include a look at Ephesians, a text that strongly emphasizes the faithfulness of the risen and exalted Lord.

One more step remains, however, before we develop our argument through close readings of the key Pauline texts. It is important to offer an account of the linguistic framework that shapes our understanding of Paul's language of πίστις, and to that issue we turn our attention in the ensuing chapter.

---

[38] For example, in Ulrichs' instructive monograph *Christusglaube*, Eph 3:12 and 2 Tim 3:15 are barely noted.

1

THE SEMANTICS OF *PISTIS*
"The Lord Is Faithful"

Already we have approached our topic in an unconventional way by proposing that the theological perspective offered in 2 Tim 2:8-13 provides a useful heuristic lens for our examination of the epistles that form the core of our study (Philippians, 1–2 Corinthians, Galatians, Romans, and Ephesians). While in the chapters that follow it will be quite apparent that our methodology is generally the same as most mainstream historical-critical biblical scholarship, in this chapter we introduce another component of our program that helps us shed new light on this seemingly stalemated debate—namely, the *linguistic framework* within which we approach the semantic and syntactical issues relating to the πίστις Χριστοῦ construction (and our readings of Paul's letters more generally). To accomplish this, the present chapter addresses the language of πίστις in 2 Thessalonians from a relevance-theoretical framework in order to illustrate the points of overlap with and divergence from other possible frameworks.

It has become axiomatic to aver that the πίστις Χριστοῦ debate "can be settled only by exegesis" and that "appeal to grammar has, in effect, run into the sand."[1] There is truth to this claim, but at the same

---

[1] Morna D. Hooker, "Another Look at πίστις Χριστοῦ," *SJT* 69 (2016): 46; see also Hooker, "Πίστις Χριστοῦ," *NTS* 35 (1989), 321. See further Stanley E. Porter and Andrew W. Pitts, "Πίστις with a Preposition and Genitive Modifier: Lexical,

time a danger that such sentiments imply a separation of "semantics" and "exegesis," as if the linguistic bit can be explored and then the results used in a second stage of interpretation. Our view is that linguistics, down to the level of individual words, is bound up with the whole process of interpreting a text.[2]

In the case of the πίστις Χριστοῦ construction in Paul's letters, linguistic arguments have been employed primarily either to disprove the subjective reading[3] or to disprove the objective reading.[4] A number of syntactical and semantic matters are regularly addressed by both camps, including uses of the genitive case, the significance of the definite article, and the question of sense disambiguation. We will address these and other linguistic matters in subsequent chapters, but here we are particularly concerned with the broader theoretical framework

---

Semantic, and Syntactic Considerations in the πίστις Χριστοῦ Discussion," in *The Faith of Jesus Christ: Exegetical, Biblical, and Theological Studies*, ed. Michael F. Bird and Preston M. Sprinkle (Carlisle, U.K.: Paternoster, 2009), 33–53. Daniel B. Wallace concludes that "on balance grammatical considerations seem to be in favor of the subjective genitive view," but offers little evidence for this position (*Greek Grammar Beyond the Basics: An Exegetical Syntax of the New Testament* [Grand Rapids: Zondervan, 1996], 116).

    [2] As Richard B. Hays writes, "Lexical semantics, insofar as it seeks to make judgments about the meanings of words in Paul's letters, must attend to larger sense units that are inescapably theological" (*The Faith of Jesus Christ: The Narrative Substructure of Galatians 3:1–4:11*, 2nd ed. [Grand Rapids: Eerdmans, 2002], xlvii). For overviews of recent work on discourse analysis within New Testament (NT) studies, see Joel B. Green, "Discourse Analysis and New Testament Interpretation," in *Hearing the New Testament: Strategies for Interpretation*, 2nd ed., ed. Joel B. Green (Grand Rapids: Eerdmans, 2010), 218–39, and Stanley E. Porter, *Linguistic Analysis of the Greek New Testament: Studies in Tools, Methods, and Practice* (Grand Rapids: Baker Academic, 2015).

    [3] See further on R. Barry Matlock, especially "Detheologizing the ΠΙΣΤΙΣ ΧΡΙΣΤΟΥ Debate: Cautionary Remarks from a Lexical Semantic Perspective," *NovT* 42 (2000): 1–23. See also Arland J. Hultgren, "The *Pistis Christou* Formulation in Paul," *NovT* 22 (1980): 248–63.

    [4] See, for example, George Howard, "On the 'Faith of Christ,'" *HTR* 60 (1997): 459–65; Hays, *The Faith of Jesus Christ*, xliv–xlvii; and Sam K. Williams, "Again *Pistis Christou*," *CBQ* 49 (1987): 157–92. Already in 1989 Stanley K. Stowers had claimed that "recent scholarship has conclusively shown that πίστεως Ἰησοῦ . . . means Jesus Christ's faith or faithfulness, not faith in Christ" ("ΕΚ ΠΙΣΤΕΩΣ and ΔΙΑ ΤΗΣ ΠΙΣΤΕΩΣ in Romans 3:30," *JBL* 108 [1989]: 667); see similarly Lloyd Gaston, *Paul and the Torah* (Vancouver: University of British Columbia Press, 1987), 12.

within which interpreters approach the πιστ- word group.[5] If, as we shall argue, πίστις Χριστοῦ is best viewed as a *concentric* expression attesting to the participation of believers in the faithfulness of the risen and exalted Christ, our assumptions about linguistic theory must be clarified lest we erroneously "strain to find our every theological initiative condensed into droplets of Pauline grammar."[6] Yet to reiterate: relevance theory is a *framework* and not a *method*. What is being "tested" in what follows is whether a relevance-theoretical framework is helpful for making sense of the interpretation that emerges from our close readings of texts from the Pauline corpus.

ΠΙΣΤΙΣ IN 2 THESSALONIANS: ΚΥΡΙΟΣ AS A REFERENCE TO CHRIST

Although 2 Thessalonians does not contain a version of the phrase πίστις Χριστοῦ and is not among the letters regularly discussed when considering this topic, the statement πιστὸς δέ ἐστιν ὁ κύριος ("But the Lord is faithful") in 2 Thess 3:3 might be viewed as an explicit statement by Paul (or an early interpreter) about the ongoing faithfulness of the risen Christ.[7] This text, therefore, not only provides us an opportunity to explore the semantics of πίστις within a relevance-theoretical framework. It also has the potential to offer important evidence to support the claim that Christ's πίστις denotes an action or attribute of the risen and exalted Lord in the Pauline corpus.

Immediately we hit a snag, however, since κύριος could be taken either as a reference to God or to Christ. Interpreters generally assert their preference rather than show how one reading or another coheres

---

[5] By "the πιστ- word group" or "the πίστις lexicon" we refer to πίστις with all its cognates, and by "lexeme" we refer to all forms of a single lexical item. Such usage is consistent with recent studies; one example is Teresa Morgan, *Roman Faith and Christian Faith: Pistis and Fides in the Early Roman Empire and Early Churches* (Oxford: Oxford University Press, 2015), 2n4.

[6] Matlock, "Detheologizing," 22–23. See also our remarks in the introduction regarding the marginalization of Pierre Vallotton's book.

[7] Here, as in the previous chapter, our discussion of 2 Thessalonians assumes no particular stance on the authorship of the letter. Our argument regarding the illustrative value of 2 Thess 3:3 does not depend on the historical identification of the epistle's author.

best with a given set of linguistic principles.[8] Our burden here, therefore, is to show how κύριος as a reference to the risen and exalted Christ makes sense when considered within a relevance-theoretical linguistic framework. On the one hand, we can make observations that any other interpreters would make about the contexts that inform a decision about the referent of κύριος. On the other, a consistent linguistic framework can provide helpful checks, at the very least as a coherent way of expressing the reasons for preferring one option over another. In this case, we might say that the semantic input of κύριος is not fixed but contributes to discourse meaning in an ad hoc fashion. Therefore, in the opening verses of the letter readers are immediately prompted to take κύριος as a reference to (and title for) Christ. Κύριος occurs twenty-two times in twenty verses in 2 Thessalonians (1:1, 2, 7, 8, 9, 12 [twice]; 2:1, 2, 8, 13, 14, 16; 3:1, 3, 4, 5, 6, 12, 16 [twice], 18). Of these, thirteen occur in the title "The Lord Jesus Christ" or "the Lord Jesus," thereby "activating" (in the sense described below) the identity and images of Christ from the reader's mental encyclopedia ("grab-bag") for κύριος.

Abraham J. Malherbe writes of 3:3 that "since the simple *kyrios* in 2:13 and 3:1 refers to God, it is natural to suppose that it also does so here."[9] This is not at all clear, however. Malherbe seems to assume that without "Jesus Christ" appended, κύριος should be assumed to refer to God. Yet the discourse already "shaped" the term by early and frequent assertions about the identity of "the Lord" as Christ. Moreover, none of the nine simple instances of κύριος in the letter signal a change of referent to God (θεός), who is repeatedly mentioned with a coordinating

---

[8] For example, Morgan simply asserts, "'The Lord' here is surely God" (*Roman Faith*, 314n28; cf. F. F. Bruce, *1 & 2 Thessalonians*, WBC 45 [Waco, Tex.: Word, 1982], 199–200), whereas Gordon D. Fee insists that "in all of his extant letters Paul uses the word *Kyrios* exclusively to refer to Christ" (*The First and Second Letters to the Thessalonians*, NICNT [Grand Rapids: Eerdmans, 2009], 318; cf. James E. Frame, *A Critical and Exegetical Commentary on the Epistles of St. Paul to the Thessalonians*, ICC [New York: Scribner, 1912], 293). Although Ulrichs provides an excursus on the πιστ- word group in 2 Thessalonians, he does not entertain the possibility that "the Lord" is a reference to Christ (*Christusglaube: Studien zum Syntagma pistis Christou und zum paulischen Verständnis von Glaube und Rechtfertigung* [Tübingen: Mohr Siebeck, 2007], 92).

[9] Abraham J Malherbe, *The Letters to the Thessalonians: A New Translation with Introduction and Commentary*, AB 32B (New York: Doubleday, 2000), 445.

conjunction (καί) along with Christ, as in 1:1 ("in God our father *and* the Lord Jesus Christ"; cf. 1:2, 8, 12; 2:16; 3:5).

In 1:9, there is a reference to those who are "separated from the presence of *the Lord* and from the glory of his might." Malherbe himself rightly states that the "presence of the Lord" in this verse, an allusion to passages like Isa 2:10, 19, 21 LXX, is clearly a reference to Jesus: "In Isaiah God is Lord; here Jesus is Lord."[10] In 2 Thess 2:2, the "day of the Lord" obviously refers to Jesus, since Paul is talking about "when the Lord Jesus is revealed" (1:7) on that "day" (1:10; cf. 2:3). In 2:13, believers are "beloved by the Lord, because God chose you (ἠγαπημέ-νοι ὑπὸ κυρίου ὅτι εἵλατο ὑμᾶς ὁ θεός)." Here, too, θεός is restated so as not to confuse God with ὁ κύριος.[11] The cluster of occurrences in 3:1-5 will be treated together below, but here we may note that in 3:1 "the word of the Lord" (another common phrase in the Old Testament that takes on a particular focus in Paul) refers to the message about Jesus Christ (cf. 1 Thess 1:8; 4:15).[12] Finally, the reference to "the Lord of peace" in the closing of the letter (2 Thess 3:16) rather than "the God of peace" (1 Thess 5:23) is an emphatic (αὐτός) and final instance in a pattern found in 2 Thessalonians in which Christ is the focus of phrases that elsewhere refer to θεός (e.g., 2:13 [cf. 1 Thess 1:4]; 3:4, 12).[13]

As we will address, the seemingly strongest argument that κύριος in 2 Thess 3:3 (πιστὸς δέ ἐστιν ὁ κύριος) is a reference to God is the close parallel with Paul's phrase "God is faithful" (πιστὸς ὁ θεός) in the Corinthian correspondence (1 Cor 1:9; 10:13; 2 Cor 1:18) and the similar phrase "the one who calls you is faithful" (πιστὸς ὁ καλῶν ὑμᾶς) in 1 Thess 5:24. It is quite clear in 1 Thessalonians that God is

[10] *Letters*, 403.

[11] Malherbe's observation that "the topic . . . is faith and God's action in relation to it" (*Letters*, 436) rightly draws attention to the collocation of κύριος and πίστις language, but this is no reason to take κύριος as a reference to God.

[12] See also the close relationship between God's faithfulness to Israel and the "word of the Lord" in passages such as Pss 32:4; 144:13; and Jer 7:28; on the phrase "word of the Lord" as a reference to the good news of Jesus Christ in the Pauline letters, see Michael W. Pahl, *Discerning the 'Word of the Lord': The 'Word of the Lord' in 1 Thessalonians 4:15*, LNTS 389 (Edinburgh: T&T Clark, 2009), 122-35.

[13] See further Jeffrey A. D. Weima, *1-2 Thessalonians*, BECNT (Grand Rapids: Baker Academic, 2014), 633-35.

the one who calls (2:12: τοῦ θεοῦ τοῦ καλοῦντος; cf. 1:4, 5), so taken by itself the reference in 1 Thess 5:24 naturally recalls God (cf. Isa 41:9; 42:6; 43:1; 45:3). With the evidence surrounding Paul's use of κύριος in 2 Thessalonians delineated earlier, however, the fact that Paul does *not* use θεός in 2 Thess 3:3 strongly suggests that this particular attribute of God is here located with Christ.

Having determined for the moment that the Lord *Jesus Christ* is called "faithful" (πιστός) in 2 Thess 3:3, we may now address the repetition that occurs in the wider passage, 3:2-3:

καὶ ἵνα ῥυσθῶμεν (*that we may be rescued*)
   ἀπὸ τῶν ἀτόπων καὶ <u>πονηρῶν ἀνθρώπων·</u> (*from wicked and evil people;*)
      οὐ γὰρ πάντων <u>ἡ πίστις.</u> (*for not of all is faith*)[14]
   <u>πιστὸς</u> δέ ἐστιν ὁ κύριος, (*but faithful is the Lord,*)
ὃς στηρίξει ὑμᾶς καὶ φυλάξει (*who will strengthen and guard you*)
   ἀπὸ τοῦ <u>πονηροῦ.</u> (*from the evil one.*)

Quite obviously, these two instances of the πιστ- word group inform one another, and "the contrast in vv. 2b and 3a is between the faithlessness of non-Christians, who act maliciously toward believers, and the abiding faithfulness of the Lord, who protects and cares for his people."[15] If the "faithful Lord" in 3:3 is the Lord Jesus, then, this passage affirms the strengthening and guarding of the risen Christ.

Interpreters often refer to such positioning as "wordplay."[16] The term "wordplay" might be misleading, however, depending upon what is implied. Below are the listed options for the sense of πίστις from some frequently consulted lexicons:

---

[14] Charles A. Wanamaker translates 3:2 as "faith is not [the response] of all to the word of God" (*The Epistles to the Thessalonians: A Commentary on the Greek Text*, NIGTC [Grand Rapids: Eerdmans, 1990], 275). An alternative paraphrase might be "not all participate in a faith relationship with Christ, but Christ is faithful."

[15] Wanamaker, *Epistles*, 276.

[16] So Fee, *Thessalonians*, 317; Weima, *1–2 Thessalonians*, 591. The phenomenon is labeled "paronomasia" in Friedrich Blass, Albert Debrunner, and Robert W. Funk (BDF), *A Greek Grammar of the New Testament and Other Early Christian Literature* (Chicago: University of Chicago Press, 1961), §488.

BDAG[17]:

1. that which evokes trust and faith, *faithfulness, reliability, fidelity, commitment*
2. state of believing on the basis of the reliability of the one trusted, *trust, confidence, faith*
3. that which is believed, *body of faith/belief/teaching*[18]

L&N[19]:

31.43 πίστιςᵃ: that which is completely believable
31.85 πίστιςᵇ: to believe to the extent of complete trust and reliance
31.88 πίστιςᶜ: the state of being someone in whom complete confidence can be placed
31.102 πίστιςᵈ⁻ᵉ: the content of what Christians believe
33.289 πίστιςᶠ: a promise or pledge of faithfulness and loyalty[20]

LSJ[21]:

I. *trust* in others, *faith*, generally, *persuasion* of a thing, *confidence, assurance,* 2. in subjective sense, *good faith, trustworthiness, honesty,* b. of things, *credence, credit,* 3. in a commercial sense, *credit,* b. *position of trust or trusteeship,* 4. Theol., *faith*
II. *that which gives confidence*: hence, 1. *assurance, pledge of good faith, guarantee,* 2. *means of persuasion, argument, proof*
III. *that which is entrusted, a trust*
IV. political *protection* or *suzerainty,* 2. in Egypt, *safe-conduct, safeguard*[22]

---

[17] Frederick W. Danker, Walter Bauer, William F. Arndt, and F. Wilbur Gingrich (BDAG), *Greek-English Lexicon of the New Testament and Other Early Christian Literature,* 3rd ed. (Chicago: University of Chicago Press, 2000).
[18] BDAG, 818–20.
[19] Johannes P. Louw and Eugene A. Nida (L&N), eds., *Greek-English Lexicon of the New Testament: Based on Semantic Domains,* 2nd ed. (New York: United Bible Societies, 1989).
[20] L&N, 371, 376, 377, 379, 421.
[21] Henry George Liddell, Robert Scott, Henry Stuart Jones (LSJ), *A Greek-English Lexicon,* 9th ed., rev. suppl. (Oxford: Clarendon, 1996).
[22] LSJ, 1408. See also *TDNT* (Gerhard Kittel and Gerhard Friedrich, eds., *Theological Dictionary of the New Testament,* trans. Geoffrey W. Bromiley, 10 vols (Grand Rapids: Eerdmans, 1964–1976), which lists several distinct definitions (6:208–14).

With these options and the assumption of polysemy that often attends such categorizations, in 2 Thess 3:2, πίστις is taken to denote the underlined glosses and rendered *faith/ Glaube/foi* (as opposed to *faithfulness/ Treue/fidélité*; cf. New Revised Standard Version [NRSV], New International Version [NIV], Common English Bible [CEB], Lutherbibel, Segond, and others), and by a similar process πιστός in 3:3 is rendered *faithful/ treu/fidèle*.[23] The wordplay occurs, in this account, because the two distinct Greek words "are spelled virtually the same (they differ in only one letter) and [are] placed immediately beside each other."[24] Or as Charles Wanamaker puts it, "The transition from the thought of v. 2 to that of v. 3 seems somewhat abrupt even though a word link exists in the use of πίστις/πιστός ('faith-faithful')."[25] The two words have different "meanings" ("belief" and "trustworthiness") and thus are somewhat artificially juxtaposed, according to Bruce: "There is an intended contrast between the πίστις of God and the ἀπιστία of the opponents of the gospel, even if the πίστις of God is his faithfulness while their lack of πίστις is their unbelief."[26] Further examination of these assumptions is needed.

A First Look at Linguistics: R. Barry Matlock and Lexical Semantics

Bemoaning the shift away from linguistics proper in the πίστις Χριστοῦ debate, Stanley Porter and Andrew Pitts declare in a 2009 essay that the "only genuine bright spot on the horizon" is the work of R. Barry Matlock.[27] Indeed, Matlock's series of essays on the topic remain the most carefully considered linguistic treatment in recent years,[28] and

---

[23] BDAG, 820

[24] Weima, *1–2 Thessalonians*, 591. It is unclear why Weima refers to this noun and adjective as "two nouns."

[25] Wanamaker, *Epistles*, 276.

[26] Bruce, *1 & 2 Thessalonians*, 200. See also Morgan's critique in *Roman Faith*, 13, cited earlier.

[27] Porter and Pitts, "Πίστις," 35.

[28] See Matlock, "Sins of the Flesh and Suspicious Minds: Dunn's New Theology of Paul," *JSNT* 72 (1998): 67–90; esp. 87; "Detheologizing"; "'Even the Demons Believe': Paul and πίστις Χριστοῦ," *CBQ* 64 (2002): 300–318; "ΠΙΣΤΙΣ in Galatians 3:26: Neglected Evidence for 'Faith in Christ'?" *NTS* 49 (2003): 433–39; "The Rhetoric

nearly every study of the πίστις Χριστοῦ debate appeals to or interacts with Matlock's work.[29] For a variety of reasons, Matlock advocates the objective reading:

> The effect of [Paul's words] . . . upon each other, in the particular case of πίστις Χριστοῦ, is clearly to select the sense, the subject, and the object of πίστις as according to the objective genitive reading. In arguing thus, I have offered what proponents of the subjective genitive reading have not (and I suspect cannot): concrete linguistic-contextual evidence, precisely of the requisite sort.[30]

Of interest here is Matlock's reliance on lexical semantics to demonstrate how the context contributes to the "selection" of one particular "sense" (*belief, faith, trust*) over another (*faithfulness*). Words are assumed to have multiple senses (polysemy), so interpretation is largely a question of disambiguating between a relatively fixed set of possible senses.

Such an understanding of lexical semantics draws on the work of David A. Cruse[31] and was popularized for biblical study by Eugene A. Nida.[32] Matlock is well aware that "the illegitimate imposition of our own sense distinctions is a real concern,"[33] yet the notion of *selection from a list of possible meanings* is pervasive in Matlock's analysis. For instance, Matlock states regarding Phil 3:9 that the presence of the

---

of πίστις in Paul: Galatians 2:16, 3:22, Romans 3:22, and Philippians 3:9," *JSNT* 30 (2007): 173–203; and "Saving Faith: The Rhetoric and Semantics of πίστις in Paul," in *The Faith of Jesus Christ: Exegetical, Biblical, and Theological Studies*, ed. Michael F. Bird and Preston M. Sprinkle (Peabody: Hendrickson, 2009), 73–89.

[29] See recently Francis Watson, *Paul and the Hermeneutics of Faith*, 2nd ed. (London: Bloomsbury T&T Clark, 2016), xlii n66, 66; and John M. G. Barclay, *Paul and the Gift* (Grand Rapids: Eerdmans, 2015), 380–83.

[30] Matlock, "Saving Faith," 89.

[31] David A. Cruse, *Lexical Semantics*, CTL (Cambridge: Cambridge University, 1986).

[32] Eugene Nida, *Exploring Semantic Structures*, ILL 11 (Munich: Fink, 1975). See also Johannes P. Louw, *Semantics of New Testament Greek* (Atlanta: Scholars, 1982); John Lyons, *Semantics*, 2 vols. (Cambridge: Cambridge University Press, 1977); and Peter Cotterell and Max Turner, *Linguistics and Biblical Interpretation* (Downers Grove, Ill.: IVP, 1989), 77–89.

[33] Matlock, "Detheologizing," 3.

term γινώσκω "further contributes to the *selection* of the semantically contiguous sense of πίστις ('belief, faith, trust', not 'faithfulness')."[34] The practice is reinforced by the numbered entries in standard lexicons such as BDAG, LSJ, and L&N and has been practiced by influential interpreters for decades.[35] Yet the practice of sense selection with an assumption of polysemy is problematic, because it prematurely imposes restrictions on word usage.[36] The key issue, then, is to articulate an alternative approach that challenges the assumption that "πίστις is a polysemous word,"[37] or more accurately, that the πιστ- word group is best viewed as polysemous.

Although appreciative of Matlock's contributions and himself an advocate of polysemity (importantly, *pervasive* polysemity), F. Gerald Downing's recent study identifies "sense selection" as a prime weakness of Matlock's approach.[38] Downing laments that interpreters "still . . . discern distinct senses in words," rightly arguing that efforts to discern precise lexicon-style "meanings" do not cohere with what we know about ancient writers.[39] After a survey of semantic assumptions apparent in ancient writers such as Cicero, Quintilian, Aristotle, Philo, Seneca, and Plutarch, Downing concludes:

> In Paul's world, trust in someone was itself founded in, and displayed and presupposed belief in their trustworthiness (as well as, most likely, their willingness to trust you): faith in Jesus would

[34] Matlock, "Saving Faith," 78, italics added; cf. Matlock, "Rhetoric," 183.

[35] For example, C. F. D. Moule: "The distinction between 'faith' and 'faithfulness' should [not] be ignored—a distinction of which writers in Hebrew and Greek were evidently well aware" (review of Pierre Vallotton, *Le Christ et La Foi*, *SJT* 14 [1961]: 420).

[36] See, for example, Thomas D. Bontley, "Modified Occam's Razor: Parsimony, Pragmatics, and the Acquisition of Word Meaning," *Mind and Language* 20 (2005): 288–312.

[37] Matlock, "Saving Faith," 74.

[38] F. Gerald Downing, "Ambiguity, Ancient Semantics, and Faith," *NTS* 56 (2010): 140.

[39] Downing, "Ambiguity," 144. See also Jonathan R. R. Tallon, "Faith in Paul: The View from Late Antiquity" (paper presented at the Annual Meeting of the British New Testament Society, Manchester, U.K., September 5, 2014), and "Faith in John Chrysostom's Preaching: A Contextual Reading" (Ph.D. diss., University of Manchester, 2015), 45–52.

necessarily imply (unless explicitly denied) at the least a trust in his faithfulness. *Ancient expectations of words have them carry much of their semantic baggage with them*, whatever part of their range appears in context to be foregrounded; that is, unless some elements of their range have been specifically discarded.[40]

The instinct that "the Greek πίστις does not require the writer or reader to make the distinction between '*Treue*' and '*Glaube*'" has often been promoted by advocates of the subjective reading,[41] but Downing's demonstration of this fact in ancient writers suggests the possibility of (and need for) a theoretically sophisticated challenge to Matlock's approach to semantics.[42]

ΠΙΣΤΙΣ IN 2 THESSALONIANS: WORDPLAY OR MEANING-MAKING?

We return, then, to the wordplay involving πίστις/πιστός in 2 Thess 3:2–3: interpreters often speak of this as a link between two words that have different "meanings" ("belief" and "trustworthiness"). Yet this is not the most helpful way to understand what happens when readers engage with Paul's discourse in 3:1–5. As we detail in the next section, a relevance-theoretical framework shifts the focus *away* from concern about which sense of the word best fits a given instance

[40] Downing, "Ambiguity," 160, emphasis added.

[41] Richard B. Hays, "ΠΙΣΤΙΣ and Pauline Theology," in *Pauline Theology*, vol. 4, *Looking Back, Pressing On*, ed. E. Elizabeth Johnson and David M. Hay (Atlanta: Scholars, 1997), 42. See also J. Haussleiter, "Der Glaube Jesu Christi und der christliche Glaube," *NKZ* 2 (1891): 136.

[42] A passage from Athanasius' *Orations contra Arianos* (2.6) regarding the depiction of Jesus as πιστός in Heb 3:2 seemingly presents a challenge to Downing's claim that ancient writers show little appetite for precise definitions. Matlock claims that Athanasius lays out "two senses of πιστός . . . 'believing' (πιστεύων) and 'trustworthy' (ἀξιόπιστος)" as confirmation of the semantic distinction that he believes should be made ("Saving Faith," 87). It is true that Athanasius speaks of the saints'"acknowledged two senses" (ἐγίνωσον διπλοῦν εἶναι τὸν νοῦν), but Athanasius is here concerned to protect the distinction between humans and God, and, as Ian G. Wallis points out, in the very next passage passage (2.9) Athanasius "changes tack" and exploits the very ambiguities of πιστός he had supposedly ruled out (*The Faith of Jesus Christ in Early Christian Traditions*, SNTSMS 84 [Cambridge: Cambridge University Press, 1995], 204–5).

("disambiguation") and *toward* descriptions of the way a given mental encyclopedia for the πιστ- word group has been shaped and activated in the letter. Context shapes the contents that are activated, as well as the grab-bag itself. The reader's assessment of πίστις is not determined by disambiguation ("What sense does the author mean here?") but by meaning-making ("What is the relationship of those who have πίστις here? What does it mean for me to have πίστις?").[43]

A Second Look at Linguistics: Πιστισ as a Univocal Lexical Input in Pauline Usage

Downing remains committed to the assumption that words are polysemous, but his central insights would find firmer theoretical footing if approached using a "monosemic bias" articulated within a relevance-theoretic understanding of ad hoc meaning construction.[44] While it is true that what Downing describes as "pervasive polysemity" has much

---

[43] Since the inception of relevance theory (RT), which will be described below, Deirdre Wilson and Dan Sperber have insisted that poetic elements can be accounted for within RT as "weak" pragmatic effects (see, e.g., *Meaning and Relevance* [Cambridge: Cambridge University Press, 2012], 84–96). When a reader offers an interpretation of, say, a poem that deliberately opens itself to multiple interpretations, he or she is simply drawing on these weak effects. Often, though, not least in the NT, explicit and identifiable (thus "strong") pragmatic effects are made present by the interpretive process. Interpreters have always devoted attention to these effects (this is what is often meant when we speak of "exegesis") but have not always had a framework within which to articulate the way these effects shape meaning all the way down to the level of individual words. As Regina Blass has described the "search for contexts" described by a relevance-theoretic account of communication: "The text alone rarely encodes enough information to determine the intended logical relations among propositions in a discourse; nor is the role of context simply one of enabling coherence relations to be established . . . it is relevance relations between text and context (in the sense of Sperber and Wilson, 1986) which are paramount in successful interpretation" ("Are There Logical Relations in a Text?" *Lingua* 90 [1993]: 93).

[44] Charles Ruhl argues for a monosemic bias in his classic monograph *On Monosemy: A Study in Linguistic Semantics* (Albany: State University of New York, 1989). For a review of recent scholarship drawing on some form of monosemy, including extensive interaction with Lappenga's approach to monosemy used in the present book, see Ryder A. Wishart, "Monosemy in Biblical Studies: A Critical Analysis of Recent Work" (*BAGL* 6 [2017]: 99–126). Wishart offers some critiques of both our relevance-theoretic approach and an alternative framework within which monosemy might be

in common with a monosemic approach, in practice the assumption of polysemy still veers in the direction of identifying specific "uses."[45] A more-comprehensive warrant for our monosemic approach to Paul's use of the πιστ- word group is needed, to which we now turn.[46]

Paul Grice insisted that "senses are not to be multiplied beyond necessity."[47] Grice's maxim stands behind recent linguistic frameworks that take seriously the need to account for how human brains process language (cognitive linguistics)[48] as well as the fact that the concept communicated by a given occurrence of a word very often (or always) differs from the encoded semantic sense (lexical pragmatics).[49] That is, the fixed contribution of a word in a given discourse is small ("semantic

---

understood (systemic functional linguistics) but enthusiastically commends the continued pursuit of a monosemic bias within biblical studies.

[45] For a defense of pervasive polysemy, see, for example, D. Geeraerts, "Polysemization and Humboldt's Principle," in *La Polysémie: Lexicographie et Cognition*, ed. R. Jongen (Louvain-la-Neuve: Cabay, 1985), 29–50. For a response, see Lappenga, *Paul's Language of Ζῆλος: Monosemy and the Rhetoric of Identity and Practice*, BINS 137 (Leiden: Brill, 2016), 53–65. Downing casts aside monosemy as undesirable, but we will argue below that a monosemic approach values what Downing values ("that usages may merge, unbounded, may flow into one another, implicate one another"; "Ambiguity," 141) and has the additional benefit of accounting for nonsemantic inputs.

[46] What follows draws on the framework developed in Lappenga, *Paul's Language*, 5–78.

[47] Paul Grice, *Studies in the Way of Words* (Cambridge: Harvard University Press, 1991), 47. Grice calls this "modified Occam's razor" (MOR). Grice's seminal contribution is found in his 1967 William James lectures at Harvard University, later revised and published as *Studies in the Way of Words*. For a summary of the contributions of Grice, see Stephen Neale, "Paul Grice and the Philosophy of Language," *Linguistics and Philosophy* 15 (1992): 509–59.

[48] That is, our minds do not determine meaning by retrieving linguistically expressible components of words; see further, for example, Reinhard Blutner, "Lexical Pragmatics," *Journal of Semantics* 15 (1998): 139.

[49] Cf. Deirdre Wilson, "Relevance and Lexical Pragmatics," *Italian Journal of Linguistics* 15 (2003): 273–74. In an effort to be more precise than Charles Morris' definition of pragmatics as the study of "the relation of signs to interpreters," Jeffrey C. King and Jason Stanley endorse the view that "the pragmatic content is what the speaker communicates over and above the semantic content of the sentence he uttered" ("Semantics, Pragmatics, and the Role of Semantic Content," in *Semantics versus Pragmatics*, ed. Zoltán Gendler Szabó [Oxford: Clarendon, 2005], 117; cf. Charles Morris, *Foundations of a Theory of Signs* [Chicago: University of Chicago Press, 1938], 6).

underspecification"), and the meaning of that word can be determined only by attending to a number of other contextual factors.

More technically, semantic underspecification lies at the heart of *relevance theory* (RT), initiated by Deirdre Wilson and Dan Sperber and further refined by Robyn Carston.[50] The fundamental insight of RT is that "human cognition tends to be geared to the maximisation of relevance."[51] Specifically, human cognition occurs as a balance between minimal processing effort and maximum cognitive effect.[52] Since very little of a communicator's conceptual repertoire is lexicalized, pragmatic enrichment of encoded meaning (semantics) takes place at every level, and, importantly, concept construction is ad hoc. That is, "words uttered in a particular context provide access to concept schemas but, in any and every particular utterance, the concepts themselves shift and morph."[53] In a given context, the hearer or reader is constantly creating meaning, down to the level of the very words themselves.

Relevance theorists maintain that a fixed semantic value is only a small (or even nonexistent) part of what a word contributes to the process of interpretation; more important is the *nonsemantic* part,

---

[50] The standard works are Dan Sperber and Deirdre Wilson, *Relevance: Communication and Cognition*, 2nd ed. (Oxford: Blackwell, 1995 [1986]); and Robyn Carston, *Thoughts and Utterances: The Pragmatics of Explicit Communication (Malden, Mass: Wiley-Blackwell, 2002)*. In addition, see Wilson and Sperber, *Meaning and Relevance*, and the digest in Wilson and Sperber, "Relevance Theory," in *The Handbook of Pragmatics*, ed. Laurence Robert Horn and Gregory Ward (Malden, Mass.: Blackwell, 2004), 607–32. See also the online bibliography maintained by Francisco Yus (http://personal.ua.es/francisco.yus/rt.html). On relevance theory in biblical interpretation, see Ernst-August Gutt, *Translation and Relevance: Cognition and Context*, 2nd ed. (Manchester, U.K.: St. Jerome, 2000); and Gene L. Green, "Relevance Theory and Biblical Interpretation," in *The Linguist as Pedagogue: Trends in the Teaching and Linguistic Analysis of the Greek New Testament*, ed. Stanley E. Porter and Matthew Brook O'Donnell (Sheffield: Sheffield Phoenix Press, 2009), 217–40.

[51] Sperber and Wilson, *Relevance*, 260.

[52] Sperber and Wilson, *Relevance*, 265.

[53] Gene L. Green, "Lexical Pragmatics and the Lexicon," *BBR* 22 (2012): 321. Carston herself states that the term *ad hoc concept* "is used to refer to concepts that are constructed pragmatically by a hearer in the process of utterance comprehension. . . . The description of such concepts as '*ad hoc*' reflects the fact that they are not linguistically given, but are constructed on-line (on the fly) in response to specific expectations of relevance raised in specific contexts" (*Thoughts and Utterances*, 322).

an "encyclopedia" of concepts associated with the word. Robyn Carston describes the encyclopedia as containing "general knowledge and individual beliefs about the things they denote, cultural knowledge, including stereotypes, which the individual may or may not endorse, imagistic representations, and perhaps also episodic memories."[54] In a similar vein, Agustín Rayo has referred to the encyclopedia as a "grab-bag" of mental items: "memories, mental images, pieces of encyclopedic information, pieces of anecdotal information, mental maps, and so forth."[55] Rayo provides the example of the color *blue*, which a hearer might associate with some particular shades of blue, the information that blue represents the sky on a clear day, the memory of a blue piece of clothing, and so on.

Some relevance theorists would be comfortable with what Downing has described as pervasive polysemy, but a growing number have concluded that a monosemic bias is preferable.[56] With the caveat that RT is a *framework* for the understanding of utterances and not a *method*, our approach to the meaning of πίστις Χριστοῦ operates from a relevance-theoretic account of communication: by writing, Paul seeks to modify the cognitive environment of his readers, and his readers' interpretive process is constrained by the search for relevance.[57]

---

[54] Robyn Carston, "Word Meaning and Concept Expressed," *Linguistic Review* 29 (2010): 612; cf. Carston, *Thoughts and Utterances*, 321.

[55] Agustín Rayo, "A Plea for Semantic Localism," *Noûs* 47 (2013): 648; cited in Carston, "Word Meaning," 620–21. Rayo's take on semantic content is essentially eliminativist (there is no semantic input per se).

[56] This includes Carston herself ("I am far from sure that any such distinction [between monosemic and allegedly polysemic words] should be made" ["Word Meaning and Concept Expressed," 609n2]), but has been taken up most directly by Thorstein Fretheim, who argues that "a single parsimonious lexical definition designed to cover all uses, in combination with massive reliance on contextual enrichment in actual conversational dialogue, is superior to an account in terms of lexical polysemy and disambiguation in context" ("In Defense of Monosemy," in *Pragmatics and the Flexibility of Word Meaning*, ed. Enikö Németh T. and Károly Bibok [Amsterdam: Elsevier Science, 2001], 83–84). Given the ubiquitous practice of choosing between senses by biblical scholars, monosemy has the added benefit over polysemy of pushing against such a practice.

[57] Our task in this book cannot be completed apart from the reader's chosen posture in relation to the text. By "reader," then, we find most helpful Umberto Eco's definition of a "model reader" as a *real* reader who *takes on the character* of the author's

The obvious question, then, is just how we might account for the contents of the grab-bag associated with and activated by πίστις in specific instances. In the case of some terms used in the New Testament, it is somewhat easy to grasp the difference that adopting a relevance-theoretical monosemic bias makes. In these cases, the same Greek word group (e.g., the ζῆλος word group) is regularly translated with two or more differing English words (*zeal* or *jealousy*), which artificially separates the repeated occurrences of the Greek word group. When approached from a monosemic framework, interpreters resist the connotations of predetermined "senses" (e.g., *jealousy* as totally distinct from *zeal*) and thereby are freed to recognize the subtle but careful rhetorical strategies at work in Paul's text.[58]

ΠΙΣΤΙΣ IN 2 THESSALONIANS: THE CONTINUING MINISTRY OF THE EXALTED CHRIST

What might a monosemic framework allow us to say, then, about how πίστις has been used throughout 2 Thessalonians? Paul has collocated the faithful advocacy of the risen Lord (especially eschatological, soteriological faithfulness) with the term πίστις. Whether 2 Thessalonians is authentically Paul's or the work of a later Paulinist, it has much in common with 1 Thessalonians and should not, in our determination, be considered in isolation from the earlier letter of Paul to the church in Thessalonica. In 1 Thessalonians, Paul makes extensive use of the πιστ- word group.[59] At the beginning of the letter, whatever we

---

"implied reader" (or better, "authorial reader") (*The Role of the Reader: Explorations in the Semiotics of Texts* [Bloomington: Indiana University Press, 1979], 7). Eco is concerned with linguistic "presupposition pools" that help determine meaning at the level of a whole text, which fits well with a relevance-theoretic framework and its interest in the communicative event.

[58] For instance, few notice that "love is not jealous" (ἡ ἀγάπη οὐ ζηλοῖ) in 1 Cor 13:4 is bookended by references to "having zeal" (ζηλοῦτε) in 12:31 and 14:1 and that Paul's use of the same term participates in the letter's efforts to subvert the Corinthians' notion of ζῆλος (thus moving the Corinthians from status distinctions brought about by the misuse of tongues toward community-edifying gifts like prophecy practiced in love). See further Lappenga, *Paul's Language*, 152–57.

[59] See especially the excellent analysis of 1 Thessalonians in Morgan, *Roman Faith*, 212–46.

make of the notoriously thorny phrasing and intriguing genitive constructions in 1:3,[60] it is abundantly clear that πίστις in the "Lord Jesus Christ" (1:3) means awaiting God's "Son from heaven, whom he raised from the dead—Jesus, who rescues us from the coming wrath" (1:10). Christ's (and God's) ongoing faithfulness to the Thessalonians, particularly regarding their eschatological salvation, is repeatedly on display throughout the letter (e.g., their faith is preserved from the work of the tempter [3:5] and trust is grounded in Jesus' resurrection [4:14]), culminating with Paul's benediction: "May the God of peace himself sanctify you completely; and may your spirit and soul and body be kept blamelessly at the coming of our Lord Jesus Christ. Faithful is the one who calls you, and he will do it" (5:24; cf. 2 Tim 2:13).

In 2 Thessalonians itself, the collocation of πίστις with "endurance" (ὑπομονή)[61] in awaiting the coming Lord is continued and expanded:

> **1 Thess 1:2-3**: We give thanks to God always concerning all of you, and mention you in our prayers, constantly remembering your work of *faith* (πίστεως) and labor of love and *endurance* (ὑπομονῆς) in hope of our Lord Jesus Christ.

> **2 Thess 1:3-4, 8-11**: We must give thanks to God for you always, brothers, as is fitting, since your *faith* (πίστις) grows abundantly, and the love of each one of all of you for one another increases. Therefore, we ourselves boast of you among the churches of God for your *endurance* (ὑπομονῆς) and *faith* (πίστεως). . . . Those who do not obey the gospel of our Lord Jesus will undergo the punishment of eternal destruction, separated from the presence of the Lord and from the glory of his strength, when he comes to be glorified by his saints and to be admired on that day among all who have *believed* (τοῖς πιστεύσασιν), because our testimony to you was

---

[60] See the helpful discussion of this passage in Karl Friedrich Ulrichs, *Christusglaube: Studien zum Syntagma pistis Christou und zum paulinischen Verständnis von Glaube und Rechtfertigung* (Tübingen: Mohr Siebeck, 2007), 71–93. Intriguingly, Fee mentions (but dismisses) the possibility that in light of 1:10, the phrase ἔμπροσθεν τοῦ θεοῦ καὶ πατρὸς ἡμῶν in 1:3 could be a reference to the Lord Jesus Christ now in the Father's presence (*Thessalonians*, 22).

[61] In the Septuagint, the Lord is sometimes characterized as *being* one's ὑπομονή; for example, "you are my endurance Lord" (Ps 70:5 LXX; cf. Jer 14:8; 17:13). See further F. Hauck, "μένω, ἐμ-, κτλ," *TDNT* 4:583–84.

believed (ἐπιστεύθη). To this end we always pray for you, asking that our God will make you worthy of his call and will fulfill every good desire and work of *faith* (πίστεως) by his power.[62]

Christ himself, who will destroy the lawless one on the last day (2 Thess 2:8) and even now protects believers from the "activity of Satan" (2:9), actively provides comfort and gives hope during this period of patient endurance:

And may *our Lord Jesus Christ himself* and God our Father, who loves us and gives us eternal comfort and good hope through grace, comfort your hearts and *strengthen* (στηρίξαι) them in every good work and word. (2:16-17)

In addition, the Thessalonians' faith is contrasted sharply from others' lack of belief:[63]

And on account of this God sends them a strong delusion, in order that they *believe* (πιστεῦσαι) what is false, so that all who have not *believed* (οἱ μὴ πιστεύσαντες) the truth but enjoyed unrighteousness will be judged. But we must always give thanks to God concerning you, brothers beloved by the Lord, because God chose you as the first fruits for salvation through the sanctification of the Spirit and through *faithfulness* (πίστει) with respect to the truth. (2:11-13)

Both of these elements are brought together in the important section in 3:1-5, part of which we already considered:

Finally, pray for us, brothers, so that the word of the Lord may advance and be glorified, just as also among you, and that we

---

[62] In 2 Thess 3:5 Paul refers to the ἀγάπην τοῦ θεοῦ and the ὑπομονὴν τοῦ Χριστοῦ. It is tempting in light of 2 Thess 3:2 to read this as a subjective genitive that expresses the endurance that the risen Christ exhibits on behalf of the faithful, but as Jan Lambrecht points out, this would be the only reference in the New Testament to the endurance of Christ himself ("Loving God and Steadfastly Awaiting Christ [2 Thessalonians 3,5]," *ETL* 76 [2000]: 439).

[63] Nijay Gupta has argued that echoes of Psalm 78 (Ps 77 LXX), which provides a sharp contrast between those who believe and those are not faithful to God (e.g., 78:7-8, 22, 32), are prevalent in 3:1-5 as well ("An Apocalyptic Reading of Psalm 78 in 2 Thessalonians 3," *JSNT* 31 [2008]: 179–94).

may be delivered from inappropriate and evil people; for not all have *faith* (πίστις). But the Lord is *faithful* (πιστός); he will go on *strengthening* (στηρίξει) *you and guarding you* from the evil one. And we trust (πεποίθαμεν) in the Lord concerning you, that you are doing and will continue to do the things that we command. May the Lord direct your hearts to the love of God and to the *endurance* (ὑπομονή) of Christ. (3:1-5)

In summary, we may consider these observations with regard to the πιστ- language in 2 Thess 3:1-5:

1. In 2 Thessalonians, the faithfulness of God is attributed to the Lord Jesus Christ.[64]
2. This faithfulness is unequivocally the ongoing faithfulness of the risen Christ.[65]
3. This faithfulness is demonstrated toward those who participate "in Christ" (1:1) by placing their trust in the one who is faithful.[66]

---

[64] James D. G. Dunn rightly points out that Paul puts the risen Lord Jesus in places reserved for the scriptural YHWH: "It is clear that the resurrection was understood as the decisive event in [Christ's] becoming Lord. . . . Paul seems to have had no qualms about transferring God's role in eschatological salvation to the risen Jesus" (*The Theology of Paul the Apostle* [Grand Rapids: Eerdmans, 1998], 245, 250). This is especially clear in Rom 10:13 (citing LXX Joel 2:32); see also Rom 8:34; 1 Cor 2:16 (Isa 40:13); 2 Cor 10:17-18 (Jer 9:24); and Phil 2:9-11 (Isa 45:23). In 2 Thess 3:3, Paul has done this as well, possibly drawing on texts such as Deut 7:9 LXX ("and you shall know that the Lord your God, he is God, the faithful God [κύριος ὁ θεός σου, οὗτος θεός, θεὸς πιστός]); Prov 15:27-28; and Pss. Sol. 14:1 (πιστὸς κύριος); 17:10 (πιστὸς ὁ κύριος); 17:40.

[65] This is especially clear if we take "strengthen" and "guard" in 2 Thess 3:3 as progressive futures ("will continue strengthening and guarding"); see, for example, Wanamaker, *Epistles*, 275.

[66] The faith of the Thessalonians expresses their being "in" Christ: "For we now live, if you continue to stand firm in the Lord (ἐν κυρίῳ)" (1 Thess 3:8); "we ask and urge you in the Lord Jesus (ἐν κυρίῳ Ἰησοῦ)" (4:1); "through Jesus, God will bring with him those who have died" (4:14); "the dead in Christ (ἐν Χριστῷ) will rise first" (4:16); "preserving salvation through our Lord Jesus Christ" (5:9); "[Christ] died for us, so that whether we are awake or asleep we may live with him" (5:10); "respect those who labor among you and have charge of you in the Lord (ἐν κυρίῳ) and admonish you" (5:12); "to the church of the Thessalonians in God our Father and the Lord Jesus Christ (ἐν θεῷ πατρὶ ἡμῶν καὶ κυρίῳ Ἰησοῦ Χριστῷ)" (2 Thess 1:1); "now may the Lord of peace himself give you peace at all times in all ways. The Lord be with all of you" (3:16).

4. The result is the Thessalonians' own faithfulness to and in Christ in the face of opposition and persecution.

A FINAL LOOK AT LINGUISTICS: THE CONTRIBUTION OF THE LEXICAL INPUT ΠΙΣΤΙΣ IN PAUL

The preceding analysis of πίστις in 2 Thessalonians has provided an example of the way a relevance-theoretical framework and a mono-semic bias can bring interpretive clarity, in this case revealing the importance for the author of the letter that Christ is recognized as the faithful preserver of his people. As a final consideration of linguistics, it will be helpful to draw attention to the important recent study by Teresa Morgan on the way πίστις/*fides* in the ancient world operates as a quality that is "inherently relational and characteristically expressed in action towards other human beings."[67] Morgan's study offers useful data pertaining to the cultural presuppositions that contribute to the grab-bag for πίστις (e.g., it is always social in Greek and Roman usage), but her study also serves as a test case for the methodological framework outlined earlier.

Morgan, like Downing, offers a rebuke of Matlock's reliance on sense disambiguation. Yet Morgan also falls short of adopting a linguistic approach (such as relevance theory) that would better account for her findings:

> To try to separate "faithfulness" from "faith" or other meanings of *pistis* is problematic. Those who used the term need not have intended, and those who heard or read it may not have expected, to understand a single meaning in any one context. Rather than trying to isolate specific meanings of the lexicon in particular passages, we should do better to work with the elasticity and multivalency of the concept.[68]

---

[67] Morgan, *Roman Faith*, 472.

[68] Morgan, *Roman Faith*, 13. Likewise Downing: "Faith, belief, trust, and . . . faithfulness and trustworthiness cannot be separated. . . . To clear every use [Paul] made of πίστις, πιστεύω of overtones of faithfulness, faithful trust lived out in faithful behaviour, would have been nigh on impossible. The terms in ancient use were too rich, the ideas they would evoke too readily elicited together. It is not appropriate for

From a relevance-theoretical perspective, Morgan is in a sense correct that "the multivalency of *pistis/fides* language is constantly exploited wherever it is used."[69] Morgan's practice, however, shows that a monosemic approach might make better sense of the realities. Rather than labeling such exploitation *polysemy* (which implies selecting from a variety of lexical "options," even if one is aware of bleed and ambiguity), it is better to recognize that this exploitation is precisely at the heart of *monosemy*, properly understood.

For instance, Morgan regularly discusses matters in terms of polysemy,[70] but must then strain to explain her results: "Sometimes the most satisfactory interpretation of a passage will depend on there being more than one meaning involved. . . . *Pistis* and *fides* are nouns derived from verbs which abandon distinctions of transitivity. . . . We might assume that active and passive meanings cannot be in play at the same time, but in practice they often are."[71] Indeed, πίστις (like many other Greek and Latin terms) can be described as an "action nominal" that encompasses both active and passive meanings of its cognate verb.[72] For Morgan's actual findings, however, a monosemic approach would allow her to speak with greater confidence of the significance of the fact that both "trust" and "trustworthiness" are regularly implicated in Paul's construction. She writes the following in her consideration of πίστις in Galatians:

> Paul uses the language of *pistis* . . . to capture his sense of the doubly reciprocal relationship of Christ with God and humanity, his sense of the place of Christ in the overarching relationship between God and humanity, and his sense of the quality of Christ, his faithfulness, trustworthiness, and trustedness by God and human beings, which makes his saving activity possible. No other term in Greek

us to impoverish in Paul's writing something his text sees fit to retain in its ordinary richness" ("Ambiguity," 158–59).

[69] Morgan, *Roman Faith*, 273.

[70] E.g., "In many passages . . . we will talk of multiple meanings being in play" (Morgan, *Roman Faith*, 30).

[71] Morgan, *Roman Faith*, 30–31.

[72] See further B. Comrie and S. Thompson, "Lexical Nominalization," in *Language Typology and Syntactic Description*, vol. 3, 2nd ed., ed. T. Shopen (Cambridge: Cambridge University Press), 334–76.

could have captured the nature and complexity of this quality and relationship in the same way.[73]

Further, after discussing the centrality of "trust" to the concept of *pistis/ fides*, Morgan describes how social interactions such as the administration of a "trust" or delivery of an emperor's letter participate in a web of social interactions. She concludes that "new meanings of *pistis* and *fides* evolve."[74] Thus, Morgan shows that Paul has effectively *shaped* the term:

> Paul use[s] *pistis* language in some distinctive ways. . . . What is clear is that it resonates with a wide range of common operations of *pistis* and *fides* in the world around him, and so may have been intuitively easy for first-century listeners, whether Greek, Roman, or Jewish, to understand. The process of developing this model also leads Paul to *develop his use of pistis* in some other passages: not dramatically, but in ways which will significantly shape later Christian thinking. In places in these letters the relationship of divine–human trust becomes something more like a bond of trust, a community of trust, the assurance created by the sacrifice of Christ. . . . This *gradual semantic shift* will lead to Christians defining the nature of their community, the content of its proclamation, and eventually the cult itself by the name *hē pistis*.[75]

This gets to the heart of another aspect of discourse that is best explained in terms of monosemy: the constant *shaping* of words (and thereby readers) that occurs in a given discourse. If we speak in terms of polysemy, senses (even if there are many of them) remain fixed (*faith*, *faithfulness*, and so on.). A single grab-bag for πίστις, by contrast, is never static, and is inherently and radically shaped by the surrounding discourse.[76] The most promising attempts to account for

---

[73] Morgan, *Roman Faith*, 272–73.

[74] Morgan, *Roman Faith*, 21.

[75] Morgan, *Roman Faith*, 305, emphasis added.

[76] Whether words contribute *little* or *no* semantic input to meaning is vigorously debated. For our purposes in establishing relevance theory as a framework for reading Paul, it still seems useful to acknowledge that individual words carry something with them (discrete words exist, for one thing, and the standard tools for grammar and lexicography are still indispensable, even if subject to revision). For a recent treatment

the meaning of πίστις gesture toward just such "shaping," but because of the assumption of polysemy, they stop short of describing matters in these terms.[77] Matlock can speak of "selecting," Downing can speak of "activating," but both of these are limited to semantic inputs. From a cognitive perspective, the items activated from the grab-bag include a wider range of associations, such as the kind of trust associations brought to the fore in Morgan's study.

In the chapters that follow, we will demonstrate that a relevance-theoretical approach to the πιστ- word group in the Pauline literature helps illumine our reading of the πίστις Χριστοῦ construction, not least by drawing attention to the *shaping* of the term that occurs in a given letter and by eliminating the perceived need to *disambiguate* between lexical choices.[78] In the process, we also aim to demonstrate that in each instance in the Pauline letters in which πίστις is an action or attribute of Christ, the one who is faithful to those who place their trust in him is not merely the earthly Jesus who suffered and died on the cross but also the risen and exalted Lord.

---

of encoded semantic meaning (specifically, a referentialist account of the content and an atomistic account of concepts), see Jerry A. Fodor, *LOT 2: The Language of Thought Revisited* (Oxford: Clarendon Press, 2008). For the eliminativist view, see Rayo, "Plea," 647–79; see also Carston's discussion of the relevance-theoretic conception of linguistic semantics (*Thoughts and Utterances*, 56–57).

[77] For example, Shuji Ota rightly laments that the various nuances of πίστις cannot be expressed by a single equivalent term in English but then expresses that in Japanese it is possible because there is a "polysemous word" that more closely encompasses the various nuances of the Greek term ("Absolute Use of ΠΙΣΤΙΣ and ΠΙΣΤΙΣ ΧΡΙΣΤΟΥ in Paul," *AJBI* 23 [1997]: 72).

[78] This approach sharply diverges from the recent claims of Kevin W. McFadden, who argues for a clear distinction between the "meanings" of πίστις in Paul ("Does Πίστις Mean 'Faith[Fulness]' in Paul?" *TynBul* 66 [2015]: 251–70).

2

PHILIPPIANS
"To Know Him and the Power of His Resurrection"

In Phil 3:8-9 Paul expresses his hope that he might "gain Christ and be found in him, not having a righteousness of my own that comes from law but a righteousness that comes through the faithfulness of Christ, the righteousness from God on the basis of faithfulness." Within the debate about the meaning of the phrase πίστις Χριστοῦ in the undisputed letters of Paul, the concise reference to Christ's πίστις in Phil 3:9 often takes a backseat to the seemingly more substantive discussions found in Galatians and Romans.[1] There is good reason for this scholarly focus on passages from Galatians and Romans, for among the πίστις Χριστοῦ constructions in the undisputed letters, Phil 3:9 does stand in "greater isolation" when compared to the clustering of the πίστις lexicon in Galatians 2 and Romans 1–3.[2] In this chapter, we ourselves will adopt the position that the language

---

[1] See the helpful orientation in Paul Foster, "Πίστις Χριστοῦ Terminology in Philippians and Ephesians," in *The Faith of Jesus Christ: Exegetical, Biblical, and Theological Studies*, ed. Michael F. Bird and Preston M. Sprinkle (Peabody, Mass.: Hendrickson, 2009), 91–109, esp. 94.

[2] Foster, "Πίστις Χριστοῦ," 94. Morgan similarly suggests that "it is possible to take a view of [the meaning of *pistis* language in Philippians 3] by comparison with Galatians and Romans, but it would be difficult to develop a view based on this letter alone" (Teresa Morgan, *Roman Faith and Christian Faith:* Pistis *and* Fides *in the Early Roman Empire and Early Churches* [Oxford: Oxford University Press, 2015], 263).

of πίστις in Phil 3:9 can be fruitfully interpreted in light of material
from Paul's letter to the church in Rome, regardless of the question
of the chronological order of Philippians and Romans.[3] Yet it is also
the case that a relevance-theoretical framework used in analyzing the
πίστις lexicon in Philippians, prior to and including its usage in 3:9,
can make an important contribution to the conversation, for such an
analysis will problematize the common limitation of πίστις in 3:9 to
Christ's faithful and obedient death.

To be clear, in this chapter (and throughout the book) we are not
arguing that the phrase διὰ πίστεως Χριστοῦ in Phil 3:9 refers, subjectively, to Christ's own πίστις. It is not the burden of this chapter to
make the case for a subjective genitive in Phil 3:9, for such an argument
has been made, convincingly in our view, by others.[4] We shall assume
that the locution διὰ πίστεως Χριστοῦ in Phil 3:9 indicates that, in
some way, God's righteousness is made known or available through
Christ's πίστις. What we aim to question, however, is the common
assumption that Christ's πίστις in Phil 3:9 is manifested exclusively
in his death. Instead, we argue that the faithfulness of Christ through
which righteousness comes is the faithfulness of the risen and exalted
Christ.

---

[3] In point of fact, we are inclined toward the view that Philippians, as a unified
literary composition, was written before Romans, although such a position does not
significantly affect our interpretation of either letter; for a discussion, see Douglas A.
Campbell, *Framing Paul: An Epistolary Biography* (Grand Rapids: Eerdmans, 2014),
122–54.

[4] Notably: Pierre Vallotton, *Le Christ et la foi: Etude de théologie biblique*, Nouvelle
série théologique 10 (Geneva: Labor et Fides, 1960), 85–91; Foster, "Πίστις Χριστοῦ,"
93–100; Markus Bockmuehl, *The Epistle to the Philippians*, BNTC (London: A&C
Black, 1997), 206–13; Douglas A. Campbell, *The Deliverance of God: An Apocalyptic
Rereading of Justification in Paul* (Grand Rapids: Eerdmans, 2009), 897–911; Thomas
Schumacher, *Zur Entstehung christlicher Sprache: Eine Untersuchung der paulinischen
Idiomatik und der Verwendung des Begriffes* πίστις, BBB 168 (Göttingen: V&R unipress; Bonn: Bonn University Press, 2012), 446–60; Morgan, *Roman Faith*, 302–4. For
a thorough argument on behalf of the view that the phrase διὰ πίστεως Χριστοῦ
in Phil 3:9 should be understood as an objective genitive, see Karl Fredrich Ulrichs,
*Christusglaube: Studien zum Syntagma pistis Christou und zum paulinischen Verständnis
von Glaube und Rechtfertigung*, WUNT 2/227 (Tübingen: Mohr Siebeck, 2007), 222–47.

PAUL'S ΠΙΣΤ- LANGUAGE IN PHILIPPIANS 1–2

From a relevance-theoretical perspective, it is necessary to consider how πίστις and its cognates are employed in Philippians prior to the twice-repeated use of the noun in 3:9. Admittedly, the terminology is not used with great frequency in the letter.[5] Fortunately, however, a cluster of πιστ- terms in 1:25-29 and a singular instance in 2:17 shed light on how the discourse has shaped the terminology by the time of its appearance in 3:9.[6]

Philippians 1:25

After the imprisoned Paul (Phil 1:7, 13, 14, 17) wrestles with the possibility of his own death—weighing the advantage of dying against the fruit of his ministry for others, including the Philippians, through the continuation of his life (1:21-23)—Paul concludes that "to remain in the flesh is more necessary" for his readers (1:24). Although a departure to be with Christ might be better for Paul (1:23), the apostle's concession that he will remain in this life for the sake of the Philippians is of a piece with the emphasis on self-giving, other-centered love throughout the epistle (1:24-25; cf. 2:3-11; 2:19-24; 2:25-30; 4:10-18).[7] Convinced that he will not pursue death, Paul indicates that he will "remain and continue with all of you *for your progress and joy in the faith* (εἰς τὴν ὑμῶν προκοπὴν καὶ χαρὰν τῆς πίστεως), so that, because of me, your confidence in Christ Jesus might overflow when I am present

---

[5] Πίστις is found in Phil 1:25, 27; 2:17; and 3:9 (twice); πιστεύω occurs in 1:29.

[6] To consider the cluster in 1:25-29 is not to suggest that 1:25-29 is itself a coherent textual unit. A helpful division of the letter is proposed by Loveday Alexander ("Hellenistic Letter-Forms and the Structure of Philippians," *JSNT* 37 [1989]: 87–101): Phil 1:12-26 offers reassurance about Paul and 1:27–2:18 requests reassurance about the recipients of the letter. See also Christof Landmesser, "Der paulinische Imperativ als christologisches Performativ: Eine begründete These zur Einheit von Glaube und Leben im Anschluß an Phil 1,27–2,18," in *Jesus Christ als die Mitte der Schrift: Studien zur Hermeneutik des Evangiums*, ed. C. Landmesser, H. J. Eckstein, H. Lichtenberger, BZNW 86 (Berlin: de Gruyter, 1997), 543–77.

[7] See N. Clayton Croy, "'To Die Is Gain' (Philippians 1:19-26): Does Paul Contemplate Suicide?" *JBL* 122 (2003): 517–31.

with you again" (1:25).[8] The genitive τῆς πίστεως here can refer subjectively to the Philippians' own practice of πίστις (cf. 1:29, τὸ εἰς αὐτὸν πιστεύειν) or objectively to the content of their trust (cf. 1:27, τῇ πίστει τοῦ εὐαγγελίου). Because both elements of πίστις are activated in the ensuing uses of the lexeme in 1:27 and 1:29, it may well be the case that both associations are present in the phrase "for your progress and joy in the faith" in 1:25: Paul's continuing presence will help the Philippians to advance and rejoice in their own πίστις (1:29), a πίστις characteristic of the gospel message that they have received (1:27).[9] Moreover, as Paul goes on to indicate, the purpose of this progress and joy in πίστις is that, on account of Paul (ἐν ἐμοί), the Philippians might grow in their confidence in the risen Christ Jesus (1:26), a goal that links their shared joy and progress in πίστις with an increase in their communal trust in the risen Lord.[10]

Philippians 1:27

At the beginning of the opening exhortation of the letter (1:27–2:18), the language of πίστις is featured again. Paul initially charges his readers, "Only let your civil conduct be worthy of the gospel of Christ, so that, whether I come and see you or am absent and hear about you, it will be evident that you are standing in one spirit, with one mind training together in the faithfulness of the gospel" (1:27).[11] Paul's instruction

---

[8] The accusative nouns προκοπήν and χαράν are both governed by the prepositional phrase εἰς τὴν ὑμῶν, and the genitive τῆς πίστεως qualifies both nouns (so Gordon D. Fee, *Paul's Letter to the Philippians*, NICNT [Grand Rapids: Eerdmans, 1995], 154–55; cf. Phil 2:19; 2 Thess 2:17). This translation understands the prepositional phrase ἐν Χριστῷ Ἰησοῦ to modify the noun καύχημα; see Constantine R. Campbell, *Paul and Union with Christ: An Exegetical and Theological Study* (Grand Rapids: Zondervan, 2012), 104.

[9] So Bockmuehl, *Epistle to the Philippians*, 94; G. Walter Hansen, *The Letter to the Philippians*, PNTC (Grand Rapids: Eerdmans, 2009), 91.

[10] As Fee observes, the noun καύχημα "has to do first with putting 'one's trust or confidence in' something or someone and thus, second, in 'glorying' in that someone or something" (*Paul's Letter to the Philippians*, 154).

[11] We have translated τῇ πίστει τοῦ εὐαγγελίου as a dative of *sphere*, indicating the view that it is in the realm of the gospel's faithfulness that the Philippians train together. A case can be made that τῇ πίστει τοῦ εὐαγγελίου is instead a dative of

in 1:27a for the Philippians to live worthily of the gospel hearkens back to the first reference to "the gospel" in the letter—namely, Paul's thanksgiving for the Philippians' "partnership in the gospel" in 1:5. Although Paul does not provide a clear definition of "the gospel" in the letter to the Philippians—unlike, say, in the creedal statements in 1 Cor 15:1-8 and Rom 1:1-4—elsewhere in the letter "the gospel" is something in which Paul and his readers share (Phil 1:5; 2:22; 4:3), something defended and confirmed in connection with God's grace (1:7, 16), and something advanced from a beginning point (1:12; 4:15).[12] Thus, there is a marked emphasis in Philippians on activity associated with the sharing and advancement of the gospel.[13] Elsewhere in the letter, Paul alludes to himself and others boldly and without fear speaking the "word" (λόγος, 1:14) and urges the Philippians to "hold forth the word of life (λόγον ζωῆς ἐπέχοντες) so that I can boast on the day of Christ that I did not run in vain or labor in vain" (2:16).[14] The "word (of life)" that is the subject of this missionary activity should be seen as "a designation for the gospel message."[15] Elsewhere within

---

advantage, which is how most English language translations render the phrase (e.g., NIV: "striving together as one for the faith of the gospel").

[12] On 1 Cor 15:1-8 and Rom 1:1-4 as definitional statements, see Robert Matthew Calhoun, *Paul's Definitions of the Gospel in Romans 1*, WUNT 2/316 (Tübingen: Mohr Siebeck, 2011); on the importance of the gospel, mission, and preaching in Philippians, see James P. Ware, *The Mission of the Church in Paul's Letter to the Philippians in the Context of Ancient Judaism*, NovTSup 120 (Leiden: Brill, 2005), 165–71; Peter O'Brien, "The Importance of the Gospel in Philippians," *God Who Is Rich in Mercy*, ed. Peter O'Brien and David G. Peterson (Grand Rapids: Baker, 1986), 213–33; G. W. Peterman, *Paul's Gift from Philippi: Conventions of Gift Exchange and Christian Giving*, SNTSMS 92 (Cambridge: Cambridge University Press, 1997), 90–120.

[13] So Ware, *Mission of the Church*, 166: "Moreover, in most of these instances the word εὐαγγέλιον does not refer merely to the gospel message, but is a *nomen actionis* referring to the *gospel work*, the activity of extending the gospel. If one takes into account the references to preaching (e.g., τὸν λόγον λαλεῖν [1:14]; κηρύσσειν [1:15]; καταγγέλλειν [1:17, 18]) and other associated terms (e.g., 1:22; 2:25; 2:30; 3:2; 4:3; 4:17) in the letter, it is clear that Philippians reveals an extraordinary level of interest in the preaching of the gospel."

[14] Some manuscripts (א, A, B, D*, P, Ψ) read λογον του θεου in 1:14, whereas others read λογον κυριου (F, G). Yet P46, D², and K omit any qualifier.

[15] Ware, *Mission of the Church*, 270; cf. Christoph W. Stenschke, "'Holding Forth the Word of Life' (ΛΟΓΟΝ ΖΩΗΣ ΕΠΕΧΟΝΤΕΣ): Philippians 2:16A and Other

the letter, the so-called Christ hymn in 2:5-11 offers a narrative summary of key parts of Paul's gospel, and this story of good news centers
on Christ's earthly descent (2:6-7), his obedient death upon a cross
(2:8), and his heavenly exaltation (2:9-11).[16] Thus, while there is no
explicit definition of "the gospel" in Philippians, the εὐαγγέλιον proclaimed by Paul and his partners no doubt centered on a narrative of
Jesus' incarnation and earthly life, his crucifixion, and his exaltation.

Interpreters have often puzzled over the unusual expression
ἡ πίστις τοῦ εὐαγγελίου at the end of Phil 1:27, a phrase that is typically rendered "the faith of the gospel" (English Standard Version
[ESV], NIV, NRSV). Proposals have maintained that the genitive τοῦ
εὐαγγελίου is objective ("human πίστις in the gospel"), appositional
("faith that is the gospel"), or descriptive ("gospel-faith").[17] We would
like to suggest, however, that here Paul is referring to the faithfulness
(or trust-relationship) that is characteristic of the gospel message itself,
a message centered on the narrative of the death, resurrection, and
exaltation of the Messiah.[18] That is, for Paul the gospel message of

---

References to Paul's Understanding of the Involvement of Early Christian Communities in Spreading the Gospel," *JECH* 3 (2013): 61–82.

[16] Michael J. Gorman has called Phil 2:6-11 Paul's "master story": "not only the
most fundamental and significant telling of the Christ-story itself, but also the controlling narrative of his own existence," as well as "the controlling narrative for life in
Christ for all believers, both individually and corporately, and it is such both for their
internal life together and for their external, public life in the world" (*Becoming the
Gospel: Paul, Participation, and Mission*, GOC [Grand Rapids: Eerdmans, 2015], 62).

[17] After considering the possibility that the phrase is either an objective, appositional, or subjective genitive, Hansen states, "Since the differences between these
options are not really substantial, it may not be necessary to make a distinction
between them" (*Letter to the Philippians*, 98). John C. Poirier's claim that πίστις in
Phil 1:27 means "stewardship" rests on an assumption of lexical polysemy, and Poirier's
assertion that πίστις should be rendered "stewardship" in Rom 12:3, 6 is unconvincing
("The Meaning of Πίστις in Philippians 1:27," *ExpTim* 123 [2012]: 334–37). Yet Poirier
does helpfully draw attention to a number of Pauline texts in which a passive form of
the verb πιστεύω is employed in connection with oversight or entrusting of the gospel
(Gal 2:7; 1 Thess 2:4; 1 Tim 1:11; cf. Rom 3:2; 1 Cor 9:17; Titus 1:3; Luke 16:11).

[18] Thus, we read τοῦ εὐαγγελίου as a subjective genitive; cf. the phrase διὰ τῆς
πίστεως αὐτοῦ in Eph 3:12. Christopher Zoccali has also recently interpreted the
phrase ἡ πίστις τοῦ εὐαγγελίου in Phil 1:27 as a subjective genitive, arguing that
"the faithfulness of the gospel" in 1:27 is "both enabled by and the very manifestation

Christ's crucifixion, God's raising of Jesus from the dead, and Christ's heavenly exaltation is a message of faithfulness or trustworthiness.

That Paul in 1:27 refers to the faithfulness that characterizes the gospel itself can be seen in a related and equally important question—namely, the role of the participle συναθλοῦντες ("training together") in 1:27 and its relationship to the dative phrase τῇ πίστει τοῦ εὐαγγελίου. The verb συναθλέω occurs in the New Testament only in Phil 1:27 and 4:3, and it is not commonly found in other ancient sources. Following the suggestion of BDAG, which avers that the verb reflects "military imagery," most English translations render the verb "strive/struggle together."[19] It is not at all clear, however, that ancient readers would have understood the term in such a conflictual way. Two recent studies have argued that the verb, especially in its literary context in Philippians, reflects athletic rather than military imagery.[20] Indeed, in the few instances in which συναθλέω occurs outside of the New Testament, it appears to communicate notions of mutual practice, or shared training, rather than martial conflict.[21] In Diodorus Siculus (first century BCE), for example, the historian writes with reference to Egyptian hieroglyphics that the system of writing expresses an intended concept "by means of the significance of the objects that

of God's *hesed* to Israel and the nations (cf. Phil 1:6; 2:13)" (*Reading Philippians after Supersessionism: Jews, Gentiles, and Covenant Identity*, NTAS [Eugene, Ore.: Cascade, 2017], 35). Morgan rightly notes that πίστις in 1:27 does not refer to the "content of the kerygma," per se, but rather to "'the relationship of trust' (or even the 'bond of trust') between God, Christ, and Christ's followers" that the kerygma proclaims (*Roman Faith*, 266).

[19] The NRSV, ESV, NIV, and New American Standard Bible (NASB) all translate the participle "striving side by side/together" in 1:27 and variations of "struggled beside" (NRSV), "labored side by side" (ESV), "shared my struggle" (NASB), and "contended at my side" (NIV) in 4:3. LSJ similarly suggests that συναθλέω is a synonym of συναγωνίζομαι and renders 4:3 "struggle together," although also LSJ offers a secondary gloss, "impress by practice upon," citing Diodorus Siculus 3.4.2.

[20] Bradley Arnold, *Christ as the Telos of Life: Moral Philosophy, Athletic Imagery, and the Aim of Philippians*, WUNT 2/371 (Tübingen: Mohr Siebeck, 2014), 160–71; Dominika Kurek-Chomycz, "Fellow Athletes or Fellow Solders? συναθλέω in Philippians 1.27 and 4.3," *JSNT* 39 (2017): 279–303.

[21] The argument here draws upon that of Bradley Arnold (*Christ as the Telos of Life*, 165–68), although Arnold does not consider the use of συναθλέω in Ignatius of Antioch.

have been copied and by a figurative meaning that has been impressed upon the memory by shared practice" (3.4.2).²² Similarly, Ignatius of Antioch, in his letter to Polycarp, employs the verb συναθλέω in a string of imperatives, all with the συν- prefix, that entreats unified obedience to the bishop, presbyters, and deacons: "Work together with one another, train together (συναθλεῖτε), run together, suffer together, rest together, and rise together as God's overseers and assistants and attendants" (Ign. Pol. 6.1).²³ Viewing συναθλέω as connoting athletic

---

²² The Greek text is ἀλλ' ἐξ ἐμφάσεως τῶν μεταγραφομένων καὶ μεταφορᾶς μνήμῃ συνηθλημένης.

²³ The Greek text is συγκοπιᾶτε ἀλλήλοις, συναθλεῖτε, συντρέχετε, συμπάσχετε, συγκοιμᾶσθε, συνεγείρεσθε, ὡς θεοῦ οἰκονόμοι καὶ πάρεδροι καὶ ὑπηρέται (Michael W. Holmes, *The Apostolic Fathers: Greek Texts and English Translations*, 3rd ed. [Grand Rapids: Baker, 2007], 266). That Ignatius immediately follows this athletic imagery with a military metaphor (6.2: "please the one whom you serve as soldiers, the one from whom you receive your wages; let none of you be found to be a deserter; let your baptism serve as a shield, your faith as a helmet, your love as a shield, your endurance as armor") is an indication that the metaphorical fields of athletics and martial conflict often overlap with one another. Also relevant, although the date of the material is disputed and probably late, are comments attributed to Aristophanes of Byzantium (third/second century BCE) but mediated by the fifth-century CE writer Timotheus of Gaza. In describing a doe's care for her fawns, the text states, "A female deer, therefore, gathers her offspring upon a steep slope, and she leads them to an uphill location, and she trains them for a run, and she, sweating with pleasure, takes part with them, and when they are laboring *she practices together with each one*" (ἔλαφος μὲν οὖν θήλεια τὰ τέκνα παραλαβοῦσα ἐπὶ κρημνοὺς ἄγει καὶ τόπους ἀνάντεις, καὶ γυμνάζει αὐτὰ πρὸς δρόμον, καὶ ἰδρώτων ἡδέως αὐτοῖς κοινωνεῖ, καὶ πονουμένοις παρ' ἕκαστα συναθλεῖ, *Historiae Animalium Epitome* 2.511); the text is from Spyridon Lambros, *Excerptorum Constantini de natura animalium libri duo. Aristophanis historiae animalium epitome subjunctis Aeliani Timothei aliorumque eclogis* (Berlin: Reimer, 1885). As Kurek-Chomycz comments on this passage, "We could almost envisage this deer as a teacher in a gymnasium, yet a teacher who not only makes sure that the ephebes prepare well for their civic responsibilities by sufficient exercise, but also participates in their toil" ("Fellow Athletes," 283n8). The noun συναθλητής is found in two inscriptions commemorating fellow-athletes: first, a decree of consolation commemorating deceased athlete Marcus Alfidius in Naples in 2 BCE (G. E. Bean, "Inscriptions of Elaea and Lebedus," *Belleten. Türk Tarih Kurumu* 29 [1965]: 585–97); second, a second-century (117–138 CE) honorific inscription from Aphrodisias remembers a certain Kallikrates, who is honored by an association of fellow athletes (*LBW* 1620 = *MAMA* 8.417). These inscriptions are discussed in Kurek-Chomycz, "Fellow Athletes," 295–96.

imagery also makes sense of Paul's use of the verb in Phil 4:3. Having framed his own pursuit of union with Christ in terms of a runner who strives for the finish line and the prize at the conclusion of the race (3:12-14; cf. 2:16), and having imaged the Philippians themselves as the reward that Paul will receive at the conclusion of his own race (4:1), Paul remembers that Euodia and Syntyche have "trained together with me in the gospel" (4:3, ἐν τῷ εὐαγγελίῳ συνήθλησάν μοι).²⁴ In both 1:27 and 4:3, therefore, the emphasis is not on the Philippians' shared struggle *for* the gospel but on their mutual training together *in* the gospel. Already in 1:5 Paul has referred to the Philippians' "partnership in the gospel" (ἐπὶ τῇ κοινωνίᾳ ὑμῶν εἰς τὸ εὐαγγέλιον) in such a way that indicates that the gospel is something in which believers participate. Later in the epistle it becomes clear that the "partnership" (κοινωνία) of the Philippians "in the gospel" was especially manifested in their material support of Paul's missionary work (cf. 2:25-30; 4:14-18).²⁵

With the parallels between Paul's (past) training together with Euodia and Syntyche "in the gospel" (ἐν τῷ εὐαγγελίῳ) and the locution συναθλοῦντες τῇ πίστει τοῦ εὐαγγελίου in 1:27, it seems likely that the dative τῇ πίστει indicates the realm in which the Philippians are to train together. Elsewhere, Paul will frame the gospel as "a sphere in which the power of salvation is operative" (e.g., 1 Cor 15:1-2; 2 Tim 2:9).²⁶ Yet τῇ πίστει in Phil 1:27 could also function as a dative of means, indicating that the Philippians are to join together in mutual

---

²⁴ As Arnold writes, "Paul uses the aorist form of the verb συναθλέω (which contrasts with the present participle used in 1:27) in calling attention to how these women once struggled as co-athletes in the gospel. Given how Paul has previously used athletic imagery in this epistle, the force of the verb is to emphasize how they were once struggling together in a contest to live virtuously, i.e. to live a life worthy of the gospel, pursuing Christ as the τέλος of life" (*Christ as the Telos of Life*, 209).

²⁵ See Julien M. Ogereau, "Paul's κοινωνία with the Philippians: *Societas* as a Missionary Funding Strategy," *NTS* 60 (2014): 360-78; Mark A. Jennings, *The Price of Partnership in the Letter of Paul to the Philippians: "Make My Joy Complete"*, LNTS 578 (London: Bloomsbury, 2018), 30-39.

²⁶ Robert L. Plummer, *Paul's Understanding of the Church's Mission: Did the Apostle Paul Expect the Early Christian Communities to Evangelize?* PBM (Eugene, Ore.: Wipf & Stock, 2006), 64.

practice by means of the gospel's faithfulness.[27] Readers of the letter would then be instructed to train together with one mind, empowered by the faithfulness that characterizes the gospel. Either way, it appears that the phrase τῇ πίστει τοῦ εὐαγγελίου in 1:27 denotes the faithfulness or trustworthiness characteristic of the gospel message—that is, the kerygma of Jesus' incarnation, death, resurrection, and exaltation.

Philippians 1:29

The final instance of the πιστ- word group in Philippians 1 is Paul's use of the verb πιστεύω in the explanatory clause in 1:29-30[28]: "For it has been graciously granted to you that for the sake of Christ you should not only trust in him (οὐ μόνον τὸ εἰς αὐτὸν πιστεύειν) but also suffer for his sake, since you are having the same struggle that you saw in me and now you hear that I still have." Here, as is the case elsewhere in the Pauline letters, the verb πιστεύω has human beings as its subject and Christ as its object, indicating that, however the phrase πίστις Χριστοῦ in Paul's epistles is to be interpreted, there can be no doubt that Paul does speak of humans expressing πίστις in or toward Jesus.[29] It should be noted, however, that in 1:29 the act of human πίστις in Christ is the result of God's gracious gift (ὑμῖν ἐχαρίσθη) for the sake of Christ. Moreover, the gift of trust in, or allegiance to, Christ for the sake of Christ is accompanied, in Paul's framing of the experience of the Philippians, by the divine gift of suffering for Christ as well (1:29b).

---

[27] It is difficult to understand why the CEB translates the phrase "as you struggle together to remain faithful to the gospel."

[28] It is grammatically possible that the antecedent of the pronoun ἥτις in 1:28 is πίστις from 1:28. If that is the case, then Paul would be stating that the faithfulness of the gospel is not evidence of the destruction of opponents in Philippi but is instead a sign of the salvation of the Philippians. Yet ἥτις may also be feminine because of its attraction to ἔνδειξις.

[29] This point is reiterated by Foster, "Πίστις Χριστοῦ," 98–99; cf. Matthew W. Bates, *Salvation by Allegiance Alone: Rethinking Faith, Works, and the Gospel of Jesus the King* (Grand Rapids: Baker Academic, 2017), 84. Other Pauline texts in which Christ is clearly the object of the verb πιστεύω include Rom 9:33; 10:11; Gal 2:16; Eph 1:13, 15; 1 Tim 1:16; for other texts that assume or refer to human πίστις in or toward Christ, see Rom 1:16; 3:22; 4:24; 10:4, 14; Gal 3:22; 1 Tim 3:13, 16; 2 Tim 1:12; Col 1:4; 2:5.

Paul does not here, as he will in 3:10 with reference to his own hope, speak directly of the Philippians' suffering as participation in the death of Christ. The Philippians suffer on behalf of Christ (ὑπὲρ αὐτοῦ), according to 1:29. Yet in the following verse Paul correlates his own struggles with those of the Philippians' (1:30), and this connection comes in a letter in which the apostle has already framed his own difficult imprisonment as taking place "in Christ" (1:13), in which he summons readers to imitate the crucified Christ (2:4-11), and in which he will speak of his hope of sharing in Christ's sufferings (3:10, τὴν κοινωνίαν τῶν παθημάτων αὐτοῦ).[30] It is reasonable to assume, therefore, that when the Philippians suffer *for* Christ they also suffer *with* Christ, a point that highlights the connection in 1:29-30 among πίστις, suffering, and participation in Christ.

Philippians 2:17

There is one additional instance of πίστις in Philippians before 3:9. At the end of the exhortation that runs from 1:27 to 2:18, Paul urges his readers to be glad and rejoice with him in spite of his own suffering: "But even if I am being poured out like a drink offering upon the sacrifice and service coming from your faithfulness (τῆς πίστεως ὑμῶν), I am glad and rejoice with all of you, and in the same way you also should be glad and rejoice with me" (2:17-18). The cultic imagery suggests that the Philippians themselves make an offering (θυσία καὶ λειτουργία) and Paul is prepared to have his own life poured out as a drink offering upon the sacrifice of the Philippians.[31] Paul's later comments, using similar sacrificial language, in 2:25-30 and 4:14-18 indicate

---

[30] For a thoughtful exploration of the differences between suffering "in Christ" and "with Christ" in Philippians in comparison with other letters from Paul, see L. Ann Jervis, *At the Heart of the Gospel: Suffering in the Earliest Christian Message* (Grand Rapids: Eerdmans, 2007), 37–62.

[31] See the discussion in Xavier Paul B. Viagulamuthu, *Offering Our Bodies as a Living Sacrifice: A Study in Pauline Spirituality Based on Romans 12,1*, TGSS 7 (Rome: Editrice Pontificia Universita Gregoriana, 2002), 281–84. The genitive τῆς πίστεως ὑμῶν, therefore, should be seen as a genitive of source (so Fee, *Paul's Letter to the Philippians*, 255; Hansen, *Letter to the Philippians*, 189).

that the nature of the Philippians' πίστις-inspired sacrifice and service consisted of their material support for him.

Summary of Paul's Πιστ- Language in Philippians 1–2

Summing up Paul's shaping of the term πίστις and its cognate πιστεύω prior to Phil 3:9, we may conclude (1) that πίστις is characteristic of the gospel, a message centered on the good news of Jesus' incarnation, life, death, resurrection, and exaltation (1:25, 27; cf. 2:5-11); (2) that πίστις is collocated with the Philippians' shared confidence in the risen Jesus (1:26); (3) that the divine gift of trusting in Christ is necessarily accompanied by suffering for (and presumably with) Christ (1:29); and (4) that the faithfulness of the Philippians has generated sacrificial care and material support for the apostle Paul in the course of his missionary labors (2:17; cf. 4:14-18).

Additionally, one negative yet important conclusion emerges from this consideration of the contextual shaping of the πιστ- word group prior to chapter 3. It is nowhere evident that a "sense" of "obedience" is activated by πίστις or its cognates in the letter. That is, in spite of frequent claims among those who favor lexical polysemy that "obedience" is one of the "senses" that can be disambiguated from the lexeme πίστις, a contextual consideration of the terminology in Philippians does not indicate that "obedience" is part of the ad hoc meaning construction associated with πιστ- language in the letter.[32] Pragmatically, this will

---

[32] On the relationship between faith and obedience in Philippians, for example, Bockmuehl writes, "And just as in Romans the believers' *hupakoe pisteós* ('obedience of faith': 1.5; cf. 10.16; 15.18; 16.19, 26) could be said to derive from Christ's own *pistis* (3.22, 26) and *hupakoé* (5.19), it is not unreasonable in Philippians to link Christ's *pistis* (3.9) and being *hupékoos* (2.8) with those same qualities in the believers (1.25, 27, 29; 2.12, 17; 3.9)" (*Epistle to the Philippians*, 211). The difficulty with Bockmuehl's claim is that, whereas Paul explicitly speaks of the "obedience of faith" in Rom 1:5 and 16:26 and connects the verb ὑπακούω with πιστεύω in Rom 10:16 (although not in Rom 15:18 or 16:19), no such lexical connection is made between the ὑπακο- word group and the πιστ- word group in any of the texts from Philippians that Bockmuehl cites. Similarly, in commenting on the meaning of the reference to Christ's faithfulness in Phil 3:9, Thomas D. Stegman writes, "In the first strophe of the Christ hymn (2:6-8), Paul has already revealed what he means by Jesus' faithfulness. Most fundamentally, it refers to Jesus' obedience to God, the obedience that led to his offering his life on

mean that a reader formed by Paul's use of πίστις and πιστεύω in the letter prior to 3:9 is not likely to associate the phrase διὰ πίστεως Χριστοῦ with the clear reference to Jesus' obedience to the point of death in 2:8. That is not to say that the "Christ hymn" in 2:5-11 has no significance for the phrase διὰ πίστεως Χριστοῦ in 3:9, however. To the extent that 2:5-11 offers a narrative recapitulation of Paul's gospel, a story marked by "faithfulness," as we have seen, it may well be the case that the "Christ hymn" evokes the story of Christ's πίστις. But there is no reason to single out the reference to Jesus' obedience in 2:8 as the full manifestation of Christ's πίστις. If Phil 2:5-11 is a summary of Paul's gospel, that particular narrative includes Christ's incarnation (2:6-7), passion (2:8), and heavenly exaltation (2:9-11). As we shall see when we turn to Phil 3:9, there is good reason to believe that among the elements of this gospel narrative, the phrase πίστις Χριστοῦ especially emphasizes the faithfulness of the risen and exalted Christ.

---

the cross. Jesus' fidelity to God, throughout his life and ministry, was accompanied by—indeed, was expressed by—his loving, humble servant-existence for the sake of others" ("Paul's Use of *Dikaio-* Terminology: Moving Beyond N. T. Wright's Forensic Interpretation," *TS* 72 [2011]: 496–524 [510]). See chapter 5 for our discussion of obedience and faith in Romans; among those who assert a connection or even an equivalence between faith and obedience in Paul's letters, see Luke Timothy Johnson, "Rom 3:21-26 and the Faith of Jesus," *CBQ* 44 (1982): 77–90; Richard B. Hays, "ΠΙΣΤΙΣ and Pauline Christology: What Is at Stake?" in *Pauline Theology*, vol. 4: *Looking Back, Pressing On*, ed. E. Elizabeth Johnson and David M. Hay, SymS 4 (Atlanta: Scholars, 1997), 35–60. The assumption that πίστις in Paul's letters means "obedience" can be traced at least as far back as Bultmann: "Paul understands faith primarily as obedience; he understands the act of faith as an act of obedience" (*Theology of the New Testament*, trans. Kendrick Grobel, 2 vols. [1951, 1955; repr., Waco, Tex.: Baylor University Press, 2007], 1:314; cf. Markus Barth, "Faith of the Messiah," *HeyJ* 10 [1969]: 366). Benjamin Schliesser helpfully points out that while Paul does speak of Christ's obedience in Phil 2:5-11 and Rom 5:15-21, Paul never refers to Christ's πίστις in these contexts ("Glauben und Denken im Hebräerbrief und bei Paulus: Zwei frühchristliche Perspektiven auf die Rationalität des Glaubens," in *Glaube: Das Verständnis des Glaubens im frühen Christentum und in seiner jüdischen und hellenistisch-römischen Umwelt*, ed. Jörg Frey, Benjamin Schliesser, and Nadine Ueberschaer, WUNT 373 [Tübingen: Mohr Siebeck, 2017], 503–60, esp. 544–48).

"A RIGHTEOUSNESS THAT COMES THROUGH THE FAITHFULNESS OF CHRIST": PHILIPPIANS 3:9

Assuming that the phrase διὰ πίστεως Χριστοῦ in Phil 3:9 describes a πίστις demonstrated by or characteristic of Christ himself, we find good reason to believe that πίστις in 3:9 refers not primarily to Jesus' faithfulness upon the cross but to the continued faithfulness of the risen and exalted Christ.

Paul begins a new section in Phil 3:2 by warning his readers about opponents whom he stamps as "dogs," "those who work evil," and "the mutilation" (3:2; cf. 1:15-17, 28; 2:15; 3:18-19). These polemical labels, followed by an affirmation that "it is *we* who are the circumcision" (3:3), suggest that in this present context Paul is concerned about the real or potential influence of Christ followers who might insist that gentile converts observe Torah, similar to the distress that prompted the apostle's letter to the Galatians.[33] Following a litany of benefits that might provide him reason to boast in his own ethno-religious identity (3:4-6), Paul rejects all of these inherited and achieved advantages, having "written off all such assets because of Christ" (3:7 Revised English Bible, rev.).

Paul then compares the loss of his previous identity with the surpassing worth of gaining Christ:

> More than that, I even regard everything as a loss because of the supreme value of knowing Christ Jesus my Lord. For his sake I have forfeited all things, and I regard them as trash, in order that I might gain Christ and be found in him, not having a righteousness of my

---

[33] The literature on Paul's opponents in Philippians is voluminous; for a basic overview of the options, see Hansen, *Letter to the Philippians*, 28–30. Even if overall in Phil 3:2-21 "the opponents function rhetorically as a foil to the example of Paul and, together with reference to other references to hostile or rival groups, as a device which aims at strengthening the cohesion and commitment of the members of the group," the particular labels used by Paul in 3:2 and 3:18-19 suggest worry about those who advocate Torah-adherence for gentiles, whether these teachers had actually come to Philippi or not and regardless of their own ethno-religious identity or identities (David A. deSilva, "No Confidence in the Flesh: The Meaning and Function of Philippians 3:2-21," *TrinJ* 15 [1994]: 27–54 [52–53]; so also Schumacher, *Zur Entstehung christlicher Sprache*, 446–51).

own that comes from law but a righteousness that comes through the faithfulness of Christ, the righteousness from God depending on faithfulness to know[34] Christ and the power of his resurrection and the partnership of his sufferings by being conformed to his death, if somehow I might attain the resurrection from the dead. (3:8-11)

As has often been observed, Paul's statement in 3:9 consists of a basic contrast between (a) *my own righteousness that comes from law* and (b) *righteousness from God that comes through the faithfulness of Christ.*[35] Without entering here into a complicated discussion about the precise nature of these two juxtaposed types of righteousness, we may initially state that there is an opposition of righteousness from a human source or action, on one hand, and righteousness from a divine source or action, on the other.[36] As Douglas Campbell states about this passage:

[34] The translation here understands the articular infinitive τοῦ γνῶναι to be explanatory rather than expressing purpose (see Jean-François Collange, *L'épître de Saint Paul aux Philippiens*, CNT 10a [Neuchâtel: Delachaux & Niestlé, 1973], 116; N. T. Wright, *Paul and the Faithfulness of God*, COQG 4 [Minneapolis: Fortress, 2013], 988: "The genitive construction [*tou gnōnai auton*] at the start of verse 10 serves actually to *define* the 'faith' which receives the divine gift of the status of 'righteous' at the end of verse 9"). Morgan translates the construction τὴν ἐκ θεοῦ δικαιοσύνην ἐπὶ τῇ πίστει τοῦ γνῶναι αὐτὸν in a way that takes the infinitive as explanatory, although without a discussion of the grammar (*Roman Faith*, 303). Koperski, along with many other interpreters, rejects this position, reasoning that "if the infinitive phrase in v. 10 explains *faith*, then faith is being defined as an experience. For Paul, on the other hand, faith generally is associated with a conscious choice, based on knowledge of the God of Jesus Christ which comes through the preached word" (*The Knowledge of Jesus Christ My Lord: The High Christology of Philippians 3:7-11* [Kampen, Neth.: Kok Pharos, 1996], 145n34; so also Gerald F. Hawthorne, *Philippians*, WBC 43, rev ed. [Grand Rapids: Zondervan, 2004], 196–97). Koperski's assumption that faith is "conscious choice" and not "an experience" is problematized by a relevance-theoretical consideration of πίστις in Philippians and elsewhere in the Pauline letters.

[35] See Veronica Koperski, "The Meaning of δικαιοσύνη in Philippians 3:9," *LS* 20 (1995): 147–69 [148].

[36] See Campbell's discussion in *The Deliverance of God*, 897–911; Schumacher, *Zur Entstehung christlicher Sprache*, 451–56. Given the function of the participle ἔχων and its implied repetition before the clause τὴν διὰ πίστεως Χριστοῦ, with δικαιοσύνη as its object in both cases, it is difficult to see how righteousness here in the second instance is not a divine gift from God received by those who are joined in union with Christ; see Charles Lee Irons, *The Righteousness of God: A Lexical Examination of the*

It can be said that the surrounding emphases on an act of God operating through Christ, over against any human activity located in and oriented by the flesh—a divine act that renders that human activity in comparative terms as the equivalent of excrement (if not *as* excrement)—incline us strongly to read the "righteous act[ivity]" and "fidelity" of v. 9 precisely *as* the act of God in Christ over against any nomistic activity of the flesh (that is, rooted in the capacities of the created and sinful human person). That act through the faithful Christ is explicated directly, in the same sentence, in participatory terms, as a sharing in his suffering and death en route to a sharing in his glorious resurrection.[37]

Campbell's observation helpfully highlights the extent to which Christ's πίστις in 3:9 is connected to the experience of participation in him. Indeed, if the infinitive τοῦ γνῶναι in 3:10 explicates πίστις from the clause τὴν ἐκ θεοῦ δικαιοσύνην ἐπὶ τῇ πίστει in 3:9b, Paul then defines "faithfulness" as knowing Christ, knowing the power of Christ's resurrection, and knowing the partnership of Christ's sufferings.[38] Πίστις, then, involves human knowledge of Christ (so 3:8), but for Paul such knowledge is only possible through participation in the resurrection and the death of Christ (3:10-11). This is a key reason that in 3:9 Christ's πίστις must be understood as directed primarily toward humanity, for it is Christ's faithfulness that enables human knowledge of him, human participation in the power of his resurrection, and human partnership in Christ's sufferings.[39]

Covenant-Faithfulness Interpretation, WUNT 2/386 (Tübingen: Mohr Siebeck, 2015), 327–29.

[37] Campbell, *Deliverance of God*, 907. Vallotton, too, emphasizes the relationship between participation in Christ's πίστις and justification: "Etre en Christ signifie ici avoir la justice qui vient de Dieu par la foi de Christ (διὰ πίστεως Χριστοῦ). Etre en Christ signifie donc être justifié" (*Le Christ et la foi*, 88).

[38] See note 34.

[39] *Pace* Vallotton (*Le Christ et la foi*, 88–89), who views Christ's πίστις as directed primarily toward God. Vallotton frames Christ's πίστις as divinely oriented because he understands "faith" and "obedience" to be the same and therefore connects Phil 3:9 with Phil 2:5-11. On the notion of Christ's πίστις as oriented *toward humanity*, see Shuji Ota, "The Holistic *Pistis* and Abraham's Faith (Galatians 3)," *HJAS* 57 (2016): 1–12; in our chapter on Galatians, we will agree with Ota's perspective on the orientation of Christ's πίστις toward humanity, but we will suggest that this extends beyond

If it is the case that the first occurrence of πίστις in 3:9 is christological (διὰ πίστεως Χριστοῦ), then Paul asserts that God's righteousness comes *through* the faith(fulness) of Christ.[40] With linguistic and thematic parallels with Gal 2:16 and Rom 3:22 (and possibly Rom 1:17), where Christ's πίστις creates the possibility of human πίστις, it is possible that the second instance of πίστις in Phil 3:9 also refers to human πίστις in Christ. Thus, Teresa Morgan interprets the phrase τὴν ἐκ θεοῦ δικαιοσύνην ἐπὶ τῇ πίστει in 3:9 as an affirmation of "Christ's faithfulness both towards God (in which God's trust and faithfulness towards Christ are also implicit) and towards human beings, which invokes human trust in both God and Christ."[41] Yet without denying the participatory dimensions of πίστις in this context, it is preferable to take the second occurrence of πίστις also as a reference to Christ's faithfulness. That is, the clause τὴν ἐκ θεοῦ δικαιοσύνην ἐπὶ τῇ πίστει is "an appositional expansion inserted to emphasize that *this* righteous activity comes from God, not humanity," repeating "the important preceding phrase with a small stylistic abbreviation and variation."[42] Morgan's interpretation imports too much into the present context, for there is little in 3:9-10 to suggest that Christ's faith is directed toward God and much to suggest that Christ's faith creates in those joined to him knowledge of Christ, the experience of his resurrection power, and conformity to his death.

As we have seen, based on the semantic shaping of the πιστ- word group in Philippians prior to chapter 3, there is no obvious reason that Christ's πίστις should be associated solely with his death upon the cross. In fact, in the immediate context of Paul's polemic against his

---

the *death* of Christ to the present faithfulness of the living Christ (cf. also Peter Oakes, "*Pistis* as Relational Way of Life in Galatians," *JSNT* 40 [2018]: 255–75 [269]).

[40] See the discussion in Foster, "Πίστις Χριστοῦ," 97–100.

[41] Morgan, *Roman Faith*, 304; so also Bockmuehl, who finds in Phil 3:9 a reference "to *two* kinds of faithfulness in relation to God's righteousness revealed in Christ: the instrumental faithfulness *of* Christ . . . (*dia pisteos Christou*), and the responding faithfulness of the believer (on the basis of faith, *epi té pistei*)" (*Epistle to the Philippians*, 211, emphasis original). There is no support for Campbell's decision to translate ἐπὶ τῇ πίστει as "on the basis of the faithful one [i.e., Christ]" (*Deliverance of God*, 906). Such a translation would require an entirely different Greek phrase (e.g., ἐπὶ τῇ πιστῷ).

[42] Campbell, *Deliverance of God*, 1169n26.

opponents and the apostle's reevaluation of his own previous identity prior to the "knowledge of Christ Jesus my Lord" in 3:1-11, Paul says nothing about Jesus' obedience and mentions Christ's death explicitly only after referring to Christ's resurrection and only in the context of the apostle's hope of sharing in Christ's sufferings and being conformed to the death of Christ on the way to resurrection from the dead (3:10-11).[43] Contextually, therefore, there is no justification for limiting the construction πίστις Χριστοῦ in 3:9 to a reference to Christ's faithful death. Instead, Christ's πίστις in 3:9 must be the πίστις of the risen and exalted Lord as that faithfulness is directed toward humans who share in his suffering, death, and resurrection.

Moreover, given Paul's contention in 3:9 that δικαιοσύνη is not his own but comes from God through Christ's πίστις, in the attempt to discern the content of Christ's πίστις and its relationship to God's righteousness in this verse, we may find assistance from Paul's letter to the church at Rome, where δικαιοσύνη from God is discussed in more detail. Often noted are the parallels between Phil 3:9 and Rom 10:3.[44] Yet a brief glance at Romans 1, together with a recent contribution to its interpretation by Joshua Jipp, offers insight into Phil 3:9 and will pave the way for a fuller discussion of God's righteousness and Christ's faithfulness in Romans in our chapter 5.

In his study of God's righteousness in Romans, Jipp draws attention to the fact that Paul declares in Rom 1:16-17 that the righteousness of God is revealed, in particular, in the gospel: "For in it (i.e., 'the gospel,' τὸ εὐαγγέλιον) the righteousness of God is revealed through faith for faith" (1:17).[45] Importantly, Paul defines "the gospel" at the very beginning of the letter (1:1-4), and in the introduction to Romans the gospel is a message focused on both the Davidic identity and the resurrection of Jesus:

> Paul, a slave of Jesus Christ, called to be an apostle, set apart for the gospel of God, which was promised beforehand through his prophets in the holy scriptures, the gospel concerning his Son, who

---

[43] Paul's opponents are identified as "enemies of the cross of Christ" in 3:18.

[44] See the discussion of Phil 3:9 and Rom 10:3 in Irons, *Righteousness of God*, 334–36.

[45] The antecedent of the pronoun αὐτῷ in Rom 1:17 is τὸ εὐαγγέλιον in 1:16.

was descended from David according to the flesh and was declared the Son of God with power according to the spirit of holiness by resurrection from the dead, Jesus Christ our Lord. (Rom 1:1-4)[46]

Paul's articulation of the gospel in 1:3-4 stresses "two *transitions* in the divine life of God's son, his coming into human existence in the line of David and his installation as 'Son-of-God-in-Power,' and it is especially these two transitions that are emphatically promised beforehand in the scriptures."[47] The reference to the declaration of the Jesus' divine sonship in 1:3-4, with God's agency implied in the passive participle τοῦ ὁρισθέντος, signals Jesus' "existence in an exalted postresurrection state, presumably in the heavenly realm" (cf. Phil 3:20-21; Rom 8:34; 2 Cor 4:14; Phil 2:9-11; Eph 1:20; Col 3:1).[48] Thus, the "gospel" in Rom 1:3-4 that was promised beforehand in the scriptures entails the announcement of Jesus' heavenly enthronement as Son-of-God-in-Power.[49]

According to the ensuing reference to "the gospel" in 1:16-17, then, God's righteousness is revealed in that gospel, a message of good news that involves the vindication of God's son through God's powerful act of resurrection and the installation of Christ to the office of "Son-of-God-in-Power." As Jipp summarizes his understanding of the relationship between the gospel and God's δικαιοσύνη in Romans:

---

[46] It is worth nothing that a definition of the gospel focused on Jesus' Davidic identity and Jesus' resurrection from the dead is also precisely what is found in 2 Tim 2:8: "Remember Jesus Christ, raised from the dead, a descendant of David—that is my gospel" (cf. Ign. *Smyrn.* 1.1; Matthew W. Bates, *The Hermeneutics of the Apostolic Proclamation: The Center of Paul's Method of Scriptural Interpretation* [Waco, Tex.: Baylor University Press, 2012], 82–83).

[47] Bates, *Hermeneutics*, 87.

[48] Bates, *Hermeneutics*, 87.

[49] Interestingly, in a famous definition of "Christian apocalyptic," Ernst Käsemann connects the revelation of God's righteousness with Christ's heavenly enthronement: "The heart of primitive Christian apocalyptic, according to the Revelation [of John] and the Synoptics alike is the accession to the throne of heaven by God and by his Christ as the eschatological Son of Man—an event which can also be characterized as proof of the righteousness of God" ("The Beginnings of Christian Theology," in *New Testament Questions of Today*, trans. W. J. Montague [London: SCM, 1969], 82–107 [105]).

God's righteousness is revealed and established over the people by means of resurrecting from the dead his righteous, faithful, and obedient Messiah, whose death had been an apocalyptic revelation of injustice. God's righteousness is on display, then, in this divine powerful activity to justify the one who is righteous, and this results in the formerly oppressed but now vindicated one having a status of righteousness, a status that is accompanied by God's actual rescue of the righteous one.[50]

We might also add that the resurrected Son is named "Jesus Christ our Lord" (1:4), with the Son's lordship implicitly linked with his heavenly exaltation at the right hand of the Father and his reign over the created order (Rom 8:34; 1 Cor 15:20-28; Eph 1:20-21; Col 3:1).

Jipp's perspective on Paul's treatment of God's righteousness at the beginning of Romans sheds light on the phrase "not having a righteousness of my own that comes from law but a righteousness that comes through the faithfulness of Christ, the righteousness from God depending on faithfulness" (μὴ ἔχων ἐμὴν δικαιοσύνην τὴν ἐκ νόμου ἀλλὰ τὴν διὰ πίστεως Χριστοῦ) in Phil 3:9. In contrast to righteous activity determined by law, and thus centered on human action, the righteous act of God comes *from* God and is effected through the faithfulness of Christ. Reading Phil 3:9 in light of Rom 1:1-4 and 1:16-17, we may suggest that it is the faithfulness of Christ that reveals God's δικαιοσύνη, and this revelation occurs through the gospel, which is a message that certainly includes Jesus' death but also centers on Jesus' resurrection from the dead. In the gospel narrative of Phil 2:5-11, resurrection is the implicit precursor to Jesus' heavenly enthronement (2:9-11; cf. 3:10-11). That is not to deny or minimize the importance of Jesus' incarnation (2:5-7) or his death (2:8) for Paul's gospel story in Philippians. The faithfulness of Christ certainly embraces these elements of the narrative. But the climax of the story is God's raising of Christ from the dead and God's installation of Christ as Lord of all. It is the faithfulness of the *risen* and *exalted* Lord Jesus that generates in Paul the hope of being found in Christ, of knowing Christ and his resurrection power, of partnering with Christ

---

[50] Joshua W. Jipp, *Christ Is King: Paul's Royal Ideology* (Minneapolis: Fortress, 2015), 215.

in suffering and being conformed to his death, and of attaining to the resurrection of the dead. It is not merely Christ crucified, but Christ risen and exalted who sustains this participatory hope: "I want to know Christ and the power of his resurrection and the partnership of his sufferings, becoming like him in his death, if somehow I may attain to the resurrection from the dead" (3:10-11). To limit the reference to Christ's πίστις in 3:9, therefore, to the faithful death of the human Jesus fails to appreciate the importance of Christ's resurrection and exaltation in the context of Paul's hope in 3:7-11.

Moreover, as Paul says later in Philippians 3, his eyes are on the "prize promised by God's heavenly call in Christ Jesus" (3:14). Here the phrase ἐν Χριστῷ Ἰησοῦ may be understood to indicate the cause or reason for God's call: "Paul pursues the prize that is grounded in God's call, which is issued *on account* of Christ."[51] The Christ on whose account God's heavenly call is issued is, in context, no doubt the resurrected and exalted Christ, for after summoning his readers to imitate him and his associates (3:17) and again warning the Philippians of false teachers (3:18-19), Paul reflects on the heavenly exaltation of Christ: "But our citizenship is in heaven, and it is from there (ἐξ οὗ) that we are expecting a Savior, the Lord Jesus Christ. He will transform our body characterized by humility so that it may be conformed to the body of his glory, by the power that also enables him to make all things subject to himself" (3:20-21).[52] Paul offers the hope that Christ followers who embrace the posture of humility that Paul has advocated in the letter (2:2-5) and that Christ demonstrated in his own incarnation and death (2:6-8) will be transformed by the power possessed by the exalted Christ. In this transformation, the Philippians will share in the glory and power of the exalted Savior. Paul, therefore, presents a vision of transformed bodily existence in which it is not merely the crucified

---

[51] Campbell, *Paul and Union with Christ*, 138 (emphasis original).

[52] This translation follows Peter Doble, "'Vile Bodies' or Transformed Persons? Philippians 3.21 in Context," *JSNT* 86 (2002): 3–27. Doble writes, "Jesus ἐταπείνωσεν ἑαυτὸν, consequently (διὸ καὶ) God exalted him (ὑπερύψωσεν). Because of this exaltation, the risen Lord's existence is spoken of as τὸ σῶμα τῆς δόξης αὐτοῦ (3.21) and it is to their participation *in*, their transformation *to* this body (σύμμορφον) that the Philippian saints are called, but for that they must first share Jesus' ταπείνωσις" (26–27, emphasis original).

body of Jesus but the glorious and ascended Lord, the ruler of all things, who is the source of hope for his readers in Philippi. It is this Christ—raised and exalted—whose πίστις makes available the righteousness of God.

CONCLUSION

We have assumed that the phrase διὰ πίστεως Χριστοῦ in Phil 3:9 refers to Christ's own πίστις. But we have differed from other interpreters who advocate a subjective genitive by suggesting that the faithfulness of Christ in 3:9 refers to the faithfulness of the risen and exalted Christ, whose resurrection makes possible God's righteousness for those united to him by πίστις. Importantly, an examination of πίστις and its cognates in Paul's letter to the church at Philippi from a relevance-theoretical perspective does not reveal any reason to limit Christ's πίστις to his death upon the cross. Indeed, the Christ whom Paul wishes to gain, the Christ in whom Paul hopes to be found, the Christ whose πίστις makes available God's righteousness is the resurrected and exalted Christ whose power makes all things subject to himself.

3

THE CORINTHIAN CORRESPONDENCE
"We Have the Same Spirit of Faithfulness"

In chapter 1, we argued that κύριος in 2 Thess 3:3 (πιστὸς δέ ἐστιν ὁ κύριος, "the Lord is faithful") refers specifically to Christ, rather than to God, even if we should not draw too fine a distinction between them in Paul's thought. In the Corinthian letters, to which we turn in this chapter, "Jesus is Lord" (1 Cor 12:3). Throughout these two epistles, Paul stresses the indissoluble bond between *God's faithfulness* (πιστὸς ὁ θεός, 1 Cor 1:9; πιστὸς . . . ὁ θεός, 2 Cor 1:18), *Christ* in whom God's promises are always kept (2 Cor 1:20), and *believers' union* with God in Christ (2 Cor 1:21). The burden of this chapter is to demonstrate that in the Corinthian letters Paul's concept and use of πίστις and its cognates assumes the risen and exalted "Christ the Lord" and not merely the crucified Jesus.

Paul's extended correspondence with the community he founded in Corinth receives relatively little attention in the context of the πίστις Χριστοῦ debate, owing to the fact that no form of the phrase occurs in these letters. Yet aspects of Paul's understanding of the faithfulness of the *risen* Christ are present in 1–2 Corinthians with particular clarity, and aspects more readily on display in other letters receive further confirmation in these missives to Corinth. Specifically, this chapter will show (1) that Paul develops the language of πίστις/πιστεύω (as well as the πειθ- lexicon) in ways that leave little doubt about the participatory, reciprocal, and relational understanding of πίστις that Paul sets out in the Corinthian letters; (2) that through this relationship, preserved by the ongoing faithfulness of the risen Christ, believers experience the faithfulness of God; and (3) that the citation of Ps 115:1 LXX in 2 Cor 4:13 not only presents a clear instance of Christ as the subject of the verb πιστεύω in Paul, but also shows that the faithful and believing Christ is none other than the risen and glorified Christ. For our project, the reference to Jesus' active πίστις in 2 Cor 4:13 is crucial, both because it locates Jesus' act of trust on the cross, which shows that the phrase πίστις Χριστοῦ cannot exclude the crucifixion, and because it demonstrates Paul's conviction that believers share "the same spirit of faithfulness" as the risen Christ through their participation in his story.

1 CORINTHIANS

There are twenty-one occurrences of the πιστ- word group in 1 Corinthians, plus an additional eleven instances of the adjective ἄπιστος describing those outside the community of faith.[1] The adjective πιστός occurs five times (1:9; 4:2, 17; 7:25; 10:13), the verb πιστεύω occurs nine times (1:21; 3:5; 9:17; 11:18; 13:7; 14:22 [twice]; 15:2, 11), and the noun πίστις occurs seven times (2:5; 12:9; 13:2, 13; 15:14, 17; 16:13).[2] In what follows, we will see that the image of *the enthroned Christ's faithfulness to believers* undergirds Paul's usage of πιστ- language throughout 1 Corinthians.

1 Corinthians 1:9 and 10:13: "God Is Faithful"

God is πιστός, Paul writes in 1 Cor 1:9 (cf. 10:13 and 2 Cor 1:18), and this faithful God calls believers into the fellowship of "Jesus Christ our Lord." The phrase "God is faithful" is repeated in 1 Cor 10:13, and this time God's faithfulness consists not only of *calling* believers,

---

[1] 1 Cor 6:6; 7:12, 13, 14 (twice), 15; 10:27; 14:22 (twice), 23, 24; see T. J. Lang, "Trouble with Insiders: The Social Profile of the Ἄπιστοι in Paul's Corinthian Correspondence," *JBL* 137 (2018): 981–1001.

[2] This compares with just eleven occurrences of the πιστ- word group in 2 Corinthians (plus three occurrences of ἄπιστος in 2 Cor 4:4; 6:14, 15). In 2 Corinthians, the adjective πιστός occurs two times (1:18; 6:15), the verb πιστεύω occurs two times (both in 4:13), and the noun πίστις occurs seven times (1:24 [twice]; 4:13; 5:7; 8:7; 10:15; 13:5).

but also of *sustaining* them through various "tests" (πειρασμοί): "He will not let you be tested beyond your strength, but he will also provide with the testing a way of escape, so that you are able to endure" (10:13). This statement echoes Num 21:4-9, when Israel was confronted with venomous snakes in the wilderness, and the Lord provided the bronze snake so that "all who have been bitten, having looked, shall *live*" (πᾶς ὁ δεδηγμένος ἰδὼν αὐτὸν ζήσεται, Num 21:8 LXX). Paul has already linked the desert experiences of Israel with *Christ* in 1 Cor 5:6-8 (Christ as the Paschal lamb) and 8:1-12 (the worship of idols is nothing because there is "one Lord, Jesus Christ," 8:6). Therefore, it is significant that just prior to the affirmation of God's continued faithfulness in 10:13, Paul uses the same language of "testing" in reference to Christ: "We must not put Christ to the test (ἐκπειράζωμεν)" (10:9).

At work in these verses, then, is a kind of christological conflation of the experiences of Israel and the believers in Corinth. One effect of this conflation is to merge the roles of God and Christ. The language of "testing" itself does not occur in the account in Numbers, so Paul's repeated use of the (ἐκ)πειρ- lexicon prompts a connection between the saying "God is faithful" and the faithfulness of *Christ* that is described using other language throughout the passage.[3] The verb ὑποφέρω ("to endure") is used only here (10:13) in the undisputed letters, but at least in 2 Timothy such endurance is understood to be enabled by the continued faithfulness of Christ: "Such persecutions I endured (ὑπήνεγκα), yet the Lord delivered me from them all" (3:11). Furthermore, in the next chapter of 1 Corinthians itself, "the Lord" is the faithful agent who preserves believers: "But when we are judged *by the Lord*, we are disciplined so that we may not be condemned along with the world" (11:32).[4]

---

[3] Psalm 77:18 LXX may refer to this event, and does use the language of "testing": "And they *tested* (ἐξεπείρασαν) God in their hearts"; cf. ἐκπειράζω also in Deut 6:16; 8:2, 16 LXX. On questions of Christology, ecclesiology, and typology in 1 Corinthians 10, Hays' treatment remains a classic (*Echoes of Scripture in the Letters of Paul* [New Haven: Yale University Press, 1989], 84–121).

[4] See Matthias Konradt, *Gericht und Gemeinde: Eine Studie zur Bedeutung und Funktion von Gerichtsaussagen im Rahmen der paulinische Ekklesiologie und Ethik im 1 Thess und 1 Kor*, BZNW 117 (Berlin: de Gruyter, 2003), 439–51.

1 Corinthians 2–9: Πίστις by the Power of God

Paul further develops this understanding of πίστις in the discourse that falls between the two overt references to God/Christ's faithfulness in 1 Cor 1:9 and 10:13. In 2:5 Paul reiterates that the Corinthians' faith relationship (ἡ πίστις ὑμῶν) is not "in/by" (ἐν) human wisdom, but is "in/by" (ἐν) the "power of God" (2:5).[5] Paul has just defined this power as *Christ* (Χριστὸν θεοῦ δύναμιν, 1:24), and at first glance it seems logical to refine further "the power of God" to mean "the message about the cross" (ὁ λόγος ὁ τοῦ σταυροῦ, 1:18).[6] Certainly the act of proclamation (λόγος/κήρυγμα) and the cross itself are crucial elements in Paul's understanding of the true nature of power.[7] Yet it is shortsighted to restrict what Paul is saying about the Corinthians' πίστις to the cross, because in what follows Paul is clear that the participatory relationship between Christ and the Corinthians depends on the resurrected and ascended Lord: "And God *raised* (ἤγειρεν) the Lord and will also *raise* (ἐξεγερεῖ) us by his power" (6:14).[8]

Such a focus on the ongoing faithfulness of the risen Jesus is evident in the way Paul makes use of the language of πίστις throughout chapters 1 through 9. The requirement of stewards of Christ is that they are "trustworthy" (πιστός, 4:2), as exemplified by both Timothy, who

---

[5] It is interesting to note that 1 Cor 2:5 has been absent from discussion of passages relating to Paul's "in Christ" motif (the verse is not cited in Constantine Campbell, *Paul and Union with Christ: An Exegetical and Theological Study* [Grand Rapids: Zondervan, 2012]; or Grant Macaskill, *Union with Christ in the New Testament* [Oxford: Oxford University Press, 2013]). BDAG (284) suggests that εἰμί plus ἐν in 1 Cor 2:5 indicates that faith does not "rest upon" or "arise from" wisdom, but we see little reason to distinguish this usage from similar instances in which Paul speaks of faith "in" Christ; e.g., πιστὸν ἐν κυρίῳ (1 Cor 4:17) (Frederick W. Danker, Walter Bauer, William F. Arndt, and F. Wilbur Gingrich [BDAG], *Greek-English Lexicon of the New Testament and Other Early Christian Literature,* 3rd ed. [Chicago: University of Chicago Press, 2000]).

[6] So Anthony C. Thiselton, *The First Epistle to the Corinthians,* NIGTC (Grand Rapids: Eerdmans), 172; Joseph A. Fitzmyer, *First Corinthians: A New Translation with Introduction and Commentary,* AB 32 (New Haven: Yale University Press, 2008), 160.

[7] See the useful discussion in Thiselton, *First Epistle,* 153–54.

[8] See Paul's continued emphasis on the power of the Lord Jesus in 1 Cor 4:19-20; 5:4. In 1 Cor 15:24 and 15:43 it is clear that Christ's power is the power of *resurrection*; see further discussion in the next section.

is "faithful in the Lord" (πιστὸν ἐν κυρίῳ, 4:17), and Paul himself, who "is trustworthy as one shown mercy by the Lord" (ὡς ἠλεημένος ὑπὸ κυρίου πιστὸς εἶναι, 7:25). Paul returns to this notion of a being a "steward" (οἰκονόμος) in speaking of being "entrusted" (πεπίστευμαι) with a "stewardship" (οἰκονομία) in 9:17. Here, too, Paul speaks of the relationship as one in which the living Christ actively places an obligation on him ("an obligation lays upon me," ἀνάγκη . . . μοι ἐπίκειται, 9:16), and in which Christ disciplines when this responsibility is not met ("woe to me if I do not proclaim the gospel!" 9:16).

1 Corinthians 11–16: "Stand Firm in Your Πίστις"

Following his second declaration of God's/Christ's faithfulness in 10:13, Paul continues to emphasize the active role of the exalted Christ in the life of the church.[9] In each instance, this role is manifested in the participatory relationship between Christ and the congregation: Paul encourages the Corinthians to become imitators of him as he is of Christ (καθὼς κἀγὼ Χριστοῦ, 11:1), and, most importantly, all relationships and ways of being are "in the Lord" (ἐν κυρίῳ, 11:11). Though the term πιστεύω occurs only once in chapter 11 (11:18, in reference to Paul's trust that the report of divisions is true), in the latter portion of chapter 11 "the risen Christ acts dramatically and concretely in the congregation, disciplining them to preserve them from the condemnation to come."[10] Christ's faithfulness can hardly be restricted to his death on the cross, given that part of his active faithfulness to believers includes judgment and discipline: "But when we are judged

[9] Also helpful on the participatory metaphors employed in this section of 1 Corinthians is Constantine R. Campbell, "Metaphor, Reality, and Union with Christ," in *"In Christ" in Paul: Explorations in Paul's Theology of Union and Participation*, ed. Michael J. Thate, Kevin J. Vanhoozer, and Constantine R. Campbell, WUNT 2/384 (Tübingen: Mohr Siebeck, 2014; repr., Grand Rapids: Eerdmans, 2018), 61–86.

[10] Peter Orr, *Christ Absent and Present: A Study in Pauline Christology*, WUNT 2/354 (Tübingen: Mohr Siebeck, 2014), 220–21. Orr helpfully shows the importance for Paul of the risen, bodily Jesus—thus Christ's presence is always *mediated* in various ways. In the case of 1 Corinthians 11, Orr points out that "even here where the presence of Christ has such dramatic, tangible effects, the absence of Christ means that this activity is still achieved through mediation in the form of sickness and death" (*Christ Absent and Present*, 221).

by the Lord we are disciplined, so that we may not be condemned along with the world" (11:32).

This sustaining presence of Jesus extends also to the equipping of believers in chapters 12 through 14. In another example of the blurring of categories that is characteristic of Paul, the one "Spirit," "Lord," and "God" activates (ἐνεργέω) these gifts (12:4-6). One of these gifts is πίστις (12:9), in this instance a more particular and effective grasp of the bond of allegiance between Christ and the believer. Even this keen understanding of πίστις must overflow into *love* to be effective, of course (13:2, 7, 13), but it is noteworthy that Paul repeatedly calls the Corinthians "believers" (οἱ πιστεύοντες, 14:22). These gifts—and the community of hope and love they are meant to produce—all persist in the πίστις relationship, where the believers' allegiance and Christ's faithfulness meet.[11]

The final cluster of references in 1 Corinthians further reinforces that for Paul the πίστις relationship, which is itself the good news (εὐαγγέλιον) that Paul has proclaimed (15:1), is wholly dependent on *the resurrection of Jesus*. An allegiance that is "thoughtless" (εἰκῇ ἐπιστεύσατε, 15:2; see also πιστεύω in 15:11)[12] fails to recognize that the participatory bond "in which you stand, through which you are also being saved" (15:1-2) is possible only because *God raised Christ* (15:15). Christ now reigns, is destroying every power, is rescuing from Sin, and will carry believers safely through in the last day when Death is finally defeated (15:24-28). An allegiance that denies this is "empty" (κενὴ καὶ ἡ πίστις ὑμῶν, 15:14) and "useless" (ματαία ἡ πίστις ὑμῶν, 15:17). True allegiance (πίστις) "in the Lord" is not empty (ὁ κόπος ὑμῶν οὐκ ἔστιν κενὸς ἐν κυρίῳ, 15:58) but rather steadfast

---

[11] Morgan—citing Tacitus, *Ann.* 15.44.4; Suetonius, *Ner.* 16.2; and Pliny, *Ep.* 10.96.5–7—shows that the designation οἱ πιστεύοντες is certainly not a reference to propositional beliefs (Teresa Morgan, *Roman Faith and Christian Faith:* Pistis *and* Fides *in the Early Roman Empire and Early Churches* [Oxford: Oxford University Press, 2015], 240n109). This coheres with its usage in the LXX for those who trust God (e.g., Prov 30:1 LXX; Wis 16:26).

[12] BDAG, 281; cf. Thiselton: "Here Paul envisages the possibility of such a superficial or confused appropriation of the gospel in which no coherent grasp of its logical or practical entailments for eschatology or for practical discipleship had been reached" (*First Epistle*, 1186).

and immovable, propelling practical labor for the gospel because the risen Jesus advocates and sustains.[13] It is not accidental, then, that the final occurrence of πίστις in the letter has Paul urging the Corinthians to live in ways that are consistent with their participation in the risen Christ: "Keep alert, stand firm in your πίστις, be brave, be strong, let all of your doings be in love" (16:13-14).

2 CORINTHIANS

The risen and faithful Christ continues to animate Paul's later correspondence with the Corinthian community. As we turn to 2 Corinthians, it is noteworthy that the emphasis on the risen Christ is also evident in the ways that Paul employs the language of πείθω/πεποίθησις in the letter (2 Cor 1:9, 15; 2:3; 3:4; 5:11; 8:22; 10:2, 7).[14] The noun πεποίθησις occurs just six times in the Pauline corpus, all but two of which (Eph 3:12 and Phil 3:4) are in 2 Corinthians (1:15; 3:4; 8:22; 10:2). The twenty-two occurrences of πείθω (nineteen in the undisputed letters) are more spread out among the letters, but the so-called present perfect form,[15] which tends to be used to emphasize and activate the mental images associated with trust and confidence in something,[16] occurs three times in 2 Corinthians (1:9; 2:3; 10:7;

---

[13] It is true that Paul does not make use of the πίστις Χριστοῦ construction in this important passage in 1 Corinthians 15, but as A. Katherine Grieb writes of Paul's core message, "Unless the faithfulness of Jesus Christ is also the righteousness of God as shown in his resurrection from the dead, then . . . 'our preaching has been in vain and your faith has been in vain' (1 Cor 15:14)" (*Romans: The Story of God's Righteousness: A Narrative Defense of God's Righteousness* [Louisville: Westminster John Knox, 2002], 37); on πίστις as "allegiance" see Matthew Bates, *Salvation by Allegiance Alone: Rethinking Faith, Works, and the Gospel of Jesus the King* (Grand Rapids: Baker Academic, 2017), esp. 77–100.

[14] The adjective form πειθός occurs in 1 Cor 2:4 but is found nowhere else (see further BDAG, 791).

[15] Cf. Friedrich Blass, Albert Debrunner, and Robert W. Funk (BDF), *A Greek Grammar of the New Testament and Other Early Christian Literature* (Chicago: University of Chicago Press, 1961), §341; A. T. Robertson, *A Grammar of the Greek New Testament in the Light of Historical Research*, 4th ed. (Nashville: Broadman, 1947), 881.

[16] See BDAG, 791. Texts such as Prov 14:16; 28:26 LXX; Sir 32:24; Wis 14:29; and Isa 28:17 LXX exemplify this sense of dependence on or trust in someone or something; see also Phil 3:3-4; Gal 5:10. For πεποίθησις, see BDAG, 796, and especially

cf. the present tense form in 5:11). For these reasons, in what follows we have given attention to instances of πείθω/πεποίθησις alongside our consideration of Paul's language of πίστις, which will help us see how and to what end 2 Corinthians nudges the πειθ- lexicon closer to the realm of πίστις.[17]

2 Corinthians 1-3: The Lord Rescues and Transforms

At the opening of his second letter to the Corinthians, Paul's immediate concern is to defend himself against the charge that the changes in his travel plans show him to be fickle (ἐλαφρία, 1:17) and therefore unworthy of their trust. In response to this critique, Paul locates his own trustworthiness in the faithfulness of God ("As surely as God is πιστός, our word to you has not been 'Yes and No,'" 2 Cor 1:18). Morna D. Hooker summarizes:

> Our trust/faith is founded in the trustworthiness/faithfulness of God, but those who trust in him become like him, trustworthy in their turn. Paul makes use of this idea in 2 Corinthians 1:15-22, where he appeals to the faithfulness of God in order to defend himself from accusations that he himself is untrustworthy. Both as a member of God's holy people—no longer because he is a Jew, but because, like the Corinthians, he is 'in Christ'—and as an apostle

---

Eph 3:12: "Christ Jesus our Lord, in whom we have boldness and access *with confidence through his faithfulness* (ἐν πεποιθήσει διὰ τῆς πίστεως αὐτοῦ)."

[17] The author of 1 Clement, relying on Paul (see, e.g., 1 Clem. 5.5-7; 32.4; 47.1), likewise draws a close connection between πίστις and πείθω/πεποίθησις. He writes, "How blessed and wonderful are the gifts of God, beloved ones. Life in immortality, splendor in righteousness, truth with boldness, faith with confidence (πίστις ἐν πεποιθήσει), self-control with holiness" (1 Clem. 35.1-2), and later stresses the importance of the *resurrection* in this regard: "Being assured by the resurrection of our Lord Jesus Christ and full of faith in the word of God (πιστωθέντες ἐν τῷ λόγῳ τοῦ θεοῦ), they went forth with the assurance that the Holy Spirit gives, proclaiming that the kingdom of God was about to come" (1 Clem. 42.3). See further the discussion in Thomas Schumacher, *Zur Entstehung christlicher Sprache: Eine Untersuchung der paulinischen Idiomatik und der Verwendung des Begriffes* πίστις, BBB 168 (Göttingen: V&R unipress; Bonn: Bonn University Press, 2012), 201-2 and Morgan, *Roman Faith*, 511.

(2 Cor 1:1-2), Paul is called to be holy as God is holy (Lev 11:45). It is no wonder, then, that he reflects the faithfulness of God himself.[18]

Yet it is not just that Paul is trustworthy because he has become a member of God's holy people by Christ's faithful *death*. Rather, well before he mentions the faithfulness of God in 1:18, Paul first focuses on the "consolation" (παράκλησις) that comes to Paul and to the Corinthians in their affliction and suffering (παράκλησις/παρακαλέω occurs nine times in 1:3-7). In 1:5 the receipt of comfort, "abundant through Christ," is paralleled with sharing Christ's sufferings. In 1:8-10, it becomes clear that such consolation is received through the active, ongoing work of the *risen* Jesus:

> For we do not want you to be ignorant, brothers and sisters, about the affliction we experienced in Asia, for we were so excessively, powerfully crushed that we despaired even of life. Indeed, among ourselves we had the sentence of death, so that we might *trust* (πεποιθότες) not in ourselves but in God who *raises the dead*. He who rescued (ἐρρύσατο) us from such great death *also will continue to rescue us* (καὶ ῥύσεται); in him we have put our hope that *he will rescue us again* (καὶ ἔτι ῥύσεται).

Paul's use of the term πείθω (and soon πίστις) continues to be shaped in what immediately follows. Paul reinforces that "on the day of our Lord Jesus" the bond between Paul and the Corinthians will have endured (1:13-14), and this is something in which Paul has "trust" (πεποίθησις, 1:15). It is finally at this point that Paul appeals explicitly to God's faithfulness (πιστὸς δὲ ὁ θεός, 1:18). In 1 Corinthians, Paul attributes the fellowship that the Corinthians share with Christ to that same faithfulness ("God is πιστός; by him you were called *into the fellowship of his Son, Jesus Christ our Lord*," 1 Cor 1:9). Likewise here, Paul says that God's promises are affirmed "in Christ" (ἐν αὐτῷ, 2 Cor 1:20), and, importantly, it is *"through* him" (δι᾽ αὐτοῦ, 1:20) that

---

[18] "Another Look at πίστις Χριστοῦ," *SJT* 69 (2016): 53; see also Hooker, "From God's Faithfulness to Ours: Another Look at 2 Corinthians 1:17-24," in *Paul and the Corinthians: Studies on a Community in Conflict: Essays in Honour of Margaret Thrall*, ed. Trevor J. Burke and J. Keith Elliott, NovTSup 109 (Leiden: Brill, 2003), 233–39.

believers' "amen" rises to God.[19] This active work of Christ on behalf of those who are "in Christ" (εἰς Χριστόν, 1:21) is evidenced by the presence of the Spirit (1:22).[20]

Then in 1:24 Paul refers twice to the Corinthians' πίστις. He first indicates that he does not mean to "lord it over you with regard to faith (κυριεύομεν ὑμῶν τῆς πίστεως)" and then declares that the faith relationship is the place where the Corinthians may "stand firm" (τῇ γὰρ πίστει ἑστήκατε). Paul closes this section with another reference to his "confidence" in them (πεποιθὼς ἐπὶ πάντας ὑμᾶς, 2:3), and in the next chapter he reinforces the point that "we have such *confidence* through Christ" (πεποίθησιν δὲ τοιαύτην ἔχομεν διὰ τοῦ Χριστοῦ, 3:4). As he moves toward the key passage about Christ's faithfulness in 2 Corinthians 4, Paul concludes by once again declaring that the presence of the Spirit is evidence of the activity of the exalted Christ: "Now the Lord is the Spirit, and where the Spirit of the Lord is, there is freedom" (3:17). The point is that the one who "*is trans-forming*" us (μεταμορφούμεθα, present tense) is "the Lord, the Spirit" (κυρίου πνεύματος, 3:18).[21]

---

[19] Thomas D. Stegman ("Ἐπίστευσα, διὸ ἐλάλησα [2 Corinthians 4:13]: Paul's Christological Reading of Psalm 115:1a LXX," *CBQ* 69 [2007]: 725–45 [741]) makes an attempt to connect Paul's use of ἀμήν (Heb. אמן) with the use of אמונה to denote "fidelity." As intriguing as this possibility might be given our interests in this book (not least because of Paul's extensive use of Hab 2:4), Stegman does not manage to avoid James Barr's trenchant critique (see *The Semantics of Biblical Language* [Oxford: Oxford University Press, 1961], 161–205).

[20] As Jerome Murphy-O'Connor argues, God has given to Paul the grace to be faithful as Jesus was faithful (*The Theology of the Second Letter to the Corinthians* [Cambridge: Cambridge University Press, 1991], 24–25). See also Stegman: "That *Paul* is anointed intimates that he now participates in the story of Jesus" ("Ἐπίστευσα," 741, emphasis original). Stegman consistently speaks of the "risen Christ," yet in his analysis he speaks almost entirely of Jesus' faithful life and death (as a model to imitate for those in Christ), even though the texts he discusses also put great emphasis on the exalted Christ.

[21] Paul's letters do not make it easy to articulate the relationship between Christ's ongoing faithfulness to believers and the work of the Spirit. Orr writes "the Spirit is the Spirit of Christ but acts as a discrete agent. In other words it is not that Christ is simply experienced *as* the Spirit. There is distinction as well as unity between the Spirit and Christ. The presence and activity of the former in *some senses* serve as a substitute for the absence of the latter" (*Christ Absent and Present*, 221, emphasis original).

2 Corinthians 4:13: "We Have the Same Spirit of Faithfulness"

The references to the activity of the Lord/Spirit in 2 Corinthians 3 prepare us for the most important passage in the Corinthian correspondence for helping us understand what Paul indicates by πίστις Χριστοῦ elsewhere in his letters: 2 Cor 4:7-15. Given what Paul has already written in 1–2 Corinthians, it should not be surprising that in this key passage we discover the *living*, resurrected Jesus as both a present reality in the bodies of believers (4:10-11) and the one with whom believers will be raised and ushered into the Lord's presence (4:14). To state clearly our reading at the outset: in 4:13, the "same spirit of faithfulness (τὸ αὐτὸ πνεῦμα τῆς πίστεως)," whether πνεῦμα is taken as the Spirit or as a human attitude, refers to the *participation believers have with the risen Christ*. In addition, even if Christ's words via the psalmist conjure up the scene involving Jesus' crucifixion, it is the risen Christ who now speaks the words of Ps 115:1 LXX ('Επί-στευσα, διὸ ἐλάλησα) and by whom those "in Christ" also are faithful and believe.

In his argument for reading Christ as the subject of the verbs ἐπί-στευσα and ἐλάλησα in the quotation of Ps 115:1 LXX in 2 Cor 4:13, Douglas Campbell marshals a preponderance of evidence in Paul's text that encourages a "participatory reading" of the passage, an interpretation that takes full account of the relationship between πίστις and participation in Paul's letters.[22] Campbell summarizes, "Because Christ has spoken *and has been resurrected and glorified*, those who participate in his steadfast believing and speaking now are guaranteed that resurrection in the future, and this should fill them with hope."[23] Yet in spite of Campbell's acknowledgment of the centrality of Christ's

---

See also Matthew Bates' argument that in 2 Cor 3:18 we hear of the Lord Jesus as functionally operative through the Holy Spirit (Matthew W. Bates, *The Hermeneutics of the Apostolic Proclamation: The Center of Paul's Method of Scriptural Interpretation* [Waco, Tex.: Baylor University Press, 2012], 160–81, 343; cf. Margaret Thrall, *A Critical and Exegetical Commentary on the Second Epistle to the Corinthians*, 2 vols., ICC [Edinburgh: T&T Clark, 2000], 1:273–97).

[22] Douglas A. Campbell, "2 Corinthians 4:13: Evidence in Paul That Christ Believes," *JBL* 128 (2009): 337–56; see also Campbell, *The Deliverance of God: An Apocalyptic Re-Reading of Justification in Paul* (Grand Rapids: Eerdmans, 2009), 914–24.

[23] Campbell, "2 Corinthians 4:13," 349, emphasis added.

resurrection in 2 Corinthians 4, Campbell fails to see how positing the *risen* Christ as the one speaking "makes sense of the narrative of trust and suffering."[24]

As will be discussed in the next chapter on Galatians, Campbell relies here on Richard Hays' influential argument about the narrative substructure at work in Paul's thought, and in particular Hays' claim that Christ's faithfulness as a reference to his self-giving *death* is "the only meaning supported by Paul's usage."[25] At the time of the publication of Campbell's article (2009), the most complete argument for reading the speaker in 2 Cor 4:13 as the risen Christ was that of Thomas Stegman.[26] Stegman's analysis is certainly helpful, but although Stegman consistently refers to the "risen Christ," in his analysis he speaks almost entirely of Jesus' faithful life and death as a model to imitate for those who are *in Christ*. Thus, Campbell was right that further work needed to be done to demonstrate (1) that in the relevant passages in 2 Corinthians, Paul emphasizes the exalted Christ, and (2) that Paul's argument depends on the identification of the speaker as the *risen* Christ.

In his important work on Paul's method of scriptural interpretation, Matthew Bates takes up this task by drawing attention to Paul's use of the technique of *prosopological exegesis* in his reading of Ps 115:1a LXX.[27] Prosopological exegesis is "a reading technique whereby an interpreter seeks to overcome a real or perceived ambiguity regarding the identity of the speakers or addressees (or both) in the divinely inspired source text by assigning nontrivial prosopa . . . to the speakers or addressees (or both) in order to make sense of the text."[28] Drawing upon the four criteria he has developed for detecting and measuring

---

[24] Campbell, "2 Corinthians 4:13," 347n25.

[25] Richard B. Hays, *The Faith of Jesus Christ: The Narrative Substructure of Galatians 3:1–4:11*, 2nd ed. (Grand Rapids: Eerdmans, 2002), 297n58.

[26] Stegman, "Ἐπίστευσα," 725–45. See also Stegman, *The Character of Jesus: The Linchpin to Paul's Argument in 2 Corinthians*, AnBib 158 (Rome: Pontico Istituto Biblico, 2005), 146–68.

[27] Bates, *Hermeneutics*, 304–28.

[28] Bates, *Hermeneutics*, 221.

the plausibility of prosopological exegesis,[29] and by examining the narrative sequence of Psalms 114–115 LXX, Bates argues that for Paul, the psalmist (through the Spirit) "was delivering an in-character speech in the person of the Christ throughout the psalm."[30] Though Paul would have understood David to be the human speaker, the "uncanny post hoc 'fit' between the circumstances the psalmist articulates and the Christ event"[31] would have induced the uncertainty that prosopological exegesis aimed to resolve.

There is no question that Paul (and many of the earliest Christians)[32] understood Christ as the real speaker of psalms that feature a righteous sufferer (e.g., Psalm 17 LXX and Psalm 68 LXX in Rom 11:9-10; 15:3, 9). Likewise, it is not difficult to see how the narrative pattern of Pss 114–115 LXX coheres with the trial–death–resurrection–exaltation sequence of the Christ event and how Paul's citation of Ps 115:1 LXX in 2 Cor 4:13 appropriately brings this narrative to bear on Paul's discourse. The speaker of the psalm has, in the past, experienced a crisis unto death ("pangs of death encompassed me," Ps 114:3), put his trust in God ("I trusted, therefore I spoke," 115:1), called out to God ("and on the name of the Lord I called: 'Lord, rescue my soul!'" 114:4), and been rescued ("he saved me . . . he delivered my soul from death," 114:6, 8), just as Paul encourages the Corinthians not to be discouraged in the midst of their present sufferings.

A key point for Bates, however, is to notice that the phrase "I trusted, and so I spoke" (Ἐπίστευσα, διὸ ἐλάλησα) is a *past* event, now recalled in the *present*:

> The speaker is presently living in God's presence, offering praise, and anticipating a life of continued praise in the future. . . . For Paul, the setting from which the prosopon of the Christ is speaking

---

[29] Bates identifies the following as "rules of thumb": (1) speech or dialogue, (2) nontriviality of person, (3) priority of introductory formulas or markers, and (4) intertextual evidence. In the case of 2 Cor 4:13, the third criterion is lacking because it is an unmarked instance.

[30] Bates, *Hermeneutics*, 309.

[31] Bates, *Hermeneutics*, 309.

[32] See especially Luke's clear indication that David could not be the real speaker of Ps 15:10 LXX in Acts 2:24-31; see Bates, *Hermeneutics*, 313.

is *after his death, resurrection, and enthronement.* The Christ speaks from the position of *exalted Lord,* where he is in the presence of God (cf. εὐαρεστήσω ἐναντίον κυρίου—Ps 114:9 LXX). . . . This is another case of what has been termed the *perfectum propheticum,* that is, an oracle spoken by a prophet in the past tense, but which really pertains to future realities with respect to the prophet. . . . Paul seems to believe that the citation is in the past tense "I believed, therefore I spoke," because within the divine economy *the enthroned Christ* is talking about events that now lie in Christ's own past—suffering, death, Hades, a decisive posture of trust, and deliverance unto life.[33]

For Bates, this reading makes sense of Paul's repeated emphasis upon the theme of resurrection life in 2 Cor 4:7-15 ("the *life* of Jesus," 4:10, 11; "*life* is at work among you," 4:12; "the one who *raised* the Lord Jesus will also *raise* us with Jesus," 4:14). With the citation of the psalm, Paul expresses his confidence in the exalted Christ's deliverance unto life, and then adds, "and *we* trust, and therefore we also are speaking (καὶ ἡμεῖς πιστεύομεν, διὸ καὶ λαλοῦμεν)." Although just prior to this passage Paul refers to his gospel proclamation and the trials that he and his fellow ministers have experienced ("we proclaim [κηρύσσομεν] Jesus Christ as Lord," 4:5), in 4:7-15 Paul clearly invites the Corinthians into the "we" (e.g., "life in you" in 4:12; "with you" in 4:14). Thus, for Paul, to say "we also speak" (καὶ λαλοῦμεν) is not a reference to *apostolic preaching,* but a powerful declaration of *all* believers' participatory sharing in Christ, who, like Christ did, cry out for deliverance in the midst of sufferings.

We find Bates' reading compelling, especially for the way it clarifies Paul's emphasis on the relationship between Jesus' πίστις and the believers' imitation of (and sharing in) that πίστις in light of the faithful presence of the risen Lord through the Spirit: "We have the same Spirit of faithfulness (τὸ αὐτὸ πνεῦμα τῆς πίστεως) . . . we know that the one who raised the Lord Jesus will raise us also with Jesus, and will bring us with you into his presence" (4:13-14). What remains is to tease out the implications of such a reading for our larger claim that πίστις is regularly used in Paul's letters to indicate the faithfulness of

---

[33] Bates, *Hermeneutics,* 316, emphasis added.

the risen and exalted Christ. If with Bates we take ἐπίστευσα (4:13) in the sense of "I trusted [God in the time of my suffering]," we have evidence of Christ believing/trusting God (something that defenders of the "objective" genitive reading of πίστις Χριστοῦ deny exists), but not necessarily evidence of Christ's πίστις in the sense of *being faithful* to those who are united to him.

Yet in the context of 2 Cor 4:7-15, this is precisely the implication. The *life* of Jesus is revealed (4:10) and is at work (4:12) among believers. When Paul says that "we also trust . . ." (4:13), this is imitative, yes, but as Campbell makes clear, it is first and foremost *participatory*.[34] As we have seen, πίστις is not a one-way event; it indicates a relationship that moves in both directions.[35] Since Paul's discourse in 4:7-14 accents specifically participatory elements of life in Christ, the use of the term πίστις activates mental images associated with bonds of trust and allegiance, far more than any notion of "obedience" to God:

> But we have this treasure in clay vessels, so that the excess of power might be of God and not from us; being afflicted in every way, but not crushed, perplexed, but not despairing, persecuted, but not forsaken, struck down, but not destroyed, always carrying the death of Jesus in the body, so that *the life of Jesus* (ἡ ζωὴ τοῦ Ἰησοῦ) in

---

[34] Bates objects to Campbell's "falsely juxtaposing" the categories of participation and imitation (*Hermeneutics*, 319n239), and Campbell does drive a wedge between a "participatory reading" and an "imitative reading" of 2 Cor 4:13-14 (*Deliverance of God*, 913–24).

[35] Campbell maintains, in line with the goals of his larger project, that 2 Cor 4:13 shows that "'faith' is a post- rather than pre-Christian phenomenon, facilitated by participation in the faithful Christ's journey" (*Deliverance of God*, 923). Again, we concur, but we do not find it accurate to limit "the faithful Christ's journey" to his death upon the cross. Campbell does helpfully demonstrate the usefulness of 4:13 for the πίστις Χριστοῦ debate: "It ought to be recognized more widely as an important contribution to the πίστις Χριστοῦ debate, if not a reasonably decisive one. The textual clues consistently seem to point toward this christocentric and ultimately apocalyptic reading of 2 Corinthians 4:13 being the correct one" (*Deliverance of God*, 924). Campbell is right to emphasize the importance of this passage for the πίστις Χριστοῦ debate because it gives a definitive example of Christ as the subject of πιστεύω, and we can now take it one step further and emphasize that the passage is also important for the debate because of its clear indicators that the faithful, believing Christ Paul has in mind is no other than the risen and glorified Christ.

our bodies may also be made visible. For we *the living* (οἱ ζῶντες) are always being delivered to death for the sake of Jesus, that also *the life of Jesus* (ἡ ζωὴ τοῦ Ἰησοῦ) *may be made visible* in our mortal flesh. So death is at work in us, *but life in you* (ἡ δὲ ζωὴ ἐν ὑμῖν). But having *the same Spirit of faithfulness* (τὸ αὐτὸ πνεῦμα τῆς πίστεως) that is in accordance with scripture—*"I believed, and so I spoke"* (ἐπί-στευσα, διὸ ἐλάλησα)—we also believe, therefore we also speak (καὶ ἡμεῖς πιστεύομεν, διὸ καὶ λαλοῦμεν), knowing that *the one who raised the Lord Jesus will raise us also with Jesus*, and will bring us with you into his presence. (2 Cor 4:7-14)

Thus, to speak of "the same Spirit of πίστις" calls to mind the dynamic relationship that encompasses Jesus' and believers' trust in the faithful God in times of trouble, the believer's allegiance to Christ/ God, and the faithfulness of the exalted Christ who sustains and pre-serves believers through his Spirit.[36]

2 Corinthians 5-13: *"Examine Whether You Are in the Πίστις"*

Paul's references to πιστ- (and πειθ-) language in the remainder of the letter also contribute to the participatory understanding of πίστις that emerges in the epistle. In 2 Cor 5:5-7, Paul acknowledges the pres-ent *perception* of the Lord's absence (ἐκδημοῦμεν ἀπὸ τοῦ κυρίου, 5:6), yet he can always be brave because of the "down payment" of the Spirit (τὸν ἀρραβῶνα τοῦ πνεύματος, 5:5; cf. 1:22). This present assurance of Christ's love is specifically called *faithfulness*: "for we walk

[36] Given the linguistic framework employed in this book, we suggest one further modification to Bates' reading. Though it is somewhat irrelevant to his particular thesis about Paul's use of prosopological exegesis in 2 Cor 4:13, with regard to the thorny debate over the referent of πνεῦμα τῆς πίστεως in 4:13 ("Spirit" or "spirit") Bates ventures that it is best rendered "disposition of trust" (*Hermeneutics*, 323). Though we agree with Bates' observation that the reference in Ps 115:1 LXX "points the reader back to the moment of crisis (Ps 114:3 LXX)," Bates' contention that the best gloss of ἐπίστευσα is "I trusted" and therefore τῆς πίστεως is best taken as "of trust" rests on linguistic assumptions that we do not share. Bates has here fallen into the trap of choosing a lexical gloss on the assumption of polysemy (see further chapter 1). For Paul, then, the use of the word "same" (αὐτό) underscores precisely the reciprocal dimension of the relationship, which fits normal Greek and Roman usage but is fur-ther strengthened by Paul's understanding of the role of the Spirit.

διὰ πίστεως, not by sight" (5:7). Immediately following, Paul reiterates the narrative of Christ's πίστις, once again highlighting the active role of the risen Christ: "For Christ's love is holding us together (ἡ γὰρ ἀγάπη τοῦ Χριστοῦ συνέχει ἡμᾶς), and we conclude this: one died for all, therefore all died; and he died for all, so that *those who live* (οἱ ζῶντες) might *live* (ζῶσιν) no longer for themselves, but for him who died and *was raised* (ἐγερθέντι) *for them*" (5:14-15).

Next, Paul uses the language of πίστις in 6:14-15 to paint a stark contrast between those who are in Christ and those who are not ("what does a *believer* share with an *unbeliever?*" τίς μερὶς πιστῷ μετὰ ἀπίστου, 6:15). This contrast is warranted by a remarkable claim about the union believers have in Christ—"we are the temple of the living (ζῶντος) God" (6:16)—and then a litany of scriptural citations that reify this union: "I will *live* in them and walk among them, and I will be their God, and they shall be my people . . . and I will be your father, and you shall be my sons and daughters, says the Lord Almighty" (6:16-18).

After making a connection between the Corinthians "abounding in fidelity (περισσεύετε πίστει)" to Christ (8:7) and the outworking of this allegiance in their participation in the collection for the saints in Jerusalem ("that also in this gift you might abound"), in ch. 10 Paul makes a connection between the "trust" (πεποίθησις; cf. 10:2) the Corinthians have of their belonging to Christ and the same bond of trust that unites them with Paul: "If you are confident [πέποιθεν] that you belong to Christ, remind yourself of this, that just as you belong to Christ, so also do we" (10:7).[37] In the same section, Paul speaks of the Corinthians' πίστις as something that can "increase" (αὐξάνω) and thereby greatly enlarge the limit (κανών) of Paul's missionary influence (10:15).

---

[37] Michael Kibbe's argument that εἰς τὴν ὑπακοὴν τοῦ Χριστοῦ in 2 Cor 10:5 should be taken as "Christ's obedience" rather than "obedience to Christ" moves in the right direction by attending to the role of Christ's narrative ("'The Obedience of Christ': A Reassessment of τὴν ὑπακοὴν τοῦ Χριστοῦ in 2 Corinthians 10:5," *JSPL* 2 (2012): 41–56 [41]). We remain somewhat unconvinced of this reading, however, because Kibbe seems to conflate "obedience" with πίστις and limits the story to Jesus' obedient death.

The final occurrence in 2 Corinthians is particularly clear about the participatory, relational understanding of πίστις Paul has set out in the letter. He writes, "Examine yourselves to see whether you are ἐν τῇ πίστει; test yourselves—or do you not recognize that Jesus Christ is in you (Ἰησοῦς Χριστὸς ἐν ὑμῖν)?" (13:5). Just as he wrote of Christ's faithfulness that sustains and forms believers through the Spirit ("we have the same Spirit of faithfulness," 4:13), at the close of the letter Paul urges the Corinthians to live in ways that are consistent with their participation in Christ.

CONCLUSION

Even though no form of the πίστις Χριστοῦ construction occurs in the Corinthian letters, these epistles contain vital information for better understanding what Paul means by Christ's πίστις. In 2 Cor 4:11, participation with Christ seems to be linked explicitly with the crucified Jesus ("we are always being delivered to death"). In addition, if (as we think) Paul's citation of Ps 115:1 LXX in 4:13 ("I believed, therefore I spoke") represents the voice of Christ, Christ's declaration likely refers to Christ's faithfulness to God *unto death* and his cry for deliverance upon the cross. Yet the shaping of the πίστις word group (as well as the πειθ- lexicon) in these letters leaves little doubt about Paul's participatory, reciprocal, and relational understanding of πίστις, and that the citation of Ps 115:1 LXX in 2 Cor 4:13 not only presents a clear instance of Christ as the subject of πιστεύω in Paul, but also shows that the faithful, believing Christ is none other than the risen and glorified Christ.

4

GALATIANS
"I Live in the Faithfulness of the Son of God"

"**P**aul's theology must be understood as the explication and defense of a *story*."[1] For Richard Hays, and thus for subsequent interpreters influenced by Hays' epochal dissertation on Galatians, the substructure of Gal 3:1–4:11 offers a prime example of the outworking of that story in Paul's writings. The burden of this chapter is to show that Galatians does indeed find its coherence as the outworking of the story of Jesus, and that the phrase πίστις Χριστοῦ is a shorthand for that story, but that the story should not be limited to "Jesus' obedience to death on the cross."[2] Any summary that adequately illumines the narrative substructure of Galatians must give attention not only to the life, suffering, and death of Jesus, but also to his resurrection.[3] What distinguishes this chapter from the majority of articles devoted to the πίστις debate in Galatians is that we will not mount yet another defense of the objective or subjective or "third way" readings of 2:16, 3:22, and 3:26. Instead, we will recast the issue as a question about the proper understanding of Paul's use of πίστις in Galatians. With this

---

[1] Richard B. Hays, *The Faith of Jesus Christ: The Narrative Substructure of Galatians 3:1–4:11*, 2nd ed. (Grand Rapids: Eerdmans, 2002), 274.

[2] Hays, *Faith of Jesus Christ*, 297n58.

[3] Paul may assume but nowhere mentions or alludes to Christ's heavenly enthronement in Galatians.

focus, it will become clear that Paul assumes the story of the faithfulness of the risen Christ, who incorporates believers "in Christ Jesus . . . through πίστις" (3:26; cf. 3:11-12, 21-22, 27-28). Attention to the role of the risen Christ lends strong support to Teresa Morgan's recent claim about 2:16-17: "'in Christ' and 'through the *pistis* of Christ' are very closely related, if not identical, in meaning."[4] Such a connection between union with Christ and the πίστις of Christ is possible precisely because the *risen* Christ is an essential part of the story that Paul utilizes in his theologizing in Galatians.

GALATIANS 2:20: THE LIVING CHRIST

In the introduction, we cited several examples of the scholarly consensus that πίστις Χριστοῦ, if taken in a subjective sense, refers solely to *Christ's obedient death*, "his faithful deed of dying on the cross in our behalf."[5] Here it will be instructive to consider an additional

---

[4] Teresa Morgan, *Roman Faith and Christian Faith: Pistis and Fides in the Early Roman Empire and Early Churches* (Oxford: Oxford University Press, 2015), 304. Morgan captures the importance of Galatians for understanding Paul's relational understanding of πίστις, which this chapter seeks to fill out: "For the first time that we know of, he uses *pistis* to articulate the tripartite relationship between God, Christ, and humanity, putting Christ in the centre of a nexus of faithfulness, trustworthiness, and trust which runs in all directions between God and Christ, Christ and humanity, and humanity and God" (*Roman Faith*, 281). As Peter Oakes has recently noted (of Gal 2:16 in particular), Morgan's "emphasis on the present relationality of πίστις reinforces the effect of the parallel with ἐν Χριστῷ which drives πίστις . . . firmly towards being an expression of current relationship" ("*Pistis* as Relational Way of Life in Galatians," *JSNT* 40 [2018]: 269).

[5] J. Louis Martyn, "The Apocalyptic Gospel in Galatians," *Int* 54 (2000): 250. See also David W. Congdon, who notes Hays' unhelpful restriction yet fails to consider the risen Christ: "This 'narrower punctiliar sense' is far too limiting, and while it makes sense within the context of Galatians alone, there are grounds for arguing that Paul is not always so limited in his other epistles. In my own exegesis of Galatians below, I seek to find a place for Jesus' life within the life of the one who lives by Christ's faith (Gal 2:20). I thus argue for a strong sense of *participatio Christi* in Paul's understanding of faith, but one that embraces the entirety of Christ's history" ("The Trinitarian Shape of πίστις: A Theological Exegesis of Galatians," *JTI* 2 [2008]: 233n5). Congdon's own use of the phrase "entirety of Christ's history" is shaped by his engagement with Barth's historicizing of christology and Barth's description of "the history of Christ as a history of 'humble obedience,' defined by the Son's obedient mission into the far

example: the recent series of articles published by Shuji Ota.[6] In his examination of Abraham's faith and what Ota calls "holistic" πίστις in Galatians, Ota makes a number of helpful observations about the way Paul's usage of the πιστ- lexicon emphasizes the faithfulness of Christ *toward humanity* (as opposed to God). Ota observes that the Lord Jesus Christ is the *subject* of the sentence in Gal 1:3-4 ("from the Lord Jesus Christ, who gave himself for our sins to deliver us from the present evil age"), just as Christ is in 2:20 ("the Son of God, who loved me and gave himself for me") and in 3:13a ("Christ redeemed us from the curse of the law by becoming a curse for us"). In each instance, the object and beneficiary of Christ's agency is not God (as in, *Christ obeyed God*), but humanity.[7] In the course of making this point, Ota repeats multiple times that the *death* of Christ is what is meant by Christ's faithfulness:

> This πίστις undoubtedly points to Christ's *death on the cross*. . . . This means that when Paul refers to *the death of Christ* using the phrase πίστις Χριστοῦ, what he means is not the objective fact of his *death on the cross* nor his deed seen as faithfulness to God, but the *faithworth*, for believers, of *Christ's death* referred to using the same phrase in this context. . . . Paul sees the deeds of Christ *culminating in his death* as totally trustworthy and truthful. . . . So the Pauline phrase πίστις Χριστοῦ, which literally means "Christ's faithfulness," denotes the *faithworth* of his specific deeds—*especially his*

---

country" (236). It seems to us that a far more accurate understanding of the phrase "entirety of Christ's history" would include the life of Christ after his resurrection from the dead.

[6] Shuji Ota, "The Holistic *Pistis* and Abraham's Faith (Galatians 3)," *HJAS* 57 (2016): 1–12, esp. 2–3; see also Ota, "Absolute Use of ΠΙΣΤΙΣ and ΠΙΣΤΙΣ ΧΡΙΣΤΟΥ in Paul," *AJBI* 23 (1997) 64–82; Ota, "ΠΙΣΤΙΣ ΧΡΙΣΤΟΥ: Christ's Faithfulness to Whom?" *HJAS* 55 (2014): 15–26; and Ota, "*Pistis* in Acts as Background of Paul's Faith Terminology," *HJAS* 56 (2015): 1–12.

[7] Thomas Schumacher also argues that for Paul Christ's πίστις is directed toward humanity, while Christ's obedience (ὑπακοή) is directed toward God: "Doch während bei der Wendung πίστις (Ἰησοῦ) Χριστοῦ die Zuwendung Jesu zu den Menschen in den Blick kommt, wird das Stichwort ὑπακοή Hinblick auf das Gottesverhältnis Jesu gebraucht" (*Zur Entstehung christlicher Sprache: Eine Untersuchung der paulinischen Idiomatik und der Verwendung des Begriffes πίστις*, BBB 168 [Göttingen: V&R unipress; Bonn: Bonn University Press, 2012], 326; see also 223 and following pages).

death on the cross—for believers; it is *a correlative of faith* in Christ *particularly in terms of his death.*[8]

It is telling that the point is emphasized so heavily. Against the consensus view that Christ's faithfulness (πίστις) toward *God* stands in contrast with human unfaithfulness (ἀπιστία) toward *God*, Ota argues instead that Christ is faithful toward *humanity*. We agree. Yet Ota's three examples, all of which certainly foreground Jesus' death, are far from the only references in Galatians to Christ's actions on behalf of those who are bound to him. It seems that Ota has prematurely rejected the possibility that πίστις Χριστοῦ indicates the ongoing faithfulness of the *risen* Jesus toward humanity. Yet once this possibility is allowed, the resurrection nearly jumps off the page in Galatians.

We will consider the importance of the resurrection in our treatment of Galatians 3–5 below, but Paul's discourse already in Galatians 1–2 has prompted his readers to consider the resurrected Jesus. The letter opening frames Paul's apostleship not in terms of Jesus' faithful death, but rather with reference to Paul's commissioning "through Jesus Christ and God the Father, who *raised him* from the dead" (1:1). Jesus is identified as the one who "gave himself" (1:3), but it is this risen Jesus who offers grace and peace through his servant Paul (1:3). After declaring that he seeks the *trust* (πείθω) of God and not humans in 1:10,[9] Paul calls attention to the revelation he received,

---

[8] Ota, "Holistic *Pistis*," 3, italics added; see also Martinus C. de Boer, *Galatians: A Commentary*, NTL (Louisville: Westminster John Knox, 2011), 150, 192–93, and subsequent pages.

[9] In chapter 3, we considered the ways Paul "shaped" not only the language of πίστις, but also that of πείθω. In Galatians, Paul employs πείθω just three times, but the occurrences are worth considering. In 1:10 ("Am I now persuading [πείθω] humans, or God?"), Paul makes clear that as a "slave of Christ," his work to "persuade" (that is, to establish a relationship of trust) is not directed toward human beings, but toward God. Just as in 2 Cor 10:7 ("If anyone is *persuaded* that he is of Christ [πέποιθεν ἑαυτῷ Χριστοῦ εἶναι], he should consider again for himself, that just as he is of Christ, so also are we"; cf. 1 Cor 1:12]), Paul emphasizes that the believer's primary identity is in Christ. Then, as we will discuss below, in Galatians 5, Paul twice uses πείθω in the context of πίστις and "in Christ" language: "For through the Spirit, by faith (ἐκ πίστεως), we eagerly await the hope of righteousness. For *in Christ Jesus*

not from God's announcement of the efficacy of Jesus' death, but from the risen Christ himself (1:12).

It is in this context—namely, Paul's proclamation of the living Son among the nations (1:16)—that Paul first uses the language of πίστις in his letter to the Galatians: "They were only hearing, 'The one once persecuting us now preaches the faith (τὴν πίστιν) that he once was destroying'" (1:23).[10] Morgan, noting that πορθέω more naturally refers to "destroying" a *relationship* rather than the content of preaching,[11] has proposed translating, "the one who was persecuting us is now proclaiming the relationship of trust [between God and human beings] which he once tried to destroy."[12] We might add that this emphasis on πίστις as *relationship* is strengthened by its proximity to Paul's reference to the churches of Judea who are "in Christ" (ἐν Χριστῷ, 1:22). Paul continually stresses the community of trust between God, Christ, and faithful humanity (see also τοὺς οἰκείους τῆς πίστεως in 6:10). At the beginning of chapter 2, Paul reiterates the importance of being "in Christ Jesus" (ἐν Χριστῷ Ἰησοῦ, 2:4) and returns to the point that he had been "entrusted (πεπίστευμαι) with the gospel" (2:7) by the risen Christ.

---

neither circumcision nor uncircumcision has any force, but rather faith (πίστις) working through love. You were running well; who prevented you from remaining persuaded by (πείθεσθαι) the truth? . . . I am persuaded (πέποιθα) about you *in the Lord* that you will not think otherwise" (5:5-7, 10).

10 Paul's language here anticipates the "hearing of faith" (ἐξ ἀκοῆς πίστεως) in 3:2, 5; see further discussion in this chapter. Most importantly, ἡ πίστις should not (here or elsewhere in Paul) be equated with the modern connotation of "the Christian faith." As is well documented, the Greco-Roman world had no concept of "religion" as a system or category that could be contrasted with "secular"; see, for example, Jörg Rüpke, *Religion of the Romans* (Cambridge: Polity, 2007), 5–12.

11 Bruce asserts that "πίστις is here practically synonymous with εὐαγγέλιον (the gospel of salvation by faith)" (F. F. Bruce, *The Epistle to the Galatians*, NIGTC [Grand Rapids: Eerdmans, 1982], 105); likewise, Longenecker ("used absolutely as a synonym for the Christian gospel"; *Galatians*, WBC 41 [Dallas: Word, 1990]) and Lightfoot ("It is striking proof of the large space occupied by 'faith' in the mind of the infant Church, that it should so soon have passed into a synonym for the Gospel" [*St. Paul's Epistle to the Galatians: A Revised Text with Introduction, Notes, and Dissertations* (London: Macmillan, 1892), 86]).

12 Morgan, *Roman Faith*, 266.

All of this prepares Paul's readers for the emergence of πίστις, δικαιοσύνη, and νόμος as key players in 2:16-20. Our interest here is not in the manifold interpretive questions raised by these verses, but in setting out the case that Paul foregrounds in 2:16-20 the faithfulness of the *risen* Jesus and the deep union shared between Christ and those "in Christ."[13] The words are among Paul's most memorable:

> We [Jews] know that a person is made righteous not by (ἐκ) the works of the law but through the faithfulness of Jesus Christ (διὰ πίστεως Ἰησοῦ Χριστοῦ), and we trusted in (ἐπιστεύσαμεν εἰς) Christ Jesus, so that we might be made righteous by the faithfulness of Christ (ἐκ πίστεως Χριστοῦ), and not by (ἐκ) works of the law, since by works of the law no one will be made righteous. . . . For through (διά) the law I died to the law, so that I might live to God. I have been crucified with Christ; and no longer do I live, but Christ lives in me; and that [life] I now live in the flesh I live in the faithfulness of the Son of God (ἐν πίστει ζῶ τῇ τοῦ υἱοῦ τοῦ θεοῦ), who loved me and gave himself for me. (2:16, 19-20)

Once again, here we need not engage in battle with the subjective versus objective camps to make the case that Paul has in view here the faithfulness of the risen Son of God. Our argument has three components: first, πίστις should not be equated with "obedience"; second, Paul's statement that "Christ lives in me" (ζῇ . . . ἐν ἐμοὶ Χριστός, 2:20)

[13] Still one of the clearest summaries of the debated issues pertaining to these verses is that of James D. G. Dunn, "Once More, ΠΙΣΤΙΣ ΧΡΙΣΤΟΥ," in Hays, *Faith of Jesus Christ: The Narrative Substructure of Galatians 3:1–4:11*, 2nd ed. (Grand Rapids: Eerdmans, 2002), 270. See also Martyn, *Galatians: A New Translation with Introduction and Commentary*, AB 33A (New York: Doubleday, 1997), 325, 530–34; "Apocalyptic Gospel," 247–51. Our view is that Dunn would be better served to read Gal 2:16 in light of 6:16, so that the discussion of πίστις, δικαιοσύνη, and νόμος is seen as irreducibly cosmic, and δικαιοσύνη accomplished by God. Congdon, for example, thinks that "Dunn's argument essentially replaces the terms 'circumcision' and 'uncircumcision' with 'works of the law' and 'faith in Christ,' where Paul's argument actually identifies 'works of the law' with both circumcision and uncircumcision (as human works) and places the 'faith of Christ' on the side of the new creation" ("Trinitarian," 245); see also Beverly Roberts Gaventa, "The Singularity of the Gospel Revisited," in *Galatians and Christian Theology: Justification, the Gospel, and Ethics in Paul's Letter*, ed. Mark W. Elliott, et al. (Grand Rapids: Baker Academic, 2014), 187–99.

is one of the clearest indicators that the *risen* Christ is the primary referent of πίστις Χριστοῦ; and third, Paul likely crafts his discourse in 2:20 as a reference to Hab 2:4, which strengthens the case that the risen Jesus is in view. We will take each of these in turn.

First, Christ's πίστις, even if taken to be directed toward God, cannot be understood as "obedience."[14] Those who claim it is must appeal to Phil 2:8 (ὑπήκοος μέχρι θανάτου, "obedient to death"), although we have already demonstrated that πίστις is not framed as obedience even in Philippians.[15] Paul does speak of the "obedience of faith" (ὑπακοὴ πίστεως) in Rom 1:5 and 16:26, and he connects the verb ὑπακούω with πιστεύω in Rom 10:16, but no such connection is made between the ὑπακο- word group and the πιστ- word group in Galatians.[16] Paul refers to a "hearing of faith" (ἀκοὴ πίστεως) in Gal 3:2, 5, but there is no suggestion that this is about obedience, and Paul never uses ὑπακούω or cognates in the letter. Thus, a reader formed

---

[14] Bultmann rather weakly defends the view that "'to believe' is 'to obey'" by referring to Hebrews 11. He then writes, "Paul in particular stresses the element of obedience in faith. For him πίστις is indeed ὑπακοή, as comparison of R. 1:8; 1 Th. 1:8 with R. 15:18; 16:19, or 2 C. 10:5 f. with 10:15, shows. Faith is for Paul ὑπακούειν τῷ εὐαγγελίῳ, R. 10:16. To refuse to believe is not to obey the righteousness which the Gospel offers for faith, R. 10:3. Paul can call believing confession of the Gospel the ὑποταγὴ τῆς ὁμολογίας εἰς τὸ εὐαγγέλιον τοῦ Χριστοῦ, 2 C. 9:13. He coins the combination ὑπακοὴ πίστεως, R. 1:5" (Rudolf Bultmann in *TDNT*, Gerhard Kittel and Gerhard Friedrich, eds., *Theological Dictionary of the New Testament*, trans. Geoffrey W. Bromiley, 10 vols. [Grand Rapids: Eerdmans, 1964–1976], 205–6).

[15] For example, Congdon: "In other words, the faith of the Son of God is made manifest in the historical act in which he gave himself up for humanity on the cross. That this is an act of obedience is clarified by Paul's introduction to the letter, in which he states that Christ 'gave himself for our sins' in accordance with 'the will of God' (το θέλημα τοῦ θεοῦ; 1:4)" ("Trinitarian," 244).

[16] In Romans, the collocation of these terms does not indicate that mental images associated with "obedience" are activated in other instances of πίστις. That is, precisely because πίστις does *not* in itself have the connotation of obedience, Paul needs to speak of the "obedience associated with faith," rather than simply πίστις, when speaking of the coming of the gentiles into faith relationship with God in Christ in Rom 1:5 and 16:26 (see further discussion in chapter 5). For Paul, obedience is something that *flows out* of and characterizes the πίστις relationship, as Morgan demonstrates so well. Somewhat puzzling is that Morgan reads ὑπακοὴ πίστεως in Rom 1:5 as a genitive of apposition, but she notes that to take it subjectively ("the obedience based on πίστις") "would not substantially alter the interpretation" (*Roman Faith*, 282–83).

by Paul's discourse prior to 2:15-21 (and specifically Paul's use of use of πίστις and πιστεύω) has not been prompted to associate the phrases διὰ πίστεως Ἰησοῦ Χριστοῦ and ἐν πίστει . . . τῇ τοῦ υἱοῦ τοῦ θεοῦ as references to Jesus' *obedience* to the point of death in 2:16 and 2:20. In addition, as noted above, to read ἐν πίστει . . . τῇ τοῦ υἱοῦ τοῦ θεοῦ as "in the obedience of the Son of God" ignores the clear statement at the end of the verse that Christ's self-giving is "for me" (ὑπὲρ ἐμοῦ) (and in 3:13, "for us" [ὑπὲρ ἡμῶν]).

Second, given that Paul's concern in 2:15-21 is the faith relationship in which the believer is *in Christ*, πίστις Χριστοῦ in 2:15-21 is not limited to Jesus' death (ἀποθνῄσκω in 2:19, 21) on the cross (συσταυρόω in 2:19; cf. σταυρόω in 3:1).[17] Paul is unambiguous about the source of the present power of this relationship: "Christ lives in me" (2:20). Paul identifies his death with the death of Christ and his life with the life of Christ. There are then two possibilities (not necessarily mutually exclusive) for the referent of Christ's life: either the *earthly* life of Jesus or the life of the *heavenly* Christ. Proponents of the subjective reading in 2:20, if they acknowledge a connection between "life" and "faithfulness" at all, speak only of the earthy life. For Hays πίστις Χριστοῦ is limited to Jesus' faithful death, but the narrative logic of Galatians also includes the (earthly) life of Jesus because "the Christian's life is a reenactment of the pattern of faithfulness revealed in Jesus."[18] Certainly, Paul envisions here a cruciform life by participation in Christ, and this life is analogous to the human Jesus' own self-giving life and death: just as Christ "loved me and gave himself for me" (τοῦ ἀγαπήσαντός με καὶ παραδόντος ἑαυτὸν ὑπὲρ ἐμοῦ, 2:20) so "in Christ Jesus" (ἐν γὰρ Χριστῷ Ἰησοῦ) the believer's life is characterized by "faith working through love" (πίστις δι᾽ ἀγάπης ἐνεργουμένη, 5:6).

---

[17] Even if Christ's "giving" (2:20) is restricted to Jesus' death, it is telling that two out of the four references are not about Jesus, but Paul's participation in the death of Jesus.

[18] Hays, *Faith of Jesus Christ*, 203; see also, for example, Congdon: "Paul's life is identified with the life of Christ—the historical life in which Jesus testified to and actualized the kingdom of God" ("Trinitarian," 248).

Yet it is strange that Hays and other interpreters ignore the clear connection in the text between death/life and cross/resurrection.[19] To *live*, as Paul makes clear in the remainder of the letter,[20] is an existence that flows exclusively and undeniably from the relationship formed by (Christ's) πίστις and maintained by the πνεῦμα of the risen Christ:[21]

> For clearly no one is made righteous before God by (ἐν) the law, for "The one who is righteous will live (ζάω) by faith (ἐκ πίστεως)." But the law is not by faith (ἐκ πίστεως); rather, "The one who does these things will live (ζάω) by (ἐν) them." (3:11-12)

> For if a law had been given that could make alive (ζωοποιέω), then righteousness would be by (ἐκ) the law. (3:21b)

> If we live (ζάω) by the Spirit, let us also follow the Spirit. (5:25)

> For the one who sows for his own flesh will reap corruption from the flesh; but the one who sows for the Spirit will reap eternal life (ζωή) from the Spirit. (6:8)

Even Paul's oft-cited emphasis on the cross in 6:14 immediately gives way to *new creation* in 6:15: "May it not be that I should boast about anything except the cross of our Lord Jesus Christ, through whom the

[19] Bultmann, *TDNT* 2:869, emphasis added: "πνεῦμα has for [Paul] the sense of the manner of the life of faith in its relationship (πίστις) to God's act of salvation in Christ. It is just because this relationship is achieved in the manner of a present existence that he can adopt the Hellenistic conception of πνεῦμα . . . and that, to bring out the fact that Christ is present and active, he can link Christ with the πνεῦμα so closely that he refers to Christ what is said of the Spirit in the OT (2 C. 3:17). As Christ is not for him an idea or a cosmic force (as in Gnosticism), so ζωή for him is not an idea or hyperphysical state, but the *present historical actuality of the believer*. For the πνεῦμα ζωοποιοῦν, expressly distinguished by him from the power of purely natural life, the ψυχὴ ζῶσα (1 C. 15:45) is indeed present. If, then, the resurrection life can come to its full development only in the future, so that ζωή is to this extent an object of hope, in some sense *it is still present already*, just as the future δόξα is already anticipated in faith (R. 8:30; 2 C. 3:6-18)."

[20] There are eleven occurrences of ζάω/ζωοποιέω/ζωή in Galatians: ζάω in 2:14, 19, 20 (four times); 3:11, 12; 5:25; ζωοποιέω in 3:21; and ζωή in 6:8.

[21] On the portrayal of the presence of the risen Christ in Paul, see Peter Orr, *Christ Absent and Present: A Study in Pauline Christology*, WUNT 2/354 (Tübingen: Mohr Siebeck, 2014).

world has been crucified to me, and I to the world. For neither circumcision nor uncircumcision is anything; rather, new creation!" The
phrase "Christ lives in me" in 2:20, then, cannot be a reference to
the earthly life of Jesus. Thus, Paul lives by the πίστις of the *resurrected*
Christ.

Finally, the case that the faithfulness of Jesus in Gal 2:20 is the
faithfulness of the risen Christ is strengthened when we consider
the likelihood that Paul here alludes to Hab 2:4. In Gal 3:11 Paul
cites the text in full (ὁ δίκαιος ἐκ πίστεως ζήσεται), but as Douglas Campbell and others have argued, the debated genitive phrases
all contain an echo of Hab 2:4,[22] and of course Paul has just written
διὰ πίστεως Ἰησοῦ Χριστοῦ and ἐκ πίστεως Χριστοῦ in Gal 2:16.[23]
Although 2:20 might be seen as an outlier because it uses ἐν πίστει
rather than διὰ πίστεως or ἐκ πίστεως, its foregrounding of the language of "living" actually strengthens the case that Hab 2:4 informs *all*

[22] Campbell seems to indicate that Paul does *not* echo Hab 2:4 in Gal 2:20, but
suggests that the echo is fully present in the wider context: "Πίστις in the debated genitive phrases is elsewhere embedded in a phrase that echoes Habbakuk 2:4, whether
as ἐκ πίστεως or its direct equivalent, διὰ πίστεως. . . . Only here, in Galatians
2:20, has Paul moved away from *both* an intertextual echo—probably because he has
just made that echo twice in 2:16—and a reference to Christ in terms of names"
(Douglas A. Campbell, *The Deliverance of God: An Apocalyptic Rereading of Justification in Paul* [Grand Rapids: Eerdmans, 2009], 1149n40). See also Hays, *Faith of Jesus
Christ*, 132–33. For an argument that Gal 2:20 does draw upon Hab 2:4, see Roy E.
Ciampa, *The Presence and Function of Scripture in Galatians 1–2*, WUNT 2/102 (Tübingen: Mohr Siebeck, 1998), 210–12. Prof. Ciampa also graciously shared with us an
unpublished paper in which he explores again the connection between Gal 2:20 and
Hab 2:4: "Habakkuk 2:4 in Paul: Echoes, Allusions, and Rewritings" (paper presented
at the Annual Meeting of the SBL, Boston, November 28, 2017).

[23] Morgan notes of Gal 2:16: "Paul's rendition of Habakkuk 2:4 as 'the *dikaios* will
live by *pistis*', avoiding both the Hebrew Bible's specification that the *pistis* is the just
man's own and that of the Septuagint that it is God's, is a master stroke. By leaving
pistis unqualified, Paul allows it to refer equally and simultaneously to the *pistis* of God
towards Christ and humanity and that of Christ towards God and humanity which
make dikaiosynē possible, and that of the human being towards God and Christ"
(*Roman Faith*, 276). Morgan captures well the concentric and expansive implications of Paul's usage here, though in our reading Christ's πίστις toward humanity is
foregrounded.

of the debated genitive texts.[24] This is true if Paul views the "righteous one" as Christ, as Campbell and others have argued, but perhaps even more so if Paul sees in Hab 2:4 a suggestive and rather elegant allusion to the blurring of identities that occurs between Christ and those who live *in him*.

Gal 2:20: ζῇ δὲ ἐν ἐμοὶ Χριστός· ὃ δὲ νῦν ζῶ ἐν σαρκί, <u>ἐν πίστει</u> ζῶ τῇ τοῦ υἱοῦ τοῦ θεοῦ τοῦ.

Hab 2:4 LXX: ὁ δὲ δίκαιος <u>ἐκ πίστεώς</u> μου <u>ζήσεται</u>.

In this reading, Paul's slight tweak toward the language of "in" (ἐν) merges the terminology of πίστις with Paul's ubiquitous language expressing his participatory soteriology.[25] In Gal 2:16 Paul refers to the faithfulness of Christ (διὰ πίστεως Ἰησοῦ Χριστοῦ) *and* believers' fidelity to Christ (εἰς Χριστὸν Ἰησοῦν ἐπιστεύσαμεν).[26] He then collates δικαιω- language (first, "no person" [οὐ δικαιοῦται ἄνθρωπος], then "we" [δικαιωθῶμεν], then "not every flesh" [οὐ δικαιωθήσεται πᾶσα σάρξ]) with yet a third reference to faith, this time with the preposition used in Hab 2:4 LXX, <u>ἐκ πίστεως</u> Χριστοῦ:

> We know that a person is *made righteous* not by (ἐκ) the works of the law but through *the faithfulness of Jesus Christ* (διὰ πίστεως Ἰησοῦ Χριστοῦ), and *we trusted in* (ἐπιστεύσαμεν εἰς) *Christ Jesus*, so that we might be *made righteous* by *the faithfulness of Christ* (ἐκ πίστεως Χριστοῦ), and not by (ἐκ) works of the law, since by works of the law no one will be *made righteous*. (Gal 2:16)

---

[24] Campbell suggests that the allusion to Hab 2:4 accounts for Paul's overwhelming lexical favoring of πιστ- over ὑπακο- terms in these texts (*Deliverance*, 613). We disagree—the notion of "obedience to God's will" is not foregrounded by Paul in the debated genitive phrases.

[25] ἐν is normally understood in an instrumental sense. See further A. J. M. Wedderburn, "Some Observations on Paul's Use of the Phrases 'in Christ' and 'with Christ,'" *JSNT* 25 (1985): 83–97, and the discussion of Gal 3:8 in Matthew V. Novenson, *Christ among the Messiahs: Christ Language in Paul and Messiah Language in Ancient Judaism* (Oxford: Oxford University Press, 2012), 124–26.

[26] For the view that it would not in fact be redundant for Paul to express "faith in" by both διὰ πίστεως Ἰησοῦ Χριστοῦ and εἰς Χριστὸν Ἰησοῦν ἐπιστεύσαμεν, see R. Barry Matlock, "The Rhetoric of πίστις in Paul: Galatians 2.16, 3.22, Romans 3.22, and Philippians 3.9," *JSNT* 30 (2007): 193–99.

Then in 2:19-20 Paul makes explicit this blurring of categories:

For through (διά) the law I died to the law, so that I might *live* to God. I have been crucified with Christ; and no longer do I *live*, but *Christ lives in me* (ζῆ . . . ἐν ἐμοὶ Χριστός); and that [*life*] I now *live* in the flesh I *live* in the faithfulness of the Son of God (ἐν πίστει ζῶ τῇ τοῦ υἱοῦ τοῦ θεοῦ), who loved me and gave himself for me.

Who is the righteous one? Christ, and now *me*, for "Christ lives in me." Whose faith is the basis for life? The faith of the loving and self-donating Son of God, in whom I *now* live, even "in the flesh," even as "sinners" (2:17), because Jesus now advocates for us as the risen Christ.[27]

To limit the reference to Christ's πίστις in Galatians 2 to the faithful death of the human Jesus therefore fails to appreciate the importance of Christ's resurrection in the context of Paul's hope in Galatians. As Paul says later in this chapter, "for you are all children of God *in Christ Jesus* through faith (διὰ τῆς πίστεως ἐν Χριστῷ Ἰησοῦ)" (3:26). Justification happens not through works of the law, and not merely through the crucifixion of Jesus, but through the faithfulness of the risen Christ. The reference to Christ's faith in 2:20, we might say, qualifies the language of Christ's faith in 2:16. As Gaventa pointedly observes, from 2:16 to 2:20,

the canvas on which Paul depicts the gospel has enlarged from legal language to existential language. The question is no longer about making things right (rectifying or justifying) and how this is done; instead, it concerns death and life. Something more is at stake than justification, for Christ is not simply the one who justifies; now Christ is the one with whom "I" am crucified, the one who lives "in me." Here the gospel's singularity comes to expression in a form that is frightening: the gospel gives life by taking it away. . . . And the gospel is also all life-giving: "Christ lives in me." The living "I"

---

[27] So Vallotton: "When Paul says that he now lives by the faith of the Son of God, this not only means that he lives by the benefit of the cross but also that the apostle takes into account the intercession of Christ, ascended and glorious" (*Le Christ et la foi: Étude de théologie biblique*, Nouvelle série théologique 10 [Geneva, Switz.: Labor et Fides, 1960], 128); on the redefinition of the self in relation to the living presence of Christ in Galatians, see also Susan Grove Eastman, *Paul and the Person: Reframing Paul's Anthropology* (Grand Rapids: Eerdmans, 2017), 151–75.

now lives in the realm of πίστις, which comes from and is given by the Son of God.[28]

And the Son of God who gives πίστις is Christ crucified *and* raised from the dead.

GALATIANS 3:1–4:11: THE STORY OF THE RISEN CHRIST

The next task of this chapter is briefly to trace the story of Jesus in Gal 3:1–4:11, so masterfully illumined by Hays' work, but to do so in a way that gives proper attention to Paul's emphasis on the risen Jesus. Hays insists that the story in 3:1–4:11 shows that for Paul, believers are saved by *participation in Christ* (not by virtue of their own faith), and therefore Abraham is a "typological foreshadowing of Christ himself, a representative figure whose faithfulness secures blessing and salvation vicariously for others."[29] While there is much to admire about Hays' reading, in what follows we will show that Hays' insightful portrayal of Paul's participationist soteriology is attenuated by his exclusive focus on the cross. The role of the *risen* Christ is indispensable in incorporating believers "in Christ Jesus . . . through faith" (3:26; cf. 3:11-12, 21-22, 27-28). To put it succinctly: *participation in Christ is inconceivable without the risen Jesus.*

Galatians 3:1-5: "The Message about Πίστις" and the Spirit of the Risen Christ

As Paul addresses the foolishness of the Galatian believers in their acceptance of the teachings of the rival teachers in Galatians 3, he appeals to their experience of having received the Spirit by responding to the message about the πίστις relationship: "From works of the law did you receive the Spirit, or from the message about faith (ἀκοῆς πίστεως)? . . . The one supplying you with the Spirit and working miracles among you—from works of the law, or from the message about faith (ἀκοῆς πίστεως)?" (3:2, 5). Our translation unsurprisingly rejects the view that by πίστις Paul means merely an act or posture of human

[28] Gaventa, "Singularity of the Gospel Revisited," 194.
[29] Hays, *Faith of Jesus Christ*, 166.

faith (though of course that dimension is present in the relationship).[30] The reason this is so, however, is strengthened by how important the *Spirit* is in this section,[31] and particularly by the evidence that readers should understand τὸ πνεῦμα as precisely *the Spirit of the risen Jesus.* As we have already shown, the ongoing faithfulness and advocacy of the risen Jesus is central to the letter. In Galatians 3, Paul gives explicit attention to the *lived experience* of Jesus' faithfulness.

The evidence may be found just a bit later in Paul's discourse, in two key verses. First, in 3:14 Paul explicitly links the coming of the Spirit with being "in Christ Jesus" (ἐν Χριστῷ Ἰησοῦ): "in order that the blessing of Abraham for the gentiles might come into being *in Christ Jesus,* so that we might receive the promise of the Spirit through πίστις." This strongly suggests that "the one supplying the Spirit and working miracles" in 3:5 is not God (so NRSV), but the risen Christ. Then, in 4:6, Paul makes the point explicit: "And because you are sons, God has sent *the Spirit of his Son* (τὸ πνεῦμα τοῦ υἱοῦ αὐτοῦ) into our hearts."[32] Therefore, when Paul speaks of the "message about πίστις," he emphasizes the ongoing work of the risen Jesus portrayed to them by

---

[30] For the view that Paul here refers to human faith, see Douglas J. Moo, *Galatians*, BECNT (Grand Rapids: Baker, 2013), 183. Moo translates "hearing accompanied by faith" (*Galatians*, 180), an attributive genitive; Martyn ("Apocalyptic Gospel," 250): "proclamation in which God exercises his power to elicit faith"; David A. de Silva (*Galatians: A Handbook on the Greek Text*, BHGNT [Waco: Baylor University Press, 2014], 51): "the message about trust/faithfulness"; and Hays (*Faith of Jesus Christ*, 129): "the message of faith."

[31] Interpreters often downplay the importance of the Spirit in Gal 3:2-5; for example, C. K. Barrett (*The Holy Spirit and the Gospel Tradition* [London: SPCK, 1977], 2) and John W. Drane (*Paul, Libertine or Legalist? A Study in the Theology of the Major Pauline Epistles* [London: SPCK, 1975], 24) consider 3:1-5 to be merely an interlude that interrupts Paul's main argument. See further Longenecker, *Galatians*, 101–2.

[32] Martyn comments that the Spirit "draw[s] its characteristics from [the Son]" (*Galatians*, 391), but in light of Paul's formulations elsewhere (notably 2 Cor 3:17: ὁ δὲ κύριος τὸ πνεῦμά ἐστιν) this seems too weak. Better is something along the lines of Schweizer: "It is thus maintained that the exalted Christ is the πνεῦμα and that turning to Him entails entry into the sphere of the πνεῦμα. . . . In so far as Christ is regarded in His significance for the community, in His powerful action upon it, He can be identified with the πνεῦμα. . . . Paul is contending that the resurrection (or exaltation) sets Christ in the sphere of the Spirit, and that union with Him ensures believers of spiritual life, which is life in the community" (*TDNT* 6:419–20).

Paul (προγράφω in 3:1) and in whom the Galatians have been joined by their baptism. They *received* and are being *supplied with* the Spirit (3:2, 5). Having *begun* with the Spirit (3:3) and *experienced* so much (3:4), they obviously should be continuing as such. They presently have *miracles* worked among them (3:5). All of this is the work of their risen Lord, faithfully working among them and on their behalf.

Galatians 3:6-12: "Living" and the Resurrected Christ

Next, Paul shows that πίστις has its origins in Abraham, "who, believing God, entered and remained in a relationship of faith with God."[33] Paul writes in 3:6-9:

> Just as Abraham "trusted God (ἐπίστευσεν τῷ θεῷ), and it was reckoned to him as righteousness" [Gen 15:6], therefore, you see that the ones from faith (οἱ ἐκ πίστεως) are the descendants of Abraham. And the scripture, foreseeing that from faith (ἐκ πίστεως) God would justify the gentiles, declared the gospel beforehand to Abraham, saying, "All the gentiles will be blessed in (ἐν) you" [Gen 12:3]. Thus, the ones from faith (οἱ ἐκ πίστεως) are blessed with faithful Abraham (σὺν τῷ πιστῷ Ἀβραάμ).[34]

As in our discussion above regarding "living" in 2:19-20, here we observe again that Paul's repeated use of πιστ- and δικαιο- language is consistent with and stems from Paul's focus on Christ's resurrection.[35] This becomes explicit in the verses that follow (3:11-12):

> Clearly no one is justified before God by (ἐν) the law, for "The one who is righteous will live from faith (ἐκ πίστεως)" [Hab 2:4]. The law is not from faith (ἐκ πίστεως); rather, "The one who does them will live by (ἐν) them" [Lev 18:5].

---

[33] Ota, "Holistic *Pistis*," 2.

[34] Many commentators prefer to translate something like "believing Abraham" or "Abraham who believed," but the adjectival form is significant here, contra Longenecker: "The translation 'believing' more exactly expresses its meaning (certainly not 'trustworthy' as in Sir 44:20 or 'faithful' as in KJV and NEB)" (*Galatians*, 114).

[35] See further Joshua Jipp, *Christ Is King: Paul's Royal Ideology* (Minneapolis: Fortress Press, 2015), 213–15, on the resurrection as central to the "royal narrative" in Romans 1, and the discussion in our chapter on Philippians.

In Habakkuk and Leviticus, the contextual meaning of "to live" (חיה/ ζάω) is imprecise, though we may assume that it involves having a secure and healthy existence in the land. In some targumic texts, *eternal life* is in view: "if a person does them, he shall live in eternal life (בחיי עלמא) through them."[36] A more particular sense is certainly in view for Paul, given the way he has just spoken of "life" in 2:20: Paul *lives* by the πίστις of the resurrected Christ, the "righteous one" (3:11).[37] Those who *live* (resurrection life) do so not in the law but *in Christ* (designated consistently in Galatians by the relationship Paul calls πίστις).[38]

Galatians 3:13-14: "Christ Redeemed Us"

While the story of Jesus that informs Paul's argument in Galatians and is encapsulated by the πίστις formulations includes both the cross and the resurrection, those who would restrict it to the cross may seem to find support in 3:13-14:

> Christ redeemed us from the curse of the law, becoming a curse for us—for it is written, "Cursed is everyone who hangs on a tree" [Deut 21:23]—in order that the blessing of Abraham might come to the gentiles in Christ Jesus (ἐν Χριστῷ Ἰησοῦ), so that we might receive the promise of the Spirit through faith (διὰ τῆς πίστεως).

---

[36] Tg. Ps.-J. Lev 18:5; see also Tg. Onq. Lev 18:5; Ramban, *Comm.*, 245.

[37] Hays argues that "the word ζήσεται carried for Paul eschatological connotations and . . . is used in 3:11b as a virtual synonym of δικαιοῦται in 3:11a" (*Faith of Jesus Christ*, 133).

[38] As Campbell writes, "Habakkuk 2:4 is probably related closely to Paul's use of the phrase ἐκ πίστεως everywhere else as well. The parallelism between the citation and the phrase therefore extends well beyond Romans 1:17 through many other texts in Romans and Galatians, asking for this entire data set to be mutually interpreted" ("The Faithfulness of Jesus Christ in Romans 3:22" in *The Faith of Jesus Christ: Exegetical, Biblical, and Theological Studies*, ed. Michael F. Bird and Preston M. Sprinkle [Carlisle, U.K.: Paternoster; Peabody, Mass.: Hendrickson, 2009], 58). Morgan may be right to downplay attempts to import a nebulous "mysticism" into Paul's notion of "living" in Gal 2:20, but it is not clear that this should also mean refraining from speaking of being "in Christ": "*Pistis* is, for Paul, as has been noted, a relationship which enables the power and word of God to be transmitted through the faithful to the world, but it is not marked as a relationship or a state of mind or heart which leads to mystical visions of Christ *or union with Christ*" (*Roman Faith*, 282, emphasis added).

Our analysis of Galatians has shown that the crucifixion is not in any way excluded from the story of Christ's πίστις. Yet a case can be made that Paul has Christ's resurrection in mind even when he uses the language of "redemption" (ἐξαγοράζω in 3:13; 4:5; cf. ἀγοράζω in 1 Cor 6:20; 7:23; 2 Pet 2:1; Rev 5:9; 14:3). In the following chapter, we will endeavor to show that Paul's references to the concepts of "blood" and sacrifice are inherently focused on the life of the exalted Jesus, however much the cross is mentioned. This will suggest that for Paul even sacrifice is seen primarily in terms of a *heavenly* offering. In Galatians, Paul does not use specifically sacrificial terminology (ἀπολύτρωσις occurs in 1 Cor 1:30; Rom 3:24; 8:23; Eph 1:7, 14; 4:30; Col 1:14; cf. Heb 9:15; λυτρόω occurs in Titus 2:14; cf. Heb 9:12). This does not seem to be a meaningful distinction for Paul, and in any case ἀπολύτρωσις is clearly associated with *resurrection* in Rom 3:24 and 8:23.[39]

More to the point, in Galatians Paul associates the language of "redemption" (ἐξαγοράζω) with the *cross* in 3:13: "Christ redeemed us from the curse of the law by becoming a curse for us—for it is written, 'Cursed is everyone who hangs on a tree.'" As we have seen above, however, even though Paul refers here to Jesus' death in the context of the "curse" of the law, the context is clearly about (resurrection) life (3:11), the blessing that is "in Christ Jesus" (3:14), and the promise of the Spirit "through faith" (3:14). The second reference to Christ "redeeming" comes in 4:4-6:

> But when the fullness of time had come, God sent his Son, born of a woman, born under the law, in order that he might *redeem* (ἐξαγοράσῃ) those who were under the law, so that we might receive *adoption*. And because you are sons, God has sent the Spirit of his Son (τὸ πνεῦμα τοῦ υἱοῦ αὐτοῦ) into our hearts.

As he does in Rom 8:23, Paul collocates "redemption" language with the image of adoption (υἱοθεσία). And as we considered above, the Spirit of the heavenly Jesus (Gal 4:6), actively working on behalf of those

---

[39] Rom 3:24: "through the *redemption* that is in Christ Jesus (διὰ τῆς ἀπολυτρώσεως τῆς ἐν Χριστῷ Ἰησοῦ)"; Rom 8:23: "and not only the creation, but we ourselves, who have the first fruits of the Spirit, groan inwardly while we wait for adoption, the *redemption* (ἀπολύτρωσις) of our bodies."

who are in him, is what characterizes the promise of the Spirit through
πίστις (3:14). The story of *redemption* includes the fact of Jesus' death,
to be sure, but is also the story of the faithfulness of the heavenly Jesus.

Galatians 3:19-22: The Promise of Christ's Faithfulness
Is Life (ἐκ πίστεως Ἰησοῦ Χριστοῦ, 3:22)

To this point in Galatians 3 (a section littered with the language of
πίστις/πιστός/πιστεύω: Gal 3:2, 3, 5, 6, 7, 8, 9 [twice], 11, 12, 14), Paul
has drawn attention to the Spirit of the resurrected Jesus, he has once
again spoken of "living" in ways that suggest resurrection life, and he
has made the first of two references to "redemption" that are closely
tied to Paul's participatory understanding of the way believers are
adopted into the story of the risen Jesus. Paul's use of πιστ- language
continues in 3:21-22 with yet another reference to "making alive" (3:21),
followed by the much-discussed construction in 3:22:

> Is the law then against the promises of God? May it not be! For
> if a law was given that was able to make alive (ζῳοποιῆσαι), then
> indeed righteousness would be from the law (ἐκ νόμου). But the
> scripture imprisoned all things under sin, so that what was prom-
> ised ἐκ πίστεως Ἰησοῦ Χριστοῦ might be given to those who
> believe (τοῖς πιστεύουσιν).

If the faithfulness described here is Christ's,[40] it makes little sense to
limit πίστις in 3:22 to the obedient death of Christ on the cross.[41] Both

---

[40] Oakes favors an objective genitive reading ("on the basis of trust in Jesus Christ"),
yet beautifully articulates the intimate relation between πίστις and "in Christ" language in Paul. Considering the question of how Paul can move from the promise
being given to the singular "seed" in 3:19 to the plural (τοῖς πιστεύουσιν) in 3:22,
Oakes writes, "A way for it to work would be if living *ek pisteōs Jēsou Christou* . . .
already carries a connotation of being united as a single entity in union with Christ,
that is, if *ek pisteōs Christou* is language of participation in Christ. That this is indeed
how Paul is thinking is shown by 3:14. The gentiles receive the blessing of Abraham
en Christō Jēsou . . . and the promise (of the Spirit) *dia tēs pisteōs*. . . . *Pistis* and being
in Christ are already tied firmly together in relation to gentiles receiving the promise"
(*Galatians*, PCNT [Grand Rapids: Baker Academic, 2015], 125).
[41] *Pace* Martyn, who calls this "an expression by which Paul refers to Christ's
trustful obedience to God in the giving up of his own life for us" (*Galatians*, 361; cf.

in the immediate context of Galatians 2–3 and elsewhere in Paul, to "make alive" is unquestionably the domain of the resurrected Jesus: "If the Spirit of him who raised Jesus from the dead lives (οἰκεῖ) in you, he who raised Christ from the dead will *make alive* (ζῳοποιήσει) your mortal bodies also through his Spirit that dwells in you" (Rom 8:11); "Just as all die in Adam, all will be made alive (ζῳοποιηθήσονται) in Christ" (1 Cor 15:22). Yes, for Paul the situation for all humanity, Jew and gentile, was desperate, and Hays and others are surely correct that for Paul the good news is that "God did act through Christ's faithful death to liberate us from the power of sin and the present evil age."[42] By Paul's own account, however, "what was promised ἐκ πίστεως Ἰησοῦ Χριστοῦ" and given to "those who believe (τοῖς πιστεύουσιν)" is nothing other than the "relational way of life"[43] that characterizes believers in union with the faithful heavenly Jesus Christ.

Galatians 3:23-28: "Until Christ" and
Baptism into the Risen Christ

In Gal 3:23-24, Paul seems to use the word πίστις to designate a kind of personified entity:

> Now before faith (τὴν πίστιν) came, we were imprisoned and guarded under the law until faith (πίστιν) would be revealed. Therefore the law was our disciplinarian until Christ (εἰς Χριστόν), so that we might be justified by faith (ἐκ πίστεως).

Hays' solution to what might be viewed as slight shift in Paul's shaping of πιστ- language is to say that "Paul speaks here of πίστις as a particular *event* that 'came' at a specific point in the past, the very recent past, from Paul's perspective."[44] No doubt Hays' reading is motivated

---

270–71). Martyn appeals here to Paul's reference to Christ's obedience (ὑπακοή) in Rom 5:19; see further the next chapter on Romans.

[42] Hays, "The Letter to the Galatians: Introduction, Commentary, Reflections," in *The New Interpreter's Bible*, ed. Leander E. Keck, *vol. 11* (Nashville: Abingdon, 2015), 269.

[43] Oakes is helpful in suggesting "relational way of life" over Morgan's "relationship" ("*Pistis*," 265).

[44] Hays, *Faith of Jesus Christ*, 202 (emphasis original).

by his concern to limit the referent of πίστις [Χριστοῦ] to the cross. Paul does indeed say in 3:23 that faith "came" (πρὸ τοῦ . . . ἐλθεῖν τὴν πίστιν), but most translations overemphasize the connotation that it is a "past event" by supplying the word "came" again in 3:24,[45] which merely says, "until Christ" (εἰς Χριστόν). If in 3:24 Paul uses "Christ" to indicate the continuing story of Christ's coming, death, resurrection, and exaltation (and that certainly seems to be the case), it need not diminish the event character of Christ's coming to suggest that what "came" at a specific point in the past was the *revelation* (εἰς τὴν μέλλουσαν πίστιν ἀποκαλυφθῆναι, 3:23b) of πίστις (the relational way of life *ushered in* by the Christ event), rather than that new way of life itself (which is certainly not restricted to the past).

In addition, Hays' own explication of what these verses contribute to the narrative substructure of Galatians would seem to require that the focus shift away from the punctiliar, past event of the cross and toward a recognition of the ongoing faithfulness of the risen Christ:

> Christ is the ground of faith because he is the one who, in fulfillment of the prophecy, lives ἐκ πίστεως. He thus proves to be the one true seed of the faithful Abraham and the heir of all the promises. His destiny, however, is not a merely individual one, because he acts as a universal representative figure, enacting (ἐκ πίστεως) a pattern of redemption which then determines the existence of others, to whom Paul refers as οἱ ἐκ πίστεως. These others *participate in him and in his destiny* not only vicariously but also actually: they are *baptized into Christ* (3:27) and they *receive the Spirit*, which in turn enables them to live ἐκ πίστεως, in conformity to the pattern grounded in Jesus Christ.[46]

As we have seen, union with Christ requires the risen Christ, and the reception of Christ's Spirit is a key indicator of the ongoing faithfulness of the heavenly Christ. Now, too, we may add that baptism must be baptism into the *risen* Christ.

---

[45] For example, "until Christ came" appears in such translations as the NRSV, NIV, ESV, and Elberfelder ("auf Christus hin geworden"). The accurate rendering "until Christ" appears, for example, in the CEB, NET, and KJV.

[46] Hays, *Faith of Jesus Christ*, 203, emphasis added.

Since this new, relational way of life has arrived (ἐλθούσης δὲ τῆς πίστεως, 3:25), the time of the disciplinarian is over, and "*in Christ Jesus*, you are all children of God through faith (πάντες γὰρ υἱοὶ θεοῦ ἐστε διὰ τῆς πίστεως ἐν Χριστῷ Ἰησοῦ)" (3:26).[47] Baptism, says Paul, is the signifier of this participation, where believers are "clothed" with Christ and have become part of the radical new way of life as "one in Christ Jesus (εἷς . . . ἐν Χριστῷ Ἰησοῦ)" (3:27-28). "If you are of Christ (εἰ . . . ὑμεῖς Χριστοῦ)," writes Paul in this summary of his topic for the whole of chapter 3, "you are then Abraham's seed, heirs according to the promise" (3:29). The preceding verses make clear that Χριστοῦ in 3:29 is a version of πίστις Χριστοῦ, and the present focus of all of this makes abundantly clear that to be "of Christ" is to be in that relationship of faith, sustained by none other than the living, risen Jesus.[48]

THE CONCLUSION OF THE LETTER: "THROUGH THE SPIRIT, BY ΠΙΣΤΙΣ" AND THE FAMILY OF ΠΙΣΤΙΣ

Though Paul reminds the Galatians that at his initial visit they welcomed him "as Christ Jesus" (Gal 4:14), thus reinforcing the union that exists between believers and the risen Christ, Paul does not utilize the language of πίστις until the cluster of three occurrences in 5:5, 6, and 22 and a final reference to the "family of πίστις" in 6:10. While a version of the formulation πίστις Χριστοῦ does not appear in these final occurrences, the way Paul's usage has shaped the term πίστις leads the reader to prioritize the relational and present-tense mental items associated with the term. And this is precisely what Paul provides.

---

[47] The rendering of πάντες γὰρ υἱοὶ θεοῦ ἐστε διὰ τῆς πίστεως ἐν Χριστῷ Ἰησοῦ (3:26) in the CEB is deeply misleading: "You are all God's children through faith in Christ Jesus." As David deSilva and others point out, ἐν should not be read as a subordinate descriptor of πίστεως, because Paul would then surely have written τῆς πίστεως τῆς ἐν Χριστῷ Ἰησοῦ as in 2:20 (*Galatians*, 76).

[48] Schumacher, also emphasizing the relational aspect of πίστις ("bei πίστις in besonderer Weise der Aspekt der Beziehung zur Sprache kommt"), argues that the phrase βαπτίζειν εἰς Χριστόν is to be interpreted by the term πίστις, and thus Paul is not here using βαπτίζω as a *terminus technicus* for the Christian ritual (*Zur Entstehung christlicher Sprache*, 163–64; so also BDAG, 164).

After Paul's most direct rebuke of the Galatians' desire to be circumcised in 5:2-4 ("you are estranged from Christ, you've fallen from grace"), the apostle immediately returns to the positive description of the believers' way of life using terms that he has emphasized throughout the letter and particularly in the sections where the debated genitive phrases occur (πνεῦμα, πίστις, and δικαιοσύνη):

> For by the Spirit, from faith (ἐκ πίστεως), we are awaiting the hope of righteousness (ἐλπίδα δικαιοσύνης). For *in Christ Jesus* (ἐν . . . Χριστῷ Ἰησοῦ) neither circumcision nor uncircumcision counts, but rather πίστις working (ἐνεργουμένη) through love. (5:5-6)

Little commentary is needed at this point, given what has come before in the letter. That being "in Christ" is a present-tense notion (ἐνεργουμένη, 5:6) is obvious,[49] as is the realization that the Spirit is that of the *risen* Christ.

As we considered in our examination of the Corinthian correspondence and earlier with regard to Gal 1:10, Paul sometimes makes use of the related term πείθω in connection with πιστ- language as well.[50] In the very next verse, Paul writes, "You were running well; who cut you off lest you obey (πείθεσθαι) the truth?" (5:7). Most interpreters assume polysemy and choose from a range of glosses here to translate "obey" or "follow," as often seems appropriate when the form

---

[49] See also Oakes, who rightly emphasizes the present-tense notion of πίστις and cites Gal 5:6 as a particularly clear example (*"Pistis,"* 270). On the importance of responding to the gift given in Christ in Paul's thought, see especially John M. G. Barclay's magisterial *Paul and the Gift* (Grand Rapids: Eerdmans, 2017).

[50] Schumacher thinks that etymologically the πιστ- forms are derived from the middle form of πείθω and reflect the Indo-European usage of **bheidh* (Schumacher, *Zur Entstehung christlicher Sprache*, 201–2; cf. Ernst Seidl, *Pistis in der griechischen Literatur bis zur Zeit des Peripatos* [Innsbruck: Verlag, 1952], 20). Interestingly, Homer uses the adjective πιστός but uses the middle πείθεσθαι to mean "trust," rather than πιστεύω, suggesting that πιστεύω had not yet come into use (e.g., "through lovemaking, we might trust one another [πεποίθομεν ἀλλήλοισιν]," *Od.* 10.335). In a relevance-theoretical framework that emphasizes monosemy, it is no surprise that a word group with such an etymology lends itself to exploitation of the relation between πιστ- and πειθ- language in texts like Galatians.

appears in the passive.⁵¹ Yet to isolate this verb by translating in such a way is misleading, given the shaping of both πειθ- (1:10) and πιστ-language earlier in the letter, and especially given that Paul repeats the noun form in 5:8 ("This persuasion [ἡ πεισμονή] is not from *the one calling you*") and then the verb in 5:10 ("*I* am confident [ἐγὼ πέποιθα] about you in *the Lord* [ἐν κυρίῳ] that you will not think otherwise"). Once again, Paul's discourse emphasizes the active and ongoing work of Christ and, as in Gal 4:14, stresses Paul's own authority because he is joined with Christ and the believers ("in the Lord," 5:10). The context of this cluster of πειθ- words prompts readers to activate mental items related to relationship and fidelity, even as Paul addresses questions of "persuasion" that have led to the crisis Paul addresses in the letter.

Just a few verses later, Paul encourages the Galatians to "live by the Spirit" (πνεύματι περιπατεῖτε, 5:16) and includes πίστις in the list of the Spirit's "fruit": "Rather, the fruit of the Spirit is love, joy, peace, patience, kindness, goodness, faithfulness (πίστις), gentleness, and self-control" (5:22-23). Interpreters generally distinguish the "virtue" called πίστις in 5:22 from the phrase πίστις Χριστοῦ that is so central to Galatians as a whole.⁵² In a relevance-theoretical framework, however, the inclusion of πίστις in the list may be seen simply to contribute to the shaping of the term in this crucial section of the letter, which emphasizes the life that characterizes believers who are participating in and experiencing the Spirit of the risen Christ.⁵³ It is true that along

---

⁵¹ BDAG indicates these glosses are preferred when the passive form is followed by the dative of person or thing (792). Texts like Heb 13:17 ("Obey your leaders" [πείθεσθε τοῖς ἡγουμένοις ὑμῶν] and Jas 3:3 ("If we put bits in the mouths of horses to make them obey us [εἰς τὸ πείθεσθαι αὐτοὺς ἡμῖν]") seem to support the use of these glosses. A closer parallel in Rom 2:8, however, uses the present tense and is perhaps better rendered "[mis]trust": "for those of strife who mistrust the truth and yet trust in unrighteousness (ἀπειθοῦσι τῇ ἀληθείᾳ πειθομένοις δὲ τῇ ἀδικίᾳ)."

⁵² For example, Oakes: "As a virtue partway down a list, it cannot be the *pistis Christou* to which Paul has given a vital role in the letter's soteriology" (*Galatians*, 176–77).

⁵³ Something similar occurs with the term ζῆλος in 5:20, which is often translated "jealousy" but is part of a word group that has been shaped and utilized with great importance in the letter; see further Benjamin J. Lappenga, *Paul's Language of Ζῆλος: Monosemy and the Rhetoric of Identity and Practice*, BibInt 137 (Leiden: Brill, 2016), 138.

with other terms in the list, πίστις among believers (and even toward nonbelievers) may nod toward a practice that is conducive to unity. Yet the occurrence of the word in the list also recalls readers to the ways Paul has developed πίστις as the relational way of life they experience in Christ and gives specificity to the surrounding discourse about life "by the Spirit" (5:16), connecting it with all that has come before in the letter: "And the ones *of Christ Jesus* (οἱ . . . τοῦ Χριστοῦ Ἰησοῦ) have crucified the flesh with its passions and desires. If we *live* (ζῶμεν) by the Spirit, let us also be in line with the Spirit" (5:24-25).

The final occurrence of the πίστις lexicon also serves as a fitting summary of what we have examined in this chapter on the faithfulness of the risen Christ in Galatians. At the conclusion of the paraenetic section 5:13–6:10, Paul charges his readers, "So then, as we have opportune time, let us work good toward all, and especially toward those of the family of faith (πρὸς τοὺς οἰκείους τῆς πίστεως)" (6:10). Certainly "those of the family of faith" includes fellow Christ followers, both local and outside of Galatia, who benefit from the good work toward all to which the Galatians are called. Yet given the conditional statement in 6:8—"if you sow to the Spirit, you will reap eternal life from the Spirit"—those of the family of faith must include not only humans united to Christ by πίστις but also Christ, the Son, and God, the Father, as members of this family. Morgan puts it nicely:

> One can, however, without difficulty be an *oikeios* of a community formed by a relationship. To translate this phrase "fellow members of the relationship" or "the bond of trust" again assumes relatively little evolution in the meaning of *pistis* and makes good sense in context. If the bond is understood as reified slightly further here, *hē pistis* may even mean "the community of trust." Verse 6.10 would then run: "While we have the opportunity, let us do good to all, but especially to fellow members of the relationship/community of trust [which exists between God, Christ, and faithful human beings]."[54]

This closing instruction therefore emphasizes the community of trust among God, the risen and exalted Christ, and faithful humanity.

---

[54] Morgan, *Roman Faith*, 267.

CONCLUSION

In his groundbreaking work on Galatians, Richard Hays has shown the importance of the christological narrative that serves as the basis for Paul's theologizing. Hays summarizes his own understanding of that narrative and of the role of the phrase πίστις Χριστοῦ in evoking it:

> The narrative structure of the gospel story depicts Jesus as the divinely commissioned protagonist who gives himself up to death on a cross in order to liberate humanity from bondage (Gal 1:4; 2:20; 3:13-14; 4:4-7). His death, in obedience to the will of God, is simultaneously a loving act of faithfulness (πίστις) to God and the decisive manifestation of God's faithfulness to his covenant promise to Abraham. Paul's use of πίστις Χριστοῦ and other similar phrases should be understood as summary allusions to this story, referring to Jesus' fidelity in carrying out this mission.[55]

We maintain that Paul's use of πίστις Χριστοῦ in Gal 2:16, 3:22, 26—combined with Paul's employment of πιστ- language elsewhere in the letter—does indeed evoke the story of Jesus Christ's own πίστις. But Christ's πίστις, which is directed primarily toward humanity, continues beyond the cross as the faithful Christ, particularly through the Spirit, is present with those joined to him by πίστις. As is the case elsewhere in Paul's letters, the narrative substructure of Galatians is the narrative of the crucified and risen Lord Jesus Christ.

[55] Hays, *Faith of Jesus Christ*, 274–75.

5

ROMANS
"The One Who Is Righteous Will Live by Faith"

In his *Homilies on Leviticus*, Origen writes that Jesus pours out his blood "not only in Jerusalem where that altar and its base and the Tent of Meeting were, but also that same blood itself was sprinkled on the celestial altar which is in heaven, where the 'church of the firstborn is.'"[1] According to Origen, Christ "now places himself before the face of God, interceding (*interpellans*) for us; he places himself before the altar, that he might offer a place of atonement (*repropitiationem*) for us to God."[2] In *Homily 9*, Origen writes that after Christ "penetrates the heavens" (*penetrat caelos*; cf. Heb 4:14), he goes to the Father to make atonement (*propitium faciat*) for the human race and advocates for all those who believe in him (*exoret pro omnibus credentibus in se*).[3] Origen's atonement theology throughout these sermons is undeniably and deeply influenced by the letter to the Hebrews. Yet interestingly *Homily 9* closes with a citation of Rom 3:25, a verse that Origen also believes locates Jesus' atoning work in heaven: "Paul calls to mind this place of atonement (*repropitiatione*) when he says concerning Christ, 'Whom

---

[1] *Hom. Lev.* 1.3; Gary Wayne Barkley, trans., *Origen: Homilies on Leviticus 1–16*, FC 83 (Washington, D.C.: Catholic University of America Press, 1990), 34.
[2] "Assistit nuns vultui Dei, interpellans pro nobis, assistit altari, ut repropitiationem pro nobis offeret Deo"; *Hom. Lev.* 7.2; our translation.
[3] *Hom. Lev.* 9.5.

God offered as a propitiator [*propitiatorem*] by his blood through faith [*per fidem*]."[4]

Few modern interpreters would take Origen as their methodological exemplar, but one need not embark on Origen's "flights of fancy"[5] to follow his lead in locating Paul's reference to Christ's blood in Rom 3:25 in the *heavenly realm*, rather than on the cross.[6] Our argument in this chapter is that the pervasive "in Christ" language and its collocation with references to πίστις in the letter to the Romans—not least in the mentions of Christ's πίστις in 3:22 and 3:26—place clear emphasis on the resurrection and the ongoing advocacy and intercession of the risen Christ.

ROMANS 1:17: LIFE BY CHRIST'S RESURRECTION

As we have throughout the book, in this chapter we take seriously the way the πιστ- word group is shaped throughout Romans (even if we must be selective in our coverage).[7] We begin, then, by observing the concepts that Paul collocates with πίστις early in the letter. In both 1:17 and 3:21-22, (1) the subject is δικαιοσύνη θεοῦ, (2) the predicate uses a word denoting "revelation" (ἀποκαλύπτω in 1:17 and φανερόω

---

[4] "Paulus . . . de hac repropitiatione commemorat, cum dicit de Christo: 'Quem posuit Deus propitiatorem in sanguine ipsius per fidem'" (*Hom. Lev.* 9.5; our translation of Rufinus' Latin rendering). David M. Moffitt, who alerted us to this reference in Origen, suggests that *repropitiationem* renders ἱλασμός in Origen's original ("Jesus' Heavenly Sacrifice in Early Christian Reception of Hebrews: A Survey," *JTS* 68 [2017]: 58n33), though we think ἱλαστήριον is more likely given the citation of Rom 3:25 that follows (even if Rufinus gives *propitiatorem* in the citation itself).

[5] See Charles J. Scalise, "Allegorical Flights of Fancy: The Problem of Origen's Exegesis," *GOTR* 32 (1987): 69–88.

[6] Moffitt makes passing reference to Origen's reference to Paul in "Jesus' Heavenly Sacrifice," 61. Even Pierre Vallotton, setting up a citation of Rom 3:25, emphasizes Jesus' death/sacrifice: "Jesus croit que son sacrifice ne sera pas vain pour nous, selon la promesse de Dieu" (*Le Christ et la foi: Etude de théologie biblique*, Nouvelle série théologique 10 [Geneva, Switz.: Labor et Fides, 1960], 99).

[7] πίστις/πιστεύω/ἀπιστέω/ἀπιστία terms occur sixty-six times in Romans, and the clusters are readily apparent: 1:5, 8, 12, 16, 17 (three times); 3:2, 3 (three times), 22 (twice), 25, 26, 27, 28, 30 (twice), 31; 4:3, 5 (twice), 9, 11 (twice), 12, 13, 14, 16 (twice), 17, 18, 19, 20 (twice), 24; 5:1, 2; 6:8; 9:30, 32, 33; 10:4, 6, 8, 9, 10, 11, 14 (twice), 16, 17; 11:20 (twice), 23; 12:3, 6; 13:11; 14:1, 2, 22, 23 (twice); 15:13; 16:26.

in 3:21), and (3) the vital modifier has to do with πίστις (ἐκ πίστεως εἰς πίστιν and the citation of Hab 2:4 in 1:17, and διὰ πίστεως Ἰησοῦ Χριστοῦ εἰς πάντας τοὺς πιστεύοντας in 3:22).[8] These factors are often noted in making the case that 1:17 and 3:21-22 are to be interpreted in parallel,[9] but there is a fourth significant emphasis embedded with the others: *resurrection life.*

The centrality of the resurrection for Paul's presentation of his gospel in the opening of Romans cannot be overstated. The gospel in Romans 1, which reveals the righteousness of God through πίστις for πίστις (1:17), is preeminently a message about Jesus' Davidic identity, his resurrection from the dead, and his lordship (1:3-4). The first mention of πίστις in Romans 1, the intriguing phrase "obedience of faith" (ὑπακοὴν πίστεως, 1:5),[10] immediately follows Paul's declaration that

---

[8] The formal parallel (ἐκ/διά and εἰς) makes it virtually certain that 1:17 is a concise statement denoting "from the faithfulness [of Christ] for the faith [of believers]"; see, for example, Luke Timothy Johnson, "Rom 3:21-26 and the Faith of Jesus," *CBQ* 44 (1982): 79.

[9] See, for example, Douglas A. Campbell, "The Faithfulness of Jesus Christ in Romans 3:22," in *The Faith of Jesus Christ: Exegetical, Biblical, and Theological Studies,* ed. Michael F. Bird and Preston M. Sprinkle (Carlisle, U.K.: Paternoster; Peabody, Mass.: Hendrickson, 2009), 60; Francis Watson, *Paul and the Hermeneutics of Faith,* 2nd ed. (London: Bloomsbury T&T Clark, 2016), 64-69; and Roy E. Ciampa, "Habakkuk 2:4 in Paul: Echoes, Allusions, and Rewritings" (paper presented at the Annual Meeting of the SBL, Boston, November 28, 2017).

[10] Teresa Morgan takes this phrase as a genitive of apposition (*Roman Faith and Christian Faith: Pistis and Fides in the Early Roman Empire and Early Churches* [Oxford: Oxford University Press, 2015], 282-83; cf. Dunn, *Romans 1-8,* WBC 38A [Dallas: Word, 1988], 24; and Johnson, who thinks "Paul clearly brings the two terms together as mutually interpretative" ["Rom 3:21-26," 86]). In our view, the appositional reading collapses πίστις into obedience in a way that is foreign to Paul. Here and in 16:26, it seems best to translate as a genitive of source, as in "the obedience that springs from faithfulness" or "the obedience based on faithfulness" (cf. Frederick W. Danker, Walter Bauer, William F. Arndt, and F. Wilbur Gingrich (BDAG), *Greek-English Lexicon of the New Testament and Other Early Christian Literature,* 3rd ed. (Chicago: University of Chicago Press, 2000), 1028; Daniel B. Wallace categorizes it tentatively as a "genitive of production/producer [produced by]" (*Greek Grammar Beyond the Basics: An Exegetical Syntax of the New Testament* [Grand Rapids: Zondervan, 1996], 104-6). As we have suggested already, if "obedience" was a "sense" that could be selected from the polysemous noun πίστις, there would be little need to qualify πίστις with ὑπακοή. But from the perspective of lexical monosemy, which we have adopted in this study,

Jesus Christ is *Lord* "by resurrection of the dead" (ἐξ ἀναστάσεως νεκρῶν, 1:4). In 1:6-16, Paul speaks of πίστις (1:8, 12, 16) to emphasize the bond between those who are "called of Jesus Christ" (κλητοὶ Ἰησοῦ Χριστοῦ, 1:6), the risen Lord (1:4, 7),[11] and his own apostolic ministry (διὰ τῆς ἐν ἀλλήλοις πίστεως ὑμῶν τε καὶ ἐμοῦ, 1:12).

Thus when in 1:17, often viewed as the programmatic statement of the letter,[12] Paul cites Hab 2:4, the prophetic text that pervades the language and logic of the letter's argument, the terms πίστις and ζάω have been shaped so as to signal Christ's *faithfulness* and *resurrection*.[13]

---

we may say that πίστις and ὑπακοή are collocated but not equated. Their syntactical pairing in Rom 1:5 and 16:26 is mutually informative (πίστις produces ὑπακοή; ὑπακοή is a fruit of πίστις) but not equalizing. Similarly, in 10:16 ("not all have obeyed [ὑπήκουσαν] the good news, for Isaiah says, 'Lord, who has believed [ἐπίστευσεν] our message?'"), ὑπακοή could be viewed as parallel to πίστις, but in 10:17 Paul immediately clarifies that faith flows from the hearing of the good news (ἄρα ἡ πίστις ἐξ ἀκοῆς). Except for the quotation from Isaiah, Paul tends not to use πιστ- language with objects other than Christ/God, whereas he speaks of "obeying" a message (10:16) and a form of teaching (6:17). In addition, Paul seems to use the term ὑπακοή primarily to designate the response of the gentiles: "what Christ accomplished through me for the obedience of the gentiles (εἰς ὑπακοὴν ἐθνῶν)" (15:18). For an overview of the uncertainties regarding the interpretation of 1:5, see Richard N. Longenecker, *The Epistle to the Romans: A Commentary on the Greek Text*, NIGTC (Grand Rapids: Eerdmans, 2016), 79–82, and especially Don B. Garlington, *Faith, Obedience, and Perseverance: Aspects of Paul's Letter to the Romans*, WUNT 79 (Tübingen: Mohr Siebeck, 1994), 11–15.

[11] The next section in which Paul refers to Christ as "Lord" also explicitly mentions resurrection: οἷς πιστεύουσιν ἐπὶ τὸν ἐγείραντα Ἰησοῦν τὸν κύριον ἡμῶν ἐκ νεκρῶν (4:24).

[12] See, for example, Ernst Käsemann, *Commentary on Romans*, trans. Geoffrey Bromiley (Grand Rapids: Eerdmans, 1980), 30.

[13] Douglas A. Campbell limits Christ's faithfulness to the cross, yet he can write of the citation of Hab 2:4 in Rom 1:17, "The righteous one spoken of here is plainly Christ, and this prophetic text . . . suggests that by means of his faithfulness to the point of death he will live in the sense of being vindicated and resurrected" (*The Deliverance of God: An Apocalyptic Rereading of Justification in Paul* [Grand Rapids: Eerdmans, 2009], 613). The various versions of Hab 2:4 are well known (in the Masoretic Text, the righteous one lives by his own faithfulness [וצדיק באמונתו יחיה], in the Septuagint by God's faithfulness [ὁ δὲ δίκαιος ἐκ πίστεώς μου ζήσεται], and in Gal 3:11/ Rom 1:17 no pronoun is given [ὁ δίκαιος ἐκ πίστεως ζήσεται]). In our view, some ambiguity or "slippage" as to who is righteous (Christ, human beings, God) fits Paul's participatory understanding of righteousness well, not least the phrase immediately

As Paul will reiterate in the remainder of the letter, believers live because of Jesus' life (ἐν τῇ ζωῇ αὐτοῦ, 5:10; cf. 5:17-18, 21; 6:4, 13, 22-23, 8:10-11; 14:7-9). All of this is budding in 1:17: in "it"—the good news that Jesus is the Son of God with power according to the spirit of holiness by *resurrection from the dead* (1:4)—the righteousness of God is revealed from (the risen Christ's) faithfulness for (enabling the believer's) faith,[14] as it is written: *the one who is righteous will live by* πίστις.

ROMANS 3:1-4 AND 9:1–11:36: "ENTRUSTED WITH THE ORACLES OF GOD"

We will identify more clearly what "life" entails when we examine 3:25 below, but first it will be helpful to note the way the term πίστις factors into Paul's consideration of the Jewish people in Romans. Toward the end of his depiction of humanity under the power of Sin (1:18–3:20), Paul affirms in the strongest terms available the abiding goodness of

---

preceding the citation (ἐκ πίστεως εἰς πίστιν). For the argument that the reference in 1:17 is to Christ, see J. R. Daniel Kirk, *Unlocking Romans: Resurrection and the Justification of God* (Grand Rapids: Eerdmans, 2008), 47–49; Campbell, *Deliverance*, 615; and Stephen L. Young, "Romans 1.1-5 and Paul's Christological Use of Hab. 2.4 in Rom. 1.17: An Underutilized Consideration in the Debate," *JSNT* 34 (2012): 277–85. For a helpful survey of the history of interpretation regarding the phrase ἐκ πίστεως εἰς πίστιν, see C. L. Quarles, "From Faith to Faith: A Fresh Examination of the Prepositional Series in Romans 1:17," *NovT* 45 (2003): 1–21.

[14] To translate 1:17 as we do (from the faithfulness of Jesus for human faith in Jesus) is not meant to suggest that human πίστις here is not multidirectional—that is, directed toward Christ and lived out faithful relationships with others. More broadly in Paul, πίστις is characteristic of all sorts of human actions and relationships: stewards are supposed to be trustworthy (1 Cor 4:2); faithfulness is a marker of human beings, presumably with some relation to how they relate to one another (1 Cor 4:17; 7:25; Eph 1:1; 6:21; Col 1:1, 7; 4:7, 9); "believer" becomes something of a mark of Christian identity, with implications for community formation and definition (1 Cor 7:12-15; 14:22-24; 2 Cor 6:14-15; cf. 1 Cor 6:6; 10:27; 2 Cor 4:4; Gal 6:10; Eph 4:13); πίστις is a spiritual gift to be used for the building up of the Christ-following community (1 Cor 12:9; 13:2; cf 13:7; Rom 12:6); the Corinthians are together called to stand firm in πίστις (1 Cor 16:13; 2 Cor 1:24) or live in πίστις (2 Cor 13:5; cf. Col 1:23); (human) faith works through (human) love (Gal 5:6; cf. Eph 3:17; 6:23); and πίστις is a virtue found in virtue lists (Gal 5:22). Also, Phil 2:17 refers to πίστις-inspired (human) sacrificial action.

the law and its custodians, anticipating what is to come in Romans 9–11. The Jews were "entrusted" (ἐπιστεύθησαν) with the oracles of God (3:2),[15] and their "unfaithfulness" (ἀπιστία) will not nullify the "faithfulness of God" (τὴν πίστιν τοῦ θεοῦ, 3:3). We will address below the majestic portrayal of Christ's faithfulness that follows in 3:21–8:39, but for now we may look ahead to the section in which Paul returns to the question of God's faithfulness to Israel in chapters 9 through 11.

As in chapters 1 and 3, Paul's discourse in chapters 9 through 11 places the notion of *life/resurrection* at the center of an intense cluster of references to πίστις (9:30, 32, 33; 10:4, 6, 8, 9, 10, 11, 14 [twice], 16, 17). The references to "life" occur in five key verses (9:17, 26, 10:5, 9, 11:15), three of which are citations from scripture, in line with the quotation of Hab 2:4 in Rom 1:17. Paul cites Exod 9:16 LXX in Rom 9:17 to reinforce his point that God has mercy and hardens hearts according to God's will (9:18). In light of what Paul is about to say regarding πίστις and the good news of Christ's resurrection in the remainder of chapters 9–11, it is intriguing that the two terms that appear in Paul's citation but not the Greek versions available to us are "raised up" (ἐξεγείρω) and "power" (δύναμις).[16] Whether Paul deliberately substituted those two words or not, in the context of Romans 9 the citation works as a kind of double entendre, a statement about Pharaoh but also Christ: "For this purpose I *raised you up*: so that I might show in you my *power*, and so that my name may be proclaimed in all the earth" (9:17). Paul uses these two terms in the key passage we considered earlier ("Son of God with *power* [δυνάμει] . . . by resurrection from the dead," 1:4; "for I am not ashamed of the gospel; it is the *power* [δύναμις] of God for salvation to everyone who has faith," 1:16), and 4:25 ("*raised* [ἠγέρθη] for our justification"), which we consider further later.

---

[15] The "oracles of God" were of course stored underneath the "mercy seat" [ἱλαστήριον] that Paul refers to in 3:25; see further in the section on Rom 3:21–31, as well as Karl Barth, *The Epistle to the Romans*, trans. Edwyn C. Hoskyns (Oxford: Oxford University Press, 1968), 105.

[16] Rom 9:17: εἰς αὐτὸ τοῦτο ἐξήγειρά σε ὅπως ἐνδείξωμαι ἐν σοὶ τὴν δύναμίν μου καὶ ὅπως διαγγελῇ τὸ ὄνομά μου ἐν πάσῃ τῇ γῇ; Exod 9:16 LXX: καὶ ἕνεκεν τούτου διετηρήθης, ἵνα ἐνδείξωμαι ἐν σοὶ τὴν ἰσχύν μου, καὶ ὅπως διαγγελῇ τὸ ὄνομά μου ἐν πάσῃ τῇ γῇ.

Three other references nestled within the cluster of references to πίστις in chapters 9 through 11 employ the language of "life." With a citation of Hos 2:1 LXX in Rom 9:26, Paul writes, "There they will be called sons of the living God (υἱοὶ θεοῦ ζῶντος)." In 10:5, this time in the form of a quotation from Lev 18:5, Paul again indicates that humans can share in the life made possible by the living God: "The person who does these things will live (ζήσεται) by them."[17] And in Rom 11:15 Paul applies this language to the immediate subject at hand, the Jewish people: "For if their rejection is the reconciliation of the world, what will be their acceptance but *life from the dead* (ζωὴ ἐκ νεκρῶν)?"

Finally, the most direct connection between πίστις and resurrection life in 10:9 (πιστεύσῃς . . . ὅτι ὁ θεὸς αὐτὸν ἤγειρεν), which will come into focus below, is situated at the center of the passage. With such reminders, then, that the resurrected Christ stands at the heart of Paul's gospel, we see more clearly in the references to πίστις in Romans 9–11 the centrality of Christ's faithfulness to believers and the believers' trust "in him":

> What then will we say? That gentiles, who did not pursue righteousness, attained righteousness, that is, righteousness by faith (τὴν ἐκ πίστεως), but Israel, who did pursue a law of righteousness, did not attain unto the law? Why not? Because not by faith (ἐκ πίστεως) but as though by works. They stumbled over the stumbling stone, as it is written, "See, I am laying in Zion a stone that will make people stumble, a rock of stumbling, and whoever believes in him (ὁ πιστεύων ἐπ᾽ αὐτῷ) will not be shamed" [Isa 28:16; 8:14]. (9:30-33)

---

[17] On the use of Lev 18:5 in Rom 10:5, see Preston M. Sprinkle, *Law and Life: The Interpretation of Leviticus 18:5 in Early Judaism and in Paul*, WUNT 2/241 (Tübingen: Mohr Siebeck, 2008), 165–90. It may be the case that the speaker of 10:5 is advocating life by the law, a proposition that is immediately rejected by the speech of "the Righteousness by Faith" in 10:6-9 (see Matthew W. Bates, *The Hermeneutics of the Apostolic Proclamation: The Center of Paul's Method of Scriptural Interpretation* [Waco, Tex.: Baylor University Press, 2012], 226–29). Even so, the character "the Righteousness by Faith" certainly agrees with the speaker of 10:5 that righteousness means *life* (now understood eschatologically).

For Christ is the *telos* of the law, unto righteousness (εἰς δικαιοσύ-νην) for everyone who believes (παντὶ τῷ πιστεύοντι). For Moses writes concerning the righteousness that is from the law, that "the person who does these things will *live* (ζήσεται) by them" [Lev 18:5]. But the *righteousness from faith* (ἡ ἐκ πίστεως δικαιοσύνη) says, "Do not say in your heart [Deut 9:4], "Who will ascend into heaven?" [Deut 30:12] (that is, to bring Christ down) or "Who will descend into the abyss?" (that is, to bring Christ *up from the dead* [ἐκ νεκρῶν ἀναγαγεῖν]). But what does it say? "The word is near you, on your lips and in your heart" [Deut 30:14], that is, the word of *faithfulness* (τὸ ῥῆμα τῆς πίστεως) that we proclaim. For if you confess with your lips that Jesus is Lord and believe (πιστεύσῃς) in your heart that *God raised him from the dead* (ἤγειρεν ἐκ νεκρῶν), you will be saved. For with the heart one *trusts unto righteousness* (πιστεύεται εἰς δικαιοσύνην), and with the mouth one confesses unto salvation. The scripture says, "Everyone who *trusts* in him (ὁ πιστεύων ἐπ᾽ αὐτῷ) will not be put to shame" [Isa 28:16]. . . . Therefore how are they to call unto one they have not *trusted* (ἐπίστευσαν)? And how are they to *trust* (πιστεύσωσιν) one of whom they have not heard? And how are they to hear without someone preaching? And how are they to preach unless they are sent? As it is written, "How beautiful the feet of those who bring good news" [Isa 52:7]. . . . But not all have obeyed the good news; for Isaiah says, "Lord, who has believed (ἐπίστευσεν) our message?" [Isa 53:1]. So *faith* (ἡ πίστις) comes from what is heard, and what is heard comes through the word of Christ. (10:4-11, 14, 16-17)

It would be easy to get lost in the exegetical weeds of 10:4-17.[18] We may briefly observe, however, that in 10:6-7 a character called "Righteousness by Faith" steps onto the stage of Paul's discourse to engage someone who is ostensibly inclined to ask questions about Christ's heavenly existence (10:6) and his resurrection from the dead (10:7). As Ross Wagner observes, "by reinterpreting the two questions in the quotation [from Deuteronomy] as references to bringing Christ down from heaven or up from among the dead, Paul demonstrates exegetically that the τέλος of the Law is Christ and that 'righteousness from

---

[18] For clarifying discussions, see Bates, *Hermeneutics*, 225–40; Kirk, *Unlocking*, 165–75.

faith' is, first and foremost, a matter of what God has done in the resurrection and exaltation of Christ."[19] The figure known as "Righteousness by Faith" responds to these potential queries by citing Deut 30:14 ("The word is near you, on your lips and in your heart") and glossing this scriptural text with an interpretation of "the word" (τὸ ῥῆμά) as "the word of faithfulness" that Paul and his associates proclaim. The content of this "word of faithfulness" is then the subject of Rom 10:9, and it centers on the confession of Christ's lordship and belief in his resurrection as keys to salvation: "For if you confess with your lips that Jesus is Lord and believe (πιστεύσῃς) in your heart that *God raised him from the dead* (ἤγειρεν ἐκ νεκρῶν), you will be saved."[20]

Thus, Paul's message of πίστις has to do with Christ's identity as Lord and his resurrection from the dead. At the beginning of Romans 3, Paul utterly rejects the notion that Israel could do anything to nullify God's faithfulness to them. In Paul's expansion of this argument in chapters 9 through 11, the "word of faithfulness" (10:8) addresses precisely the *life* that is enabled and sustained through the faithfulness of the resurrected Lord Jesus.

ROMANS 3:21-31: "THROUGH FAITHFULNESS, BY HIS BLOOD"

Further on in Romans 3, after Paul has established that Jew and gentile alike are under the power of Sin and thus in need of God's righteousness, the story of *the faithfulness of the risen Christ* is given concrete expression. Since we take as a starting point the subjective/concentric reading of the debated phrases in 3:22 and 3:26, our attention will fall especially on the phrase διὰ τῆς πίστεως in 3:25 and its significance for understanding Paul's emphasis on the risen Jesus in the passage as a whole. The reading we offer here draws on David M. Moffitt's important work on sacrificial logic in Leviticus and its value for understanding

---

[19] J. Ross Wagner, *Heralds of the Good News: Isaiah and Paul in Concert in the Letter to the Romans*, NovTSup 51 (Leiden: Brill, 2002), 164.

[20] Morgan cites this passage as a good example of "the interdependence of cognition, emotion, action, and relationship in Paul's conception of *pistis*" (*Roman Faith*, 285). See similarly Campbell, *Deliverance*, 817–21.

atonement language in Hebrews.[21] Significant attention has been given to Paul's lone use of the term ἱλαστήριον, with "means of atonement"[22] and "place of atonement/mercy seat"[23] as the main interpretive poles.[24] While we think "place of atonement" is a better rendering,[25] the more

---

[21] *Atonement and the Logic of the Resurrection in the Epistle to the Hebrews*, NovTSup 141 (Leiden: Brill, 2011). See also Moffitt, "Atonement at the Right Hand: The Sacrificial Significance of Jesus' Exaltation in Acts," *NTS* 62 (2016): 549–68. For a recent treatment of the language of πίστις in Hebrews and Paul, see Benjamin Schliesser, "Glauben und Denken im Hebräerbrief und bei Paulus: Zwei frühchristliche Perspektiven auf die Rationalität des Glaubens," in *Glaube: Das Verständnis des Glaubens im frühen Christentum und in seiner jüdischen und hellenistisch-römischen Umwelt*, ed. Jörg Frey, Benjamin Schliesser, and Nadine Ueberschaer, WUNT 373 (Tübingen: Mohr Siebeck, 2017), 503–60. The only other scholar we are aware of who reads Rom 3:25 as "a description of the *risen* Christ who, as the blood-cleansed bearer of pneumatic eschatological life, has become the permanent locus of the divine glory that rested upon the OT mercy seat" is David M. Westfall, "Thine Be the Glory: Christ the Mercy Seat in Romans 3:25" (paper presented at St. Andrews Symposium for Biblical and Early Christian Studies: Atonement: Sin, Sacrifice, and Salvation in Jewish and Christian Antiquity, St. Andrews, U.K., June 5, 2018). We are grateful to David for making a prepublication version of his paper available to us as we finalized our manuscript for publication.

[22] Adolf Deissmann led the shift away from a strictly cultic reading of ἱλαστήριον in Rom 3:25; see *Bible Studies: Contributions, Chiefly from Papyri and Inscriptions, to the History of the Language, the Literature, and the Religion of Hellenistic Judaism and Primitive Christianity*, trans. A. Grieve (Edinburgh: T&T Clark, 1901), 124–30.

[23] That ἱλαστήριον refers to the "mercy seat" that covers the ark of the covenant (translating כפרת frequently in the LXX, especially in Exodus, Leviticus, and Numbers) has been the dominant view throughout Christian history; see recently, for example, Daniel P. Bailey, "Jesus as the Mercy Seat: The Semantics and Theology of Paul's Use of *Hilasterion* in Romans 3:25," *TynBul* 51 (2000): 155–58; and Mark Wilson, "*Hilasterion* and Imperial Ideology: A New Reading of Romans 3:25," *HvTSt* 73 (2017): 1–9.

[24] Another way to frame the options for how best to understand Paul's use of ἱλαστήριον is to emphasize "propitiation" (in the sense of "appeasing the wrath of the deity") or "expiation" (focusing on delivering from the power of sin/Sin) (see especially C. H. Dodd's classic article "ΙΛΑΣΚΕΣΘΑΙ, Its Cognates, Derivatives, and Synonyms, in the Septuagint," *JTS* 32 [1931]: 352–60). In our reading, Rom 3:25 clearly emphasizes the latter, since expiation suggests that *sprinkling* the blood of life is the dominant image in play, rather than *shedding* blood, as is so often assumed.

[25] See likewise Morna D. Hooker, "'Who Died for Our Sins, and Was Raised for Our Acquittal': Paul's Understanding of the Death of Christ," *SEÅ* 68 (2003): 59–71; Hooker, "Raised for Our Acquittal," in *Resurrection in the New Testament:*

significant question for our project has to do with Paul's reference to Christ's *blood*. The overwhelming consensus that ἐν τῷ αὐτοῦ αἵματι is a "synonym for 'by his [Christ's] death on the cross'"[26] is based on the perceived parallel between ἐν τῷ αἵματι αὐτοῦ in 5:9 and διὰ τοῦ θανάτου τοῦ υἱοῦ αὐτοῦ in 5:10 (see below on Romans 5), as well as associations between Jesus' blood and his death elsewhere in the New Testament.[27] While there is no question that Jesus' death on the cross plays a vital role in Paul's understanding of the gospel,[28] our argument is that Paul's inclusion of the phrase διὰ τῆς πίστεως[29] strongly suggests that in 3:25 "blood" represents (resurrection) *life*, not death.

Before turning to Romans itself, we review two texts that illustrate the role and significance of blood in the sacrificial system (especially Yom Kippur) from which Paul's use of ἱλαστήριον is derived. First, a passage from Josephus indicates that the *worshiper*, rather than the priest, regularly slaughtered the animal in the late Second Temple period:

> Suppose a private man offers a burnt offering, *he* must slay either an ox, a lamb, or a kid. . . . When they are slain, the *priests* sprinkle the blood round about the altar. (*Ant* 3.226)

Second, Lev 16:15-20 LXX shows how the conveyance of the blood (which was performed by the priests at the altars) stands at the center of the process:

Festschrift J. Lambrecht, ed. R. Bieringer, V. Koperski, and B. Lataire, BETL 165 (Leuven, Bel.: University Press/Uitgeverij Peeters, 2002), 323–41.

[26] Longenecker, *Epistle to the Romans*, 432.

[27] See, for example, Matt 26:28 par.; Acts 20:28; Heb 9:12-14; 10:19, 29; 13:12, 20; 1 Pet 1:2, 19; 1 John 1:7; 5:6; Rev 1:5; 5:9; 7:14; 12:11.

[28] Moffitt writes of the significance of Jesus' death in Hebrews, "His death puts into motion the sequence of events that results in the crucial atoning moment—the presentation of his blood/life before God in heaven" (*Atonement*, 277). Whether or not this holds true in Hebrews, in our view Christ's death plays a stronger role than this in the Pauline letters: "In dying for our sins, he shared our punishment; in being raised from the dead, he enables *us* to share his righteous status before God" (Hooker, "Who Died for Our Sins," 71).

[29] For a rebuttal of the view that διὰ τῆς πίστεως is a "rough interpolation" or parenthesis inserted into a traditional formula cited by Paul, see Bruce W. Longenecker, "Πίστις in Romans 3.25: Neglected Evidence for the 'Faithfulness of Christ'?" *NTS* 39 (1993): 478–80.

And he shall slaughter the goat for sin that is for the people before the Lord and bring in its blood inside the veil and do with its blood as he did with the blood of the bull calf, and he shall sprinkle its blood on the mercy seat (ἱλαστήριον) and in front of the mercy seat (ἱλαστήριον). And he shall make the holy place ritually acceptable because of the unclean things of the sons of Israel and because of their wrongs—concerning all their sins, and so he shall do for the tent of witness, which has been established among them in the midst of their uncleanness. And no person shall be in the tent of witness, when he enters to make atonement (ἐξιλάσασθαι) in the holy place, until he comes out. And he shall make atonement (ἐξιλάσεται) for himself and for his house and for all the congregation of the sons of Israel. And he shall go out to the altar which is before the Lord and make atonement (ἐξιλάσεται) on it and shall take some of the blood of the bull calf and some of the blood of the goat and put it on the horns of the altar, round about. And he shall sprinkle some of the blood on it with his finger seven times and pronounce it clean and hallow it from the uncleanness of the sons of Israel. And he shall finish making the holy place and the tent of witness and the altar ritually acceptable, and he shall pronounce clean the things that pertain to the priests.[30]

These passages suggest not only that the death of the animal is insufficient for cleansing and for drawing near to God's presence[31] but also

---

[30] Translation adapted from Albert Pietersma and Benjamin G. Wright, eds., *A New English Translation of the Septuagint* (Oxford: Oxford University Press, 2007).

[31] Moffitt helpfully summarizes:

First, a reduction or conflation of blood sacrifice with the act of slaughtering the victim for the sake of dealing with sin is a conceptual mistake. Leviticus simply does not support either the inference that the act of slaughter achieved the atoning goals of the sacrifice, or that atonement can be reduced merely to the forgiveness of sins. Rather, the process of sacrifice was an important element for achieving both ritual and moral purity. Second, the slaughter of the victim, while a necessary step in the sacrificial process (when such a sacrifice involved an animal victim), never occurred on any of the Jewish altars, and was never by itself sufficient to procure the atoning benefits that the entire process aimed to obtain. Third, the hierarchical structure of the process suggests that the atoning benefits of sacrifice are primarily connected with the priestly activities that occurred at the altars as the priests drew near to God and conveyed the sacrificial materials into that a reference to "blood" in connection with sacrifice connotes *life* rather than death.[32] "Blood," writes Jacob Milgrom, "as *life* is what purges the sanctuary. It nullifies, overpowers, and absorbs the Israelites' impurities that adhere to the sanctuary, thereby allowing the divine presence to remain and Israel to survive."[33]

As we have already seen, Paul's articulation of the gospel in Romans is saturated with precisely such an understanding of *life*. With this in mind, we are now poised to make a series of observations about Rom 3:21-26 itself, and offer the following translation:

---

his presence. Priestly acts at the altars achieved atonement. Fourth, sacrificial atonement, which resolves the problem of sin (moral impurity) or the problem of mortality (ritual impurity)—or, as on Yom Kippur, both of these problems—was essential for enabling God and his people to dwell together. ("Atonement at the Right Hand," 557–58)

In addition to Moffitt's work, see further C. A. Eberhart, *Studien zur Bedeutung der Opferim Alten Testament: Die Signifikanzvon Blut- und Verbrennungsriten im kultischen Rahmen*, WMANT 94 (Neukirchen-Vluyn: Neukirchener, 2002); Eberhart, *The Sacrifice of Jesus: Understanding Atonement Biblically* (Minneapolis: Fortress, 2011); R. E. Gane, *Cult and Character: Purification Offerings, Day of Atonement, and Theodicy* (Winona Lake, Ind.: Eisenbrauns, 2005); and Jacob Milgrom, *Leviticus 1–16: A New Translation with Introduction and Commentary*, AB 3 (New York: Doubleday, 1991), 133–489.

[32] "The emphasis in such sacrifices is not the act of slaughtering the victim, but the application of its blood to certain appurtenances in the tabernacle/temple and the presentation of its blood before God's presence in the holy of holies. This blood did not represent or bear the victim's death; rather, the blood is identified as the life of the victim. In Levitical terms, to offer blood to God is not an act of offering death to God or of bringing death into God's presence—a notion that would be abhorrent. In fact, one of the goals of the purification effected by offering blood to God was to push back or fight against the corrupting power of death. The purification element of blood sacrifice implies that mortality cannot approach God, nor can God dwell in the presence of corruption unless the mortal first becomes ritually pure. Insofar as blood language works symbolically in a sacrificial context, it represents life, not death" (Moffitt, *Atonement*, 219; see further 257–78).

[33] *Leviticus 1–16*, 711–12, emphasis added. Stanley K. Stowers likewise observes that "sacrifice is not about death or ritual killing" (*A Rereading of Romans: Justice, Jews, and Gentiles* [New Haven: Yale University Press, 1994], 207). See also Max Botner's comments on the centrality of *life* in ritual sacrifice, with a brief reference to Rom 3:25, in "The Fragrance of Death—or of Life? Reconsidering the Sacrificial Logic of Ephesians 5:2" (paper presented at the Annual Meeting of the SBL, Denver, November 18, 2018), 3–7.

²¹But now, apart from law, the righteousness of God has been made known, attested by the law and the prophets, ²²the righteousness of God through the faithfulness of Jesus Christ (διὰ πίστεως Ἰησοῦ Χριστοῦ) for all those who believe (εἰς πάντας τοὺς πιστεύοντας). For there is no distinction, ²³for all sinned and lack (ὑστεροῦνται) God's *glory* (δόξης); ²⁴being made righteous (δικαιούμενοι) freely by his gift, through the redemption (ἀπολυτρώσεως) that is *in Christ Jesus*, ²⁵whom God put forward as a place of atonement (ἱλαστήριον), through [Jesus'] faithfulness (διὰ τῆς πίστεως), by his blood, to show his [God's] righteousness; because in the clemency of God he passed over previous sins, ²⁶for evidence for his [God's] righteousness *at the present time* (ἐν τῷ νῦν καιρῷ), so as to be righteous himself and making righteous (δικαιοῦντα) the one who is of the faithfulness of Jesus (τὸν ἐκ πίστεως Ἰησοῦ).

In 3:22 Paul declares that God's righteousness is revealed through—as we have argued throughout this book—the ascended Jesus' faithful advocacy on behalf of those who are "in him" in the bond of faith.³⁴ Specifically, Paul offers a clear statement of his participatory understanding of salvation in his declaration that "redemption" (ἀπολύτρωσις) is found "*in* Christ Jesus" (ἐν Χριστῷ Ἰησοῦ, 3:24).³⁵ In 3:23, Paul

---

³⁴ Morgan comes close to such a reading when she suggests that πίστις carries the connotation "assurance" in this passage: "The *pistis* of Jesus Christ in verse 22 may well be Christ's faithfulness, but it could also mean the 'assurance' or 'pledge' of dikaiosynē which Christ gives to the faithful by his blood. This assurance would presumably be that, as they exercise *pistis*, human beings are made *dikaioi*. An attraction of this interpretation is that it emphasizes the active role of Christ in salvation: he does not only obey and allow himself to be made an expiation; he makes an assurance or pledge by offering himself" (*Roman Faith*, 290). The linguistic framework within which we have operated in this book also helps clarify Morgan's further suggestion that Paul's usage here reifies the sense "(new) covenant." Indeed, Paul's discourse shapes the term so that in 3:21-26 such covenantal mental images are surely invoked. So Morgan: "Since the covenant is understood from very early, among followers of Christ, as made between God and humanity through the sacrifice and blood of Christ (e.g. I Cor. 11.25), Paul's use of *pistis* here in the context of the expiation performed by Christ by his blood would be wholly appropriate" (*Roman Faith*, 291).

³⁵ Paul's only other use of "redemption" language in Romans links it with adoption (υἱοθεσίαν) in 8:23. The only other use in the undisputed Pauline corpus also associates redemption with both life "in Christ Jesus" and "righteousness": "From him, you are in Christ Jesus, who became wisdom for us from God, and righteousness

indicates that all humans, Jew and gentile alike, lack access (cf. 5:2, προσαγωγή) to God's incorruptible *glory* (cf. 1:23).[36]

Thus, when in 3:25 Paul speaks of Christ's *blood*, the image conveyed is Jesus' advocacy on behalf of all those who are "in" him through the relationship Paul repeatedly describes as πίστις. (There are five occurrences of the term πίστις in the verses immediately following, 3:27-31.[37]) Sandwiched between the term ἱλαστήριον ("place of atonement") and the phrase ἐν τῷ αὐτοῦ αἵματι ("by his blood") is the phrase διὰ τῆς πίστεως, "through [Jesus'] faithfulness."[38] This imagery

---

(δικαιοσύνη) and sanctification and redemption (ἀπολύτρωσις)" (1 Cor 1:30). On Rom 3:24, Constantine R. Campbell writes, "Grace is the agent for justification, and grace effects justification through its instrument, *in-Christ-redemption*. Thus, this example demonstrates a clear connection of ἐν Χριστῷ to the language of justification: justification occurs through *in-Christ-redemption*, which is the instrument of grace" (*Paul and Union with Christ: An Exegetical and Theological Study* [Grand Rapids: Zondervan, 2012], 114, emphasis original).

[36] Westfall likewise takes ὑστερέω in the sense of "lack" (rather than "fall short"; cf. BDAG 1043), and concludes that Paul's reference to humanity's lack of God's glory amounts to "their *loss of God's incorruptible life and presence on account of sin*" ("'Thine Be the Glory,'" 5, emphasis original). Westfall rightly connects the reference to God's glory in 3:23 with Paul's allusion to the golden calf (cf. Exod 32:31; Ps 105:20 LXX) in Rom 1:23 ("they exchanged the glory [δόξαν] of the incorruptible God"), as well as with the reference in 6:4-5 to the Father's glory as the agent of Christ's resurrection and the new life for believers. See the following section for a discussion of Paul's reference to "gaining access" by πίστις to the hope of God's glory in Rom 5:2.

[37] So also Westfall: "As mercy seat, the crucified and *raised* Christ is the permanent mediator of eschatological glory to humanity. While his sacrificial death is instrumental to his fulfilment [of] this role, effecting his purification from the corruptible condition that he assumes in his incarnation and enabling the forgiveness of sins for those who draw near in faith, Paul's primary concern is with Christ's ongoing role and status as the human being in whom God's glorious presence has returned to dwell with humanity" ("'Thine Be the Glory,'" 2, emphasis original). Other interpreters are too quick to write of "shedding blood" in their readings of 3:25; for example, Johnson: "God's action of putting forth Jesus Christ as a redemption, in the expiation effected by the *shedding of his blood*. . . . The phrase *dia tēs pisteōs* here again (and awkwardly) refers to the disposition of the one who was *shedding his blood*, viz., Jesus" ("Rom 3:21-26," 79, emphasis ours).

[38] Campbell, recognizing the pervasive influence of Hab 2:4 on these verses, likewise affirms that the phrase διὰ τῆς πίστεως in 3:25 "echoes διὰ πίστεως Ἰησοῦ Χριστοῦ in v. 22, which . . . is a christological statement denoting the fidelity of Jesus Christ," and rightly translates 3:25a, "God intended Christ to be a ἱλαστήριον by

is bookended by the two πίστις Χριστοῦ phrases in Romans: "through the faithfulness of Jesus Christ" (διὰ πίστεως Ἰησοῦ Χριστοῦ) in 3:22 and the reference to "the one who is of the faithfulness of Jesus" (τὸν ἐκ πίστεως Ἰησοῦ) in 3:26.[39] As in Galatians, the story of Jesus' faithfulness denoted by πίστις Χριστοῦ is primarily directed toward human beings, but of course also represents Jesus' faithfulness to God (cf. Rom 6:10).[40] Even more clearly than in Galatians, however, the references to Christ's πίστις in Rom 3:21-26 indicate that the faithful Christ is the *risen and ascended Jesus* who offers his atoning, sacrificial life to God in the heavenly realm.

---

means of [his] fidelity, by means of his blood." Yet for Campbell the "exact reference of these claims" is "Christ's suffering and death on the cross (indicating overtly that this story of faithfulness culminated in that virtue's supreme test—death)" (*Deliverance*, 642). Our view is that for Paul the emphasis on "life" in Hab 2:4 means that the story of faithfulness *includes* the cross but culminates in the faithful advocacy of the risen and exalted Christ (see further the section "Romans 8 and Conclusion").

[39] Johnson's proposal, "the one who shares the faith of Jesus" ("Rom 3:21-26," 80), is suggestive of a possible elegant rendering, "the one who shares in Jesus' faithfulness." Campbell argues for a thoroughly christocentric reading of τὸν ἐκ πίστεως Ἰησοῦ[ν] in 3:26b, where God justifies "the one from faith, that is, Jesus" (*Deliverance*, 672–76). While the accusative variant is present in some late manuscripts such as D, L, Ψ, 33, 614, 945, 1506, 1881, and 2464, and while Campbell is right that Paul *could* speak of God justifying Jesus, it is unclear why Paul would do so in this context. As previously argued, the implications of Christ's faithfulness for those who place their trust in him (the relationship of πίστις) find succinct expression in Rom 1:17: ἐκ πίστεως εἰς πίστιν, καθὼς γέγραπται· ὁ δὲ δίκαιος ἐκ πίστεως ζήσεται.

[40] So also Morgan on πίστις Χριστοῦ in Rom 3:21-26: "This could be taken as referring solely to the faithfulness of Christ to God. It has, however, been seen many times that it is rarely possible to confine the interpretation of *pistis* to a single meaning; moreover, some of the most convincing interpretations of New Testament passages are those which decline to segregate, for instance, faith and faithfulness in their interpretations, but hear Paul as invoking both, so we should not jump to the conclusion that we are dealing here solely with Christ's *pistis* towards God. . . . Since, for Paul, God is *pistos* and practises *pistis* towards human beings, and Christ is the Son of God and Lord, it is no great stretch to see Christ as exercising *pistis* towards human beings too" (*Roman Faith*, 289–90). For the perspective that Jesus' faithfulness to believers is in view (though falling short of identifying this faithfulness as that of the risen and exalted Christ), see Shuji Ota, "ΠΙΣΤΙΣ ΧΡΙΣΤΟΥ: Christ's Faithfulness to Whom?" *HJAS* 55 (2014): 15–26.

In the second part of 3:25, Paul indicates that God puts Jesus forward to be this place of atonement "to show his righteousness"; that is to say (in continuity with the programmatic phrase in 1:17), *the good news of Jesus' resurrection demonstrates God's righteousness.* Redemption by Jesus' blood, then, is an "act of His faithfulness" (Barth).[41] So in 3:26 the action of God—*making righteous* (δικαιοῦντα) the one who is of the faithfulness of Jesus—points to the resurrection. While the death of Jesus matters a great deal in the story of his faithfulness (πίστις Χριστοῦ), Rom 3:21-26 makes clear that for Paul, the cross does not do everything.[42]

ROMANS 4–6: "RAISED FOR OUR JUSTIFICATION"

Those who disagree, and who wish to restrict the meaning of the πίστις Χριστοῦ phrases to the obedient death of Jesus on the cross, might seem at first glance to find support in Rom 5:9-10, which could be read to equate "blood" with "death."[43] Yet this passage does no such

[41] "The secret of redemption by the blood of Jesus is, and remains, the secret of God. Its manifestation also, which is the invisibility of God becoming visible, is always the action of God, *an act of His faithfulness*, or, what is the same thing, an act of faith. In so far as this occurs and *His faithfulness persists*, in so far as the hazard of faith is ventured, the dawn of the new world, the reality of the mercy of God and of our salvation, of our future being-clothed upon with our habitation not made with hands, eternal, in the heavens (2 Cor. v. I ff.), is displayed and announced, secured and guaranteed to us, *in the blood of Jesus.* We stand already, *here and now*, in the reflection of the things which are to come" (Barth, *Romans*, 106, emphasis added). On the relationship of Christ's resurrection to God's righteousness, see our discussion of Phil 3:9 and Rom 1 in light of Joshua Jipp's work (*Christ Is King: Paul's Royal Ideology* [Minneapolis: Fortress, 2015]) in chapter 2.

[42] In 1 Cor 11:24-26, for instance, Paul refers to the Lord's Supper as a proclamation of "the Lord's death" (11:26). Even here, though, the emphasis falls on Christ who will come again, and on the "new covenant in my blood"—which is about *life.*

[43] Johnson may be right that "the key to understanding Rom 3:21-26 is found in its placement between 1:17 and 5:18-19" ("Rom 3:21-26," 80), but in our view he misses what Paul conveys about resurrection in chapters 4 and 5. Johnson thinks "Rom 5:19 is the plain explication of Rom 3:21-26" ("Rom 3:21-26," 89) because Paul writes that by Christ's *obedience* "the many are made righteous" (δίκαιοι κατασταθήσονται οἱ πολλοί, 5:19). However, in 5:19 Paul contrasts παρακοή (which "makes" [καθίστημι] sinners) with ὑπακοή (which "makes" [καθίστημι] righteous), which is not the same as the contrast Paul makes between πίστις and ἀπιστία in 3:3; 4:20; 11:20; and 11:23.

thing. The language of justification by *blood* (5:9) echoes what Paul has said about the blood of life in 3:25, and in 5:10 Paul pairs reconciliation through death and salvation through life:

> Therefore much more, now being justified *by his blood* (ἐν τῷ αἵματι αὐτοῦ), will we be saved through him from wrath. For if while we were enemies, we were reconciled (κατηλλάγημεν) to God through the *death* of his Son (διὰ τοῦ θανάτου τοῦ υἱοῦ αὐτοῦ), much more, being reconciled, will we be saved *by his life* (ἐν τῇ ζωῇ αὐτοῦ). (5:9-10)[44]

This is especially clear in light of what Paul has just said in 4:24–5:2, which presents Christ as a kind of mediator or high priest:[45]

> To those trusting (τοῖς πιστεύουσιν) the one who *raised* (ἐγεί-ραντα) Jesus our Lord from the dead, who was handed over for

---

Johnson misses that Paul's words in 5:18-19 cannot be separated from what he says in 4:25, that Christ was *raised* for our justification. As Hooker notes,

> Remarkably, there is no reference in 5,12-21 to Christ's death or to his resurrection. The only oblique reference to his death is in the word "obedience," contrasted in 5,19 with Adam's disobedience. What we have in Romans 5, on the other hand, is precisely what was missing in 4,25, namely an attempt to explain the *link* between trespasses and death and between acquittal and life. If we put the two passages together, we understand *why* "our" sins led to Christ's death, and why his resurrection (or vindication) brought us acquittal and life (4,25): it is because not only sin and death but grace and life can work through "one man" (5,15-21). We also understand *how* the grace of God has replaced condemnation with acquittal, and death with life (5,15-21): it is through the death and resurrection of Christ himself (4,25). ("Raised for Our Acquittal," 329)

[44] As previously noted, this emphasis on life is reiterated in 11:15: "For if their rejection is the reconciliation of the world, what will be their acceptance but *life from the dead* (ζωὴ ἐκ νεκρῶν)." See also Paul's similar use of καταλλάσσω/καταλλαγή in 2 Cor 5:18-20, in which Paul writes that "*in Christ* God was reconciling the world to himself" (5:19). On Christ as the *place* where reconciliation between God and humans happens, see Hooker, "'Who Died for Our Sins,'" 59–71.

[45] Morgan: "Romans 5.1 does not call Christ a mediator, but clearly describes him as such: 'Therefore, since we have been acquitted by *pistis*, we have peace with God through our Lord Jesus Christ, through whom we have gained access [by *pistis*] to this grace in which we stand.' There seems no doubt that Paul conceives of Christ as a mediating figure, even if he does not use the term" (*Roman Faith*, 294).

our trespasses and was *raised* for our justification (ἠγέρθη διὰ τὴν δικαίωσιν ἡμῶν). Therefore, being justified *by faithfulness* (ἐκ πίστεως), we have peace with God through our Lord Jesus Christ, through whom we have obtained access to this grace *in which we stand*, and we boast in our hope of *the glory of God.*

Interpreters often assume that "justification" happens on or through the cross, and resurrection/life is the *result*.[46] However, to restrict all the justification language in chapter 5 to Jesus' *death*, one must read ἠγέρθη διὰ τὴν δικαίωσιν ἡμῶν in 4:25 as "raised *because of* our justification"[47] rather than "raised *for* our justification." As Morna Hooker points out, however, a causal reading of 4:25 fails to attend to what Paul goes on to say about acquittal resulting in *life* (εἰς δικαίωσιν ζωῆς, 5:18).[48] The resurrection of Jesus is the fulfillment of Hab 2:4.[49]

---

[46] Kirk writes penetratingly about resurrection and πίστις in Romans yet repeatedly limits Christ's faithfulness to his death. For example, Kirk writes, "Paul's gospel message of the Christ who was raised in keeping with God's covenant faithfulness to Israel draws his eyes to the righteous-making action in *Jesus' faithful death* (righteousness ἐκ πίστεως; cf. 3:22; 10:6), and elicits a call to the appropriate, righteous-making response in the obedience of faith (εἰς πίστιν; cf. 1:5; 3:22; 10:9-10)" (*Unlocking*, 48, emphasis added); "Paul takes up the reason (διό) why all who believe are justified through faith (3:22, his simultaneously social and religious claim), and he does not stop until he has placed the faith of justified humanity squarely on *the faithful, atoning death of Christ* as its material ground (3:26, Paul's theological claim). The paragraph that runs from 3:21-26 expounds the central act that enables God to be just in justifying anyone, Jew or Greek" (*Unlocking*, 57, emphasis added); see also *Unlocking*, 58–59, 63, and 68.

[47] See an argument for this reading in Kirk, *Unlocking*, 77–81.

[48] Hooker translates, "acquittal—resulting in life—for all," taking it as a genitive of result (cf. BDB §166), as does Longenecker: "acquittal that brings life for all people" (*Romans*, 596–97). Like the NRSV and NIV, Joseph A. Fitzmyer takes it as a genitive of apposition: "justification and life came to all human beings" (*Romans: A New Translation with Introduction and Commentary*, AB33 [New York: Doubleday, 1993], 421).

[49] So also Hooker, "Raised for Our Acquittal," 332. Ciampa connects 5:18 closely with Hab 2:4 as well: "Here Paul refers to Christ's righteous act (= his faithfulness?) as the key εἰς δικαίωσιν ζωῆς. . . . Again, it is not hard to see how Hab 2:4 could evoke such a statement that sees life as a result of righteousness (which has earlier in the letter been shown to have been realized ἐκ πίστεως)" ("Habakkuk 2:4," 28). See further on Rom 4:25 David Michael Stanley, who argues that "Paul has in mind [in 4:25] a more direct connection between Christ's rising to a new life 'with God' (Rom 6:10) and the Christian life which he here calls 'our justification'" (*Christ's*

Indeed, Romans 5 is bursting at the seams with the language of life/resurrection.[50] In addition to the reference to the "acquittal resulting in life" in 5:18, Paul writes that those who "receive the abundance of grace and the free gift of righteousness will reign in life (ἐν ζωῇ) through the one man, Jesus Christ" (5:17). And again in 5:21, "grace reigns through *righteousness unto eternal life* (διὰ δικαιοσύνης εἰς ζωὴν αἰώνιον) through Jesus Christ our Lord."[51]

Resurrection in Pauline Soteriology, AnBib 13 [Rome: E Pontificio Instituto Biblico, 1961], 173); and Michael F. Bird, "Justified by Christ's Resurrection: A Neglected Aspect of Paul's Doctrine of Justification," *SBET* 22 (2004): 72–91. For broader treatments that address Rom 4:25, see I. Howard Marshall, *Aspects of the Atonement: Cross and Resurrection in the Reconciling of God and Humanity* (Carlisle, U.K.: Paternoster, 2007), 68–97, and Daniel G. Powers, *Salvation through Participation: An Examination of the Notion of the Believers' Corporate Unity with Christ in Early Christian Soteriology*, CBET 29 (Leuven, Bel.: Peeters, 2001), 125–34.

[50] It is striking how Hays seemingly misses all the language of life/resurrection in Romans 5, even when explicitly centering Paul's story on Jesus' death and resurrection:

Paul's gospel story hinges on the death and resurrection of Jesus. Jesus' death is both an expression of God's love and Jesus' own act of fidelity. The latter emphasis comes strongly to the fore in Rom 5, where Paul refers to this self-sacrificial death as "one man's act of righteousness" (*dikaiōma*) and "one man's obedience" (5.18-19). As Luke Timothy Johnson has contended, this narrative pattern explicates the meaning of *pistis Iēsou Christou*. One implication of this "overlap" of subjects in the death of Jesus is that the *pistis* of Jesus becomes simultaneously a revelation of the divine character, and the mystery of the unity of the Father and the Son is figured in the fundamental logic of the narrative (see, e.g., Campbell, p. 107). A further implication of this narrative grammar is that, because the many are made righteous by this one act of Jesus (5.19), we can never suppose that we are saved by our own actions and choices. Such actions are always derivative, always responsive to the prior gracious initiative of God in Christ. (Hays, "Is Paul's Gospel Narratable?" *JSNT* 27 [2004]: 235)

[51] Ciampa writes of 5:21, "Another way Paul described the consequences of Christ's redemption is that grace now reigns διὰ δικαιοσύνης εἰς ζωὴν αἰώνιον διὰ Ἰησοῦ Χριστοῦ τοῦ κυρίου ἡμῶν. Here again we see righteousness leading to (eternal) life, as might/would have been suggested by Hab 2:4 (especially as we have suggested the first parts were typically read by Paul). Once again, the final clause, διὰ Ἰησοῦ Χριστοῦ τοῦ κυρίου ἡμῶν, *may subtly point to the faithfulness of Christ, which makes it all work*" ("Habakkuk 2:4," 28, emphasis added).

The close connection we have observed in Romans between Christ's faithfulness and Jesus' *lordship* (1:4; 4:25; 10:9; cf. 14:8) is made more explicit in Romans 6, where Paul continues to emphasize *life* in Christ and the incompatibility of Sin with "living" (ζήσομεν, 6:2):

> Therefore we were buried with him by baptism into death, so that, just as Christ was *raised* (ἠγέρθη) from the dead by the *glory* (δόξης) of the Father, thus also we might walk in newness of *life* (ζωῆς). For if we have become united with him in a likeness of his death, certainly too we will be in a likeness of his *resurrection* (ἀναστάσεως). . . . But if we have died with Christ, we *believe* (πιστεύομεν) that we will also *live* (συζήσομεν) with him. We know that Christ, being *raised* (ἐγερθεὶς) from the dead, will no longer die; death no longer rules over him. For the death he died, he died to Sin, once for all; but *the life he lives, he lives to God* (ὃ δὲ ζῇ, ζῇ τῷ θεῷ). So you also must consider yourselves dead to Sin and *living* (ζῶντας) with respect to God *in Christ Jesus* (ἐν Χριστῷ Ἰησοῦ). (6:4-5, 8-11)

In 3:25 and 5:9, Paul uses the imagery of Christ's life-giving *blood*.[52] Here in chapter 6, then, as in 4:24-25, "living" with and through Jesus is explicitly connected with the πίστις relationship (πιστεύομεν, 6:8) that Paul earlier summarized with the genitive phrases in 3:22 and 3:26.

ROMANS 8 AND CONCLUSION: "IT IS CHRIST JESUS WHO INTERCEDES FOR US"

At the end of the letter, Paul speaks of πίστις as something that can be apportioned in greater or lesser measure in an individual "believer" (12:3, 6; 14:1, 22, 23a). In 13:11, however, he connects believers' acts of love with the establishment of the relationship of faith (ὅτε ἐπιστεύσαμεν). And in 14:23b, Paul cleverly links his words about problematic eating practices with his larger point about God's rescue from Sin (cf. 3:9, 5:21; 6:11) through the story of Jesus' faithfulness: "But the one

---

[52] Westfall helpfully connects 4:25 with 5:9: "Paul can equally say . . . that Christ's resurrection is the basis of believers' justification (4:25) *and* that they have been 'justified by his blood' (5:9). As the risen Lord, Christ is the blood-cleansed mercy seat whose imperishable body is now fitted to be the permanent locus of God's glory" ("'Thine Be the Glory,'" 7).

who doubts is condemned if he should eat, for it is not *from faith* (ἐκ πίστεως); and all that is not *from faith* (ἐκ πίστεως) is sin."[53] Then in closing the letter Paul echoes his opening lines: "Now may the God of hope fill you with all joy and peace *in believing* (ἐν τῷ πιστεύειν), so that you may abound in hope by the *power* of the Holy Spirit" (15:13).[54]

Paul's concluding statement in 15:13 is fitting given all we have considered about the good news of Christ's faithfulness in the letter. We close, however, with a brief look at Romans 8. While Paul refrains from using the language of πίστις in chapter 8 (even if ἀγάπη may function as a synonym, as in 5:8), the chapter nonetheless captures powerfully the implications of the story Paul calls to mind with the phrase πίστις Χριστοῦ.

> *Now*, therefore, there is no condemnation for those who are *in Christ Jesus* (τοῖς ἐν Χριστῷ Ἰησοῦ). For the law of the Spirit of *life in Christ Jesus* (τῆς ζωῆς ἐν Χριστῷ Ἰησοῦ) has set you free from the law of sin and of death. (8:1-2)

> Thinking of the flesh is death, but thinking of the Spirit is *life and peace* (ζωὴ καὶ εἰρήνη). (8:6; cf. 5:1; 15:13)

> But you are not in the flesh but in the Spirit, since the Spirit of God dwells in you. If anyone does not have the Spirit of Christ, that one is not of him (αὐτοῦ). But if Christ is in you, though the body is dead because of sin, the Spirit is *life unto righteousness* (ζωὴ διὰ δικαιοσύνην). If the Spirit of him who *raised* (ἐγείραντος) Jesus from the dead dwells in you, he who *raised* (ἐγείρας) Christ from the dead will *give life* (ζωοποιήσει) to your mortal bodies also through his Spirit that dwells in you. (8:9-11)

Clearly for Paul, Christ's *Spirit* is crucial in the bond of faith that unites believers with the living Christ. Paul next says in 8:12-17 that believers are children and heirs "since we are suffering together that also we are *glorified* together (συνδοξασθῶμεν)" (8:17), and it is Christ's

---

[53] *Pace* Ciampa, who writes of 14:23, "In this case it is clearly the person's own faith that is in question, rather than Christ's faithfulness" ("Habakuk 2:4," 32).

[54] The final occurrence of πίστις in the letter is the reiteration of the phrase ὑπακοὴν πίστεως in 16:26; see earlier section on 1:5.

Spirit who "intercedes" (ὑπερεντυγχάνει) for believers in their present weakness (8:27). Paul continues:

> Who will bring any charge against God's elect? It is God who jus-tifies. Who is to condemn? It is Christ Jesus, who died, and more, who was *raised* (ἐγερθείς), who is *at the right hand of God*, who indeed *intercedes for us* (ἐντυγχάνει ὑπὲρ ἡμῶν). (8:33-34)

With this language of Christ's intercession at God's right hand, deeply resonant with all we have considered from 3:21-26 and 4:24-5:2, Paul reaches his stirring crescendo about the faithfulness of Christ: "noth-ing in all creation will be able to separate us from the love of God that is *in Christ Jesus our Lord* (ἐν Χριστῷ Ἰησοῦ τῷ κυρίῳ ἡμῶν)" (8:39). Peter Stuhlmacher incisively illuminates the connection between 4:25–5:1 ("raised for our justification, justified by faithfulness [ἐκ πίστεως]") and 8:34:

> For our justification Christ was raised from the dead, and now he intercedes for us before God. Taken together, Rom 4:25 and 8:34 give a wide eschatological span to Christology: On Good Friday Christ was delivered up to death by God, and since Easter he makes his death effective before God's judgment throne on behalf of all those who confess him as Lord (*cf.* Rom 10:9-11). If they remain true to him, he remains their advocate until the final judgment so that nothing can separate them from the love of God shown them in Christ Jesus (*cf.* Rom 8:38-39). Jesus Christ is the living guarantor of believers' justification from Easter until the end of this world.[55]

Indeed, there could hardly be a better description of the function of the references to Christ's πίστις in 3:21-26.

[55] Peter Stuhlmacher, *Revisiting Paul's Doctrine of Justification: A Challenge to the New Perspective* (Downers Grove, Ill.: InterVarsity, 2002), 58–59.

6

EPHESIANS
"In Whom We Have Boldness and Access with Confidence through His Faithfulness"

The letter to the Ephesians contains one reference to Christ's πίστις. After describing the gift of God's grace that has enabled him to bring the good news of Christ to the gentiles and to make known the plan of God's mystery, Paul states that the present revelation of the wisdom of God through the church has occurred "in accordance with the eternal purpose that [God] has carried out in Christ Jesus our Lord, in whom we have boldness and access with confidence through his πίστις (διὰ τῆς πίστεως αὐτοῦ)" (Eph 3:11-12). Perhaps because the authorship of Ephesians is disputed, and perhaps because this text qualifies the noun πίστις with a pronoun instead of the name Ἰησοῦς or the honorific Χριστός, Eph 3:12 has received less attention in debates about the πίστις Χριστοῦ construction in the Pauline epistles than texts from the undisputed epistles (Rom 3:21-26; Gal 2:16-20; 3:22; and Phil 3:9).[1] As is the case elsewhere in the Pauline corpus, we contend

---

[1] These points are both made by Paul Foster, "Πίστις Χριστοῦ Terminology in Philippians and Ephesians," in *The Faith of Jesus Christ: Exegetical, Biblical, and Theological Studies,* ed. Michael F. Bird and Preston M. Sprinkle (Peabody, Mass.: Hendrickson, 2009), 100–101. Foster also mentions the syntactical difference that "unlike the seven key texts [from the undisputed letters] which have anarthrous forms

that the faithfulness of Christ in Eph 3:12 refers primarily to the faithfulness of the risen and exalted Christ.[2] Yet the reference to the πίστις of the living Christ toward humanity in Eph 3:12 is not connected to a theology of justification, as in Romans, Galatians, and Philippians. Instead, the risen Christ's πίστις serves as a ground for hope in the midst of Paul's vicarious suffering on behalf of his readers (3:13).

We should state at the outset of this chapter that we do not consider the question of the authorship of Ephesians to be particularly relevant to our analysis of 3:12. The evidence from 3:12 either counts as a statement from Paul himself or it provides "the first extant post-Pauline use of πίστις Χριστοῦ terminology and an attempt to integrate its theological implications within a developed cosmological reflection on the work of Christ in 'the heavenlies.'"[3] We include Eph 3:12 in our study because it is part of the canonical image of Paul the letter writer, regardless of who actually penned the epistle to the Ephesians. In this chapter, therefore, we shall consider the construction διὰ τῆς πίστεως αὐτοῦ in 3:12 in its literary context within Ephesians, putting to the side questions about the historical identity of the letter's author or recipients. For the sake of convenience, we will employ the name

---

of the genitive phrase, the example in Ephesians is formulated with a definite article before the noun πίστις" (101). On the classification of Χριστός as an honorific, see Matthew V. Novenson, *Christ among the Messiahs: Christ Language in Paul and Messiah Language in Ancient Judaism* (Oxford: Oxford University Press, 2012).

[2] It is not our aim to make the case for a subjective genitive in Eph 3:12; such an argument has already been made convincingly by others, notably Paul Foster in two perceptive essays: "The First Contribution to the πίστις Χριστοῦ Debate: A Study of Ephesians 3.12," *JSNT* 85 (2002): 75–96, and "Πίστις Χριστοῦ," 91–109. For a defense of an objective interpretation of the phrase διὰ τῆς πίστεως αὐτοῦ in Eph 3:12, see Richard H. Bell, "Faith in Christ: Some Exegetical and Theological Reflections on Philippians 3:9 and Ephesians 3:12," in *The Faith of Jesus Christ: Exegetical, Biblical, and Theological Studies*, ed. Michael F. Bird and Preston M. Sprinkle (Carlisle, U.K.: Paternoster: 2009), 111–25.

[3] Foster, "First Contribution," 80. We agree with Foster's rejection of Dunn's conclusion that "the deutero-Pauline usage therefore gives us no assistance in resolving the force of the genitive constructions in Paul" ("Once More, ΠΙΣΤΙΣ ΧΡΙΣΤΟΥ," in Richard B. Hays, *Faith of Jesus Christ: The Narrative Substructure of Galatians 3:1–4:11*, 2nd ed. [Grand Rapids: Eerdmans, 2002], 255).

Paul when were refer to the author of Ephesians, for he is the implied author of the text, regardless of whether he is the real author.[4]

ΠΙΣΤ- LANGUAGE IN EPHESIANS

The pragmatic shaping of πίστις and its cognates in Ephesians begins already in the opening address of the letter: "to the saints who are in Ephesus and are *faithful in Christ Jesus*" (τοῖς ἁγίοις τοῖς οὖσιν [ἐν Ἐφέσῳ] καὶ πιστοῖς ἐν Χριστῷ Ἰησοῦ).[5] This initial descriptive designation emphasizes the trusting and/or faithful posture of those united to Christ.[6] Similarly, in Eph 1:15 the πίστις of the Ephesians is collocated with the idea that readers share in union with the

---

[4] For a recent defense of the authenticity of Ephesians (although with the qualification that it should be identified as Paul's lost letter to the Laodiceans; cf. Col 4:16), see Douglas A. Campbell, *Framing Paul: An Epistolary Biography* (Grand Rapids: Eerdmans, 2014), 309–38; an extensive consideration of questions of the authorship and provenance of Ephesians can be found in Harold W. Hoehner, *Ephesians: An Exegetical Commentary* (Grand Rapids: Baker, 2002), 1–61.

[5] Πίστις occurs in 1:15; 2:8; 3:12, 17; 4:5, 13; 6:16, 23. The verb πιστεύω is employed only twice (1:13, 19).

[6] Morgan declares that οἱ πιστοί in Eph 1:1 must mean "those who trust/the faithful," since "no Greek speaker would have coined the term *hoi pistoi* to mean 'those who believe'" (Teresa Morgan, *Roman Faith and Christian Faith:* Pistis *and* Fides *in the Early Roman Empire and Early Churches* [Oxford: Oxford University Press, 2015], 240). This is an overstatement, since Paul utilizes the adjective πιστός substantivally in 2 Cor 6:15 in contrast to someone labeled ἄπιστος (so Constantine R. Campbell, *Paul and Union with Christ: An Exegetical and Theological Study* [Grand Rapids: Zondervan, 2012], 112). Yet the use of the adjective πιστός does tip the balance in favor of viewing the phrase πιστοῖς ἐν Χριστῷ Ἰησοῦ as a characteristic of those in Christ (cf. Rom 16:10; 1 Cor 4:10; 15:31; Phil 1:26; 2:1, 5; Col 1:28; 2 Tim 1:13; 2:1; 3:12; Phlm 8; Campbell, *Paul and Union with Christ*, 101–13). Elsewhere in Paul's letters, πιστ- language is used as a designation for Christ followers in Rom 4:11 (Abraham is the father πάντων τῶν πιστευόντων), 1 Thess 1:7 (πᾶσιν τοῖς πιστεύουσιν ἐν τῇ Μακεδονίᾳ καὶ ἐν τῇ Ἀχαΐᾳ), 1 Tim 6:2 (οἱ πιστοὺς ἔχοντες δεσπότας), and probably Titus 1:6 (τέκνα ἔχων πιστά; cf. 1 Tim 4:10, where the clause μάλιστα πιστῶν may also function as a designation for Christ followers). See also instances where ἄπιστος/ἄπιστοι is used to denote those outside of the Pauline communities (1 Cor 6:6; 7:12-15; 10:27; 14:22-23; 2 Cor 4:4; 6:14-15; 1 Tim 5:8; Titus 1:15). Apart from Paul's letters, 1 Pet 2:7 also contrasts οἱ πιστεύοντες with οἱ ἄπιστοι; on this terminology see Morgan, *Roman Faith*, 234–41; Paul Trebilco, *Self-Designations and Group Identity in the New Testament* (Cambridge: Cambridge University Press, 2012), 68–121; and T. J. Lang, "Trouble with

risen Lord, for Paul reports that he has heard "of your faithfulness in the Lord Jesus" (ἀκούσας τὴν καθ᾽ ὑμᾶς πίστιν ἐν τῷ κυρίῳ Ἰησοῦ). Given the use of the adjective πιστός as a descriptor of the Ephesians in 1:1, combined with the concentration of "in Christ" language in the doxological material of 1:3-14, the phrase "πίστις in the Lord Jesus" in 1:15 likely "means faithfulness on the part of those who are in the Lord, rather than belief in Jesus as Lord. It is the news not of their conversion but of their perseverance that provokes Paul's thanksgiving."[7] Then in 1:19 readers are called οἱ πιστεύοντες in a context in which their (and Paul's) identity as "those who are faithful" is said to be made possible by the active power of God (κατὰ τὴν ἐνέργειαν τοῦ κράτους τῆς ἰσχύος αὐτοῦ), the same power that God employed in raising Christ from the dead and seating him at his right hand in the heavenly places (1:20). Thus, from the beginning of the epistle, the πιστ- word group correlates the readers' identity as faithful saints and their union with the risen and exalted Christ.

A key text for understanding the clause διὰ τῆς πίστεως αὐτοῦ in 3:12 is Paul's statement about the relationship between grace and works in 2:8: "For by grace you have been saved through faith (διὰ πίστεως[8]), and this is not from you; it is the gift of God." Reasonable arguments can be made that πίστις in 2:8 should be taken as a reference to the πίστις of those saved by grace, on one hand, or that the πίστις is God's and/or Christ's, on the other.[9] Paul's emphatic claim

---

Insiders: The Social Profile of the Ἄπιστοι in Paul's Corinthian Correspondence," *JBL* 137 (2018): 981–1001.

[7] John Muddiman, *A Commentary on the Epistle to the Ephesians*, BNTC (London: Continuum, 2001), 83. Participatory language in the doxological material of 1:3-14 includes ἐν Χριστῷ/αὐτῷ/τῷ ἠγαπημένῳ (1:3, 4, 6, 9, 10, 12) and ἐν ᾧ (1:7, 11, 13 [twice]); cf. διὰ Ἰησοῦ Χριστοῦ in 1:5.

[8] Some scribes add τῆς between the preposition and the noun in the construction διὰ πίστεως (e.g., A, D², K, L, Ψ). The shorter reading is preferred, however.

[9] The literature is voluminous, given the theological issues at stake. See Ernest Best, *A Critical and Exegetical Commentary on Ephesians*, ICC (Edinburgh: T&T Clark, 1998), 226–27, for an argument for human faith (cf. Stephen E. Fowl, *Ephesians: A Commentary*, NTL [Louisville: Westminster John Knox, 2012], 78–79). Andrew Lincoln writes, "Faith is a human activity but a specific kind of activity, a response which allows salvation to become operative, which receives what has already been accomplished by God in Christ" (*Ephesians*, WBC 42 [Dallas: Word, 1990], 111).

in 2:8 that the grace that comes by πίστις is not the result of human action (τοῦτο οὐκ ἐξ ὑμῶν) might perhaps tip the balance in favor of the view that the construction διὰ πίστεως in 2:9a should be seen primarily as a reference to faith (or faithfulness) that is not human but divine.[10] Yet such ambiguity is perhaps not to be quickly resolved. In the larger context of the letter, πίστις is a characteristic or action of humans who demonstrate faith(fulness) (1:13, 19; 4:5, 13; 6:16; cf. 1:1; 6:21), especially in connection with their union with Christ (1:15; 3:17). Yet in Ephesians, as elsewhere in the Pauline corpus, divine πίστις coexists with human πίστις. Πίστις is an action or attribute of Christ in 3:12, and in 6:23 Paul wishes πίστις, along with peace and love, *from* God the Father and the Lord Jesus Christ to his siblings in Ephesus.

If πίστις in 2:8 is not primarily human, this πίστις might be God's, Christ's, or an attribute or action of both God and Christ. Markus Barth, for example, identifies πίστις in 2:8 as a property of God, though embodied and finalized in the earthly work of Jesus:

> If Paul calls "faith" a "gift of God" at all, he cannot intend to over-look the fact that God who gives faith is himself faithful and proves his total loyalty to the covenant by the gift of his beloved, obedient, and loving son. . . . The "faith" by which you are saved would be no good if it were not first shown by God himself and then begun and completed on earth by Jesus Christ (cf. Heb 12:2).[11]

---

[10] Most modern commentators take the antecedent of the pronoun τοῦτο in Eph 2:8b as the entire statement Τῇ γὰρ χάριτί ἐστε σεσῳσμένοι διὰ πίστεως of 2:8a (so Best, *Ephesians*, 226; Hoehner, *Ephesians*, 342–43; Frank Thielman, *Ephesians*, BECNT [Grand Rapids: Baker Academic, 2010], 143). It is at least possible that πίστις is the antecedent of τοῦτο, however (so Chrysostom, *Eph* 2:8 [*PG* 62:33]; Theodoret, *Eph* 2:8 [*PG* 82:521]; cf. Markus Barth, *Ephesians*, AB 34 [Garden City, N.Y.: Double-day, 1974], 225; Matthew Olliffe, "Is 'Faith' the 'Gift of God'? Reading Ephesians 2:8-10 with the Ancients," The Gospel Coalition website, https://au.thegospelcoalition.org/article/is-faith-the-gift-of-god-reading-ephesians-28-10-with-the-ancients). Thiel-man's claim that πίστις cannot be the antecedent of τοῦτο because Paul immediately "denies that τοῦτο is ἐξ ἔργων" (2:9a) is mitigated if πίστις comes from God (*Ephesians*, 143).

[11] Barth, *Ephesians*, 225; cited in Foster, "Πίστις Χριστοῦ Terminology," 107.

Again, we might be cautious about parsing the distinction too fine-ly.[12] It is certainly possible that πίστις in 2:8 refers primarily, or even exclusively, to the faithfulness of God the Father. Paul's description of salvation by grace through πίστις as a gift of God might be taken as an indication that πίστις, too, is of God. Statements about God's own πίστις are found elsewhere in the Pauline corpus. Notably, in Rom 3:3, Paul asks if the faithfulness of some Jews will nullify the faithfulness of God (εἰ ἠπίστησάν τινες, μὴ ἡ ἀπιστία αὐτῶν τὴν πίστιν τοῦ θεοῦ καταργήσει). God the Father is not explicitly identified as πιστός in Ephesians, although this construction is found in the Corinthian correspondence, as we have discussed already (i.e., 1 Cor 1:9; 10:13; 2 Cor 1:18). Yet in Ephesians πίστις is said to come from God the Father *and* the Lord Jesus Christ at the conclusion of the letter (6:23; cf. 1 Tim 1:2). At the same time, if the phrase διὰ τῆς πίστεως αὐτοῦ in Eph 3:12 refers to Christ's own πίστις, as we believe to be the case, then that would strengthen the notion that salvation by grace through faith in 2:8 occurs through Christ's πίστις. This connection would receive additional support if the language of "salvation" διὰ πίστεως in 2:8 is functionally equivalent to the language of justification/righteousness διὰ πίστεως Χριστοῦ in the undisputed Pauline epistles (Rom 3:22–26; Gal 2:16; Phil 3:9; cf. 2 Tim 3:15).[13]

In light of this ambiguity, Teresa Morgan's gloss on Eph 2:8 is intriguing: "God saved the Ephesians by grace, through Christ, and through the doubly reciprocal *pistis* relationship of Christ with God and humanity, the whole of which is a gift from God and not brought about by the Ephesians' works."[14] Morgan explains, with reference to the use of πίστις in the undisputed Pauline letters:

> The Janus-faced quality of *pistis* enables Paul to capture the qualities and practices of both partners in each simple relationship, and of both ends of each relationship in more complicated configurations with more partners. Trust and trustworthiness, trustworthiness

---

[12] See the discussion in chapter 2 of κύριος as a designation for both God and Christ in 2 Thessalonians.

[13] See the discussion in I. Howard Marshall, "Salvation, Grace and Works in the Later Writings in the Pauline Corpus," *NTS* 42 (1996): 339–58, esp. 343–48.

[14] Morgan, *Roman Faith*, 309.

and faithfulness, are all always implicit in it. It is precisely the fact that Christ is both faithful to God and worthy of God's trust, trustworthy by human beings and trusted by them, that enables him to take those who *pisteuein* into righteousness (and human beings, in turn, to spread the word to others).[15]

Morgan's reflections on the reciprocal relationality of πίστις are helpful. Yet they do not account for the extent to which Christ's πίστις in 2:8-9 is oriented toward humanity, for salvation by grace through faith is what the Ephesians receive through Christ as a gift from God.

Moreover, and this point is important for understanding the phrase διὰ τῆς πίστεως αὐτοῦ in 3:12, the larger context of 2:8-9 makes clear that it is the risen and exalted Christ, not merely the crucified Christ, whose πίστις enables salvation. The connective γάρ at the beginning of 2:8 "has the force of providing support for the writer's stress on the surpassing richness of God's grace to believers in v. 7."[16] And the richness of God's grace displayed in the new age is itself a result (ἵνα in 2:7a) of the Ephesians' participation in God's merciful and loving act of empowering readers to share in Jesus' resurrection and heavenly exaltation: "But God, who is rich in mercy, because of his great love with which he loved us, even when we were dead in our transgressions, made us alive together with Christ—by grace you have been saved—and raised us up with him and seated us with him in the heavenly places in Christ Jesus" (2:4-6). Thus, before its appearance

---

[15] Morgan, *Roman Faith,* 273–74. We would suggest that a similar dynamic is present in the use of the noun πίστις in Eph 3:17. In this prayer-report, Paul indicates that he prays that "according to the riches of his glory, [God] may grant that you may be strengthened in your inner being with power through his Spirit, and that Christ may dwell in your hearts through faith, as you are being rooted and grounded in love" (3:16-17). As Morgan observes, "the emphasis here is on qualities which come from God and/or Christ" (310). God is the one who grants strength through his Spirit, and the love in which the Ephesians are rooted and grounded (3:17) is Christ's love that surpasses their knowledge (3:19; cf. 1:4), even as the Ephesians are called to love others (1:15; 4:2, 15-16; 5:2, 25, 28, 33) and Christ (6:24). In the same way, the πίστις through which Christ dwells in the hearts of believers in 3:17 is likely to be πίστις from God, Christ, or both. Yet the indwelling presence of Christ (and the Spirit) does not eliminate human πίστις.

[16] Lincoln, *Ephesians,* 111.

in the prepositional phrase διὰ τῆς πίστεως αὐτοῦ in 3:12, the πιστ-word group has been shaped through its connection with the theme of human participation in the story of the risen and exalted Christ and by the notion that human faithfulness is enabled by divine agency.

We should add, once again, that there is no evidence that a "sense" of "obedience" is activated by πίστις or its cognates in the epistle. As we have seen in other letters, the assumption of those who work with a concept of lexical polysemy that "obedience" is one of the "senses" of the πιστ- word group is challenged by the ad hoc meaning construction associated with πιστ- language in the letter to the Ephesians. From a relevance-theoretic perspective, this suggests that a reader shaped by Paul's use of πίστις and πιστεύω in the letter prior to (and even after) 3:12 is unlikely to limit the phrase διὰ τῆς πίστεως αὐτοῦ to Jesus' obedient death upon the cross.

THE CONTEXT OF EPHESIANS 3:12

The reference to Christ's πίστις in Eph 3:12 comes near the end of what appears to be a digression (3:2-13) on the nature of Paul's ministry to the gentiles, an excursus that interrupts the beginning of Paul's report of his prayer in 3:1 and the content of that prayer in 3:14-19. Paul's discussion of his receipt of "the administration of the grace of God" for the gentiles (3:2) is no aimless detour, however.[17] Instead, the excursus on Paul's ministry to the gentiles in 3:2-13 can be seen as emerging precisely from the apostle's claims regarding the resurrection, heavenly session, and cosmic kingship of Christ in 1:20-23. In this sense, Paul's "digression" in 3:2-13 both assumes and alludes to the empowering presence of the risen and exalted Christ.

In 1:20-23, Paul announces the cosmic triumph and rule of the resurrected and exalted Messiah:

> God put this power to work in Christ by raising him from the dead and seating him at his right hand in the heavenly places, far above

[17] Our interpretation of Eph 3:1-14 is indebted to Timothy G. Gombis, "Ephesians 3:2-13: Pointless Digression, or Epitome of the Triumph of God in Christ?" *WTJ* 66 (2004): 313–23, and "Ephesians 2 as a Narrative of Divine Warfare," *JSNT* 26 (2004): 403–18.

all rule and authority and power and dominion, and every name that is named, not only in this age but also in the age to come. And he put all things in subjection under his feet and gave him as head over all things for the church, which is his body, the fullness of him who fills all in all.[18]

Following this declaration of Christ's victorious rule in 1:20-23, the apostle expounds the triumphs of the exalted Christ in 2:1-16. Paul initially highlights Christ's deliverance of his people from their captivity in death in this age (κατὰ τὸν αἰῶνα τοῦ κόσμου τούτου), under the ruler of the power of the air (κατὰ τὸν ἄρχοντα τῆς ἐξουσίας τοῦ ἀέρος, 2:2), asserting that his readers have been made alive through their participation in the resurrection and heavenly enthronement of Christ, the faithful agent of their salvation (2:1-10). Paul then illustrates the nature of Christ's cosmic victory by proclaiming Christ's triumph over the law and his reconciliation of "the uncircumcision" and "the circumcision" through the establishment of one new humanity through his blood (2:11-16). There follows in 2:17-22 a celebration of Christ's conquest, including an affirmation of God's construction of a temple, with Jewish and gentile Christ followers both imaged as "members of the household of God" (2:19), an eternal monument to Christ's triumph.

The declaration and celebration of Christ's resurrection and heavenly exaltation in 1:20–2:22 raises important questions, however: "If Christ Jesus is exalted to the position of cosmic supremacy over the powers ruling the present evil age, then why is Paul in prison? Why has the exaltation of Christ resulted in the defeat and humiliation of

---

[18] On the kingship of Jesus in Ephesians and its relationship to the theme of participation in Christ, see the perceptive essay by Joshua W. Jipp, "Sharing in the Heavenly Rule of Christ the King: Paul's Royal Participatory Language in Ephesians," in *"In Christ" in Paul: Explorations in Paul's Theology of Union and Participation*, ed. Michael J. Thate, Kevin J. Vanhoozer, and Constantine R. Campbell, WUNT 2/384 (Tübingen: Mohr Siebeck, 2014; repr., Grand Rapids: Eerdmans, 2018), 251–79. Jipp does much to show how various aspects of Paul's participatory soteriology (i.e., sharing in the Messiah's royal rule, participating in Christ's election and body, participating in the Messiah's reconciliation and peace) emerge from Paul's royal messianism; cf. also Julien Smith, *Christ the Ideal King*, WUNT 2/313 (Tübingen: Mohr Siebeck, 2011), 174–242.

his servant?"[19] Paul's digression in 3:2-13 is directly preceded by the acknowledgment of his lowly status as a prisoner: "For this reason I, Paul, a prisoner of Christ Jesus on behalf of you gentiles . . ." (3:1). The ensuing discussion in 3:2-13 reflects Paul's attempt to explain that "at the same time that [he] occupies an utterly weak and shameful position as a prisoner, he fulfills his cosmically crucial commission as the administrator of the grace of God."[20] Thus, 3:2-13 presupposes Christ's exaltation and offers a response to Paul's imprisonment in light of the cosmic triumph of the risen Lord.

After acknowledging his status as a prisoner, Paul's initial claim in this digression is that he has been commissioned as an administrator of the grace of God for the gentiles and, importantly, that "the mystery" (τὸ μυστήριον) was made known to him by a revelation (3:2-3). In 3:6, Paul concisely yet clearly summarizes the content of that "mystery" revealed to him: "that the gentiles have become joint heirs and joint members of the body and joint sharers of the promise in Christ Jesus through the gospel." The mystery, therefore, involves the gentiles being united to the "commonwealth of Israel" (2:12) as both Jews and gentiles are united to Christ.[21] This mutual sharing in God's promise occurs "in Christ Jesus through the gospel" (ἐν Χριστῷ Ἰησοῦ διὰ τοῦ εὐαγγελίου).[22] While there is no explicit summary of "the gospel" in the letter to the Ephesians, "the gospel" is described a message of salvation and peace in 1:13 and 6:15 (cf. the reference to proclamation of τὸ μυστήριον τοῦ εὐαγγελίου in 6:19). There is no reason to doubt that the message of the gospel centers on the story of God's cosmic triumph in Christ, including Christ's death, resurrection, and heavenly

[19] Gombis, "Ephesians 3:2-13," 316.
[20] Gombis, "Ephesians 3:2-13," 316.
[21] On the language of mystery in Ephesians, see T. J. Lang, *Mystery and the Making of a Christian Historical Consciousness: From Paul to the Second Century*, BZNW 219 (Berlin: de Gruyter, 2015), 85–109.
[22] As Campbell comments on Eph 3:6, "While ἐν Χριστῷ could modify 'the same promise,' it more likely modifies the gentiles' status of co-inclusion: coheirs, members, and partners. . . . Since this status of co-inclusion is the topic modified by ἐν Χριστῷ, it is best to regard this as a local use of the phrase depicting inclusion within the realm of Christ, which is the location of such status" (*Paul and Union with Christ*, 119).

exaltation.[23] The good news, moreover, involves not merely what God has done in Christ but the fact that those "in Christ" participate in his story: "As participants in the Messiah's lordship, the king's subjects share in the benefits of his royal rule, foremost of which are: participation in the Messiah's election, participation in the Messiah's assembly where the Messiah nourishes and gives gifts to his people, and participation in the Messiah's establishment of ethnic peace and reconciliation."[24]

THE FAITHFULNESS OF THE RISEN CHRIST IN EPH 3:12

Paul has made the point that the display of God's wisdom through the church "to the rulers and authorities in the heavenly places" happened "in accordance with the eternal purpose that [God] has carried out in Christ Jesus our Lord" (3:10b-11). The ensuing clause in 3:12 elucidates the identity of the one through whom God's eternal purpose has been effected: "in [Christ Jesus our Lord] we have boldness and access with confidence through his faithfulness" (3:11-12). In 2:18, Paul employs the noun προσα-γωγή to refer to the access that both Jews and gentiles have to God the Father through Christ in one Spirit. For this reason, "access" in 3:12 must denote a way of approach to God the Father.[25]

There are at least two reasons to believe that Christ's πίστις in 3:12 refers primarily to the faithfulness of the risen and exalted Christ toward humanity. First, as we have already seen, the heavenly session of the risen Christ is a major theme in the letter to the Ephesians. At the very beginning of the letter, readers are reminded of the heavenly location of Christ now that God the Father "has blessed us in Christ with every spiritual blessing in the heavenly places" (1:3; cf. 1:10).[26]

---

[23] For a reading of Ephesians as a "gospel script," see Timothy G. Gombis, *The Drama of Ephesians: Participating in the Triumph of God* (Downers Grove, Ill.: IVP Academic, 2010).

[24] Jipp, "Sharing in the Heavenly Rule of Christ the King," 253.

[25] In Rom 5:2, προσαγωγή refers to access "by faith (ἐκ πίστεως) . . . to this grace in which we stand."

[26] On the language of "the heavenly places" in Ephesians (1:3, 20; 2:6; 3:10; 6:12), see M. Jeff Brannon, *The Heavenlies in Ephesians: A Lexical, Exegetical, and Conceptual Analysis*, LNTS 447 (Edinburgh: T&T Clark, 2011).

More explicitly, Paul closely associates, but does not collapse into a single event, Christ's resurrection and heavenly exaltation in 1:20-21: "God put this power to work in Christ by *raising him from the dead* and *seating him at his right hand in the heavenly places*, far above all rule and authority and power and dominion, and every name that is named, not only in this age but also in the age to come." Moreover, in 2:6 those incorporated into Christ are said to share in Christ's resurrection and to participate in his reign as they are seated with him in the heavenly places. Finally, whatever is to be made of the citation of Ps 68:18 (67:19 LXX) in 4:8 and the difficult gloss on this scriptural text in 4:9-10, it is clear that Paul believes that Jesus' ascent involved Christ's own victorious rule ("he made captivity itself a captive"), his provision of benefactions to others ("he gave gifts to his people"), and his cosmic lordship over all things (3:10).[27] Given the emphasis on Christ's resurrection and heavenly enthronement in Ephesians, therefore, limiting any reference to an action or attribute of Christ solely to the timeframe of Jesus' work on earth is problematic, unless the text specifically locates that action or attribute in the timeline of Jesus' earthly life (e.g., 2:16). Or, to frame the point more pithily, Christ crucified is Christ resurrected is Christ exalted.

Second, the prepositional phrase ἐν ᾧ that introduces the clause in 3:12 indicates that the boldness and access to God made available through Christ's πίστις are given to those incorporated into Christ. It is "in Christ" that these benefits are located, a phrasing that connects boldness and access to God to the concept of union with Christ, which is also a major theme in Ephesians.[28] To put the matter sharply, the motif of union with Christ in this letter and elsewhere in the Pauline corpus is incomprehensible apart from Christ's resurrection and heavenly enthronement. Therefore, to limit the reference to Christ's πίστις in 3:12 to the faithful death of the human Jesus fails to appreciate the importance of Christ's resurrection and exaltation for Paul's concept of union with Christ.[29] Paul does not believe that his readers in Ephesus

---

[27] Smith, *Christ the Ideal King*, 219.

[28] See Jipp, "Sharing in the Heavenly Rule of Christ the King," 251-79.

[29] Union with Christ in the Pauline letters cannot be reduced to a narrative, for it also includes aspects of location, identification, incorporation, and instrumentality (so

have the boldness of confident access to God merely because Jesus died on a cross. The crucifixion is essential, to be sure (2:16). But it is the fact that Jesus' death is followed by his resurrection and exaltation (1:20), and that the saints share in this resurrection life and heavenly enthronement because they are "in Christ" (2:5-6), that leads Paul to remind the Ephesians of the boldness and confident access that they have before God.

These points should be sufficient to establish the claim that Christ's πίστις in 3:12 belongs to the risen and exalted Christ, whose πίστις enables those united to him to approach God the Father with confidence. An additional yet allusive support for this position may also be found in the atonement theology of Ephesians, beginning with the linguistic and thematic parallels between 2:18 and 3:12. We have already pointed out that the use of προσαγωγή in 2:18 defines the one to whom readers are said to have access in 3:12:

> So he came and proclaimed peace to you who were far off and peace to those who were near. For *through him we have access* (δι᾽ αὐτοῦ ἔχομεν τὴν προσαγωγήν) in one Spirit to the Father. (2:17-18)

> This was in accordance with the eternal purpose that he has carried out in Christ Jesus our Lord, *in whom we have boldness and access* [to God] with confidence (ἐν ᾧ ἔχομεν τὴν παρρησίαν καὶ προσαγω-γὴν ἐν πεποιθήσει) through his faithfulness. (3:11-12)

It has been suggested that the basis for access to God is the same in both 2:18 and 3:12—namely, the *death* of Christ.[30] According to this interpretation, 2:13 can be read as an initial statement of the process by which gentiles have been reconciled to God and provided access to him: "But now in Christ Jesus you who once were far off have been

---

Campbell, *Paul and Union with Christ*, 408–9, from whom these terms are taken). Yet the notion of union with Christ as sharing in Christ's story is key: "Union with Christ involves the participation of believers in the events of Christ's narrative, including his death and burial, resurrection, ascension, and glorification. Believers are described as having died with Christ, having been raised with him, and so forth, such that the significance of these events pertain to us as it pertains to him" (Campbell, *Paul and Union with Christ*, 408).

[30] This is the view of Foster, "Πίστις Χριστοῦ Terminology," 105–7.

brought near by the blood of Christ." Paul Foster, for example, states that "the reference to Christ's blood is a vivid metaphor describing sacrificial death on the cross," so that "the access to the divine presence which gentiles now enjoy comes about through Christ's death."³¹ And this allows Foster to conclude with regard to προσαγωγή in 3:12, "If the author has been consistent in his understanding of that basis of access, then πίστεως αὐτοῦ would refer to Christ's faithfulness and obedience in undergoing a death that provides gentiles with the privileged access described both in Ephesians 2:18 and 3:12."³²

The problem with this interpretation, however, is that in 2:17-18 Paul is speaking specifically about the activity of Christ *after the resurrection*. Much ink has been spilled over the question of the timeframe for the preaching activity of Christ when "he came and proclaimed peace to you who were far off and peace to those who were near" (2:17). While some have argued that this is a reference to the earthly ministry of Jesus, such a contention is implausible.³³ For one thing, it is difficult to identify a time in Jesus' life when he preached peace to gentiles (cf. Matt 10:5-6; 15:24-27), and the discussion in 2:11-16 makes clear that the contrast between those far off and those near is between gentiles and Jews. Moreover, the soteriological logic of Ephesians 2 demands that Christ's death and resurrection stand as the basis for, rather than being equivalent to, this proclamation of peace. It is because those "who were once far off have been brought near by the blood of Christ" (2:13), and because the two groups have been made into one (2:14), and because Christ has created in himself "one new humanity in place of the two, *thus making peace*" (ποιῶν εἰρήνην, 2:15), and because both groups have been reconciled to God in one body *through the cross* (2:16) that peace can be proclaimed by the risen Christ. The dynamics of how exactly the post-resurrection Christ serves as the subject of the verb εὐηγγελίσατο are not unpacked, although perhaps Paul is thinking of

³¹ Foster, "Πίστις Χριστοῦ Terminology," 106.
³² Foster, "Πίστις Χριστοῦ Terminology," 106.
³³ Among those who argue that Jesus' coming in Eph 2:17 refers to the earthly ministry of the Messiah, see Peter Stuhlmacher, "'Er ist unser Friede (Eph 2,14): Zur Exegese und Bedeutung von Eph 2,14-18," *Neues Testament und Kirche: Für Rudolf Schnackenburg*, ed. Joachim Gnilka (Freiburg: Herder, 1974), 337-58.

Christ as the agent of this preaching in the sense that the risen Christ speaks through his apostles by the power of the Spirit (cf. 3:5-6).[34]

And if it is the living, post-resurrection Christ who has proclaimed peace to those who were far off and those who were near, this clarifies that it is the risen Christ, too, through whom both groups "have access in one Spirit to the Father" (2:18). That is to say, Paul *is* being consistent in his understanding of the basis of the access to God described in both 2:18 and 3:12. Access to God is not merely possible because of Christ's death, although the crucifixion plays a key role in the soteriology of 2:11-16. Instead, readers are said to be able to approach God through the risen Christ in one Spirit in 2:18 and through the faithfulness of the risen Christ in 3:12.

This interpretation of "access" (προσαγωγή) to God in 3:12 made possible by the living Lord Jesus also coheres with the atonement theology of Ephesians more broadly, although a full exploration of this point is not possible here.[35] Given our discussion of atonement and blood in the previous chapter, it is doubtful that "the blood of Christ" in 2:13 should be viewed as a synecdoche for the crucifixion. Certainly the reference to the "blood of Christ" implies and includes Christ's death, and the reconciliation of both Jews and gentiles to God is said to happen "through the cross" (διὰ τοῦ σταυροῦ) in 2:16. At the same time, in Ephesians a constellation of images suggests that the reference to the reconciling power of Jesus' blood in 2:13 is not simply to be equated with his death, but instead denotes the resurrection *life* of Jesus.

[34] So Hoehner, *Ephesians*, 385; cf. Barth, *Ephesians*, 293–95; Michael Gese, *Das Vermächtnis des Apostels: Die Rezeption der paulinischen Theologie im Epheserbrief*, WUNT 2/99 (Tübingen: Mohr Siebeck, 1997), 117–24.

[35] While the main lines of thought in this section were sketched before we learned of a paper that Max Botner gave on this very topic at the 2018 annual meeting of the Society of Biblical Literature, we are grateful that Dr. Botner kindly shared a copy of his paper with us shortly after the conference: Max Botner, "The Fragrance of Death—or of Life? Reconsidering the Sacrificial Logic of Ephesians 5:2," paper presented at the Annual Meeting of the SBL, Denver, November 18, 2018. On the motif of sacrifice in Ephesians, see also John Frederick, "The Perpetual Sacrifice of the Ecclesial Christ: Atonement as Moral Transformation in Ephesians and Second Temple Judaism," in *Spiritual Formation in the Global Context*, ed. John Frederick and Ryan Brandt (Downers Grove, Ill.: IVP Academic, 2019), forthcoming.

Already in 2:1-6, the elimination of human sins and trespasses is connected to humanity's sharing in the resurrection life and heavenly installation of Christ. Deliverance from fleshly passions and liability to God's wrath (cf. 5:6), that is, comes from participation in Christ's resurrection and enthronement. Moreover, while it is difficult to load a detailed theology of atonement into the avowal that "in Christ Jesus" gentiles "have been brought near by the blood of Christ" (2:13), it is notable that the locative phrase ἐν Χριστῷ Ἰησοῦ in 2:13 introduces a series of ἐν Χριστῷ statements and images in 2:13-22 that contrast the gentiles' former state of alienation with their present location "in the new realm of Christ."[36] In 2:14-16, for instance, the parallel phrases "in his flesh" (ἐν τῇ σαρκὶ αὐτοῦ, 2:14), "in himself" (ἐν αὐτῷ, 2:15), and "in one body" (ἐν ἑνὶ σώματι, 2:16) all reflect the location "in Christ" in which an activity takes place: "The doing away of commandments is conducted in the sphere of his flesh; the creation of one new man is conducted in the sphere of himself; the reconciliation of the two is conducted in the sphere of one body."[37] In no way is the cross unrelated or incidental to these activities "in Christ," and the breaking down of the dividing wall "in his flesh" (2:14) must refer to the crucified body of Jesus, since σάρξ is never used in the Pauline epistles to refer to resurrection existence and is even contrasted with resurrection life (e.g., 1 Cor 15:50). The point is that the narrative soteriology of Eph 2:13-16 assumes the location of believers in the realm of the risen Christ.[38] Indeed, the language of "access" (προσαγωγή) to

---

[36] Campbell, *Paul and Union with Christ*, 88. As Campbell suggests, the phrase ἐν Χριστῷ Ἰησοῦ in Eph 2:13a should not be taken instrumentally, which would then create a tautology with the instrumental clause ἐν τῷ αἵματι τοῦ Χριστοῦ in 2:13b.

[37] Campbell, *Paul and Union with Christ*, 278.

[38] Additionally, in Eph 5:1-2, Paul exhorts his readers, "Therefore be imitators of God, as beloved children, and live in love, as Christ loved us and gave himself up for us, a fragrant offering and sacrifice to God" (NRSV). This text, too, is almost universally interpreted as a reference to Jesus' atoning death. For example, Barth writes, "The author designates Jesus Christ's death as an atoning sacrifice offered by the pouring out of blood. Sacrifice is not just a metaphor, but here—as much as in Rom 3 and Hebrews—its essence and fulfillment are declared as presented on the cross" (*Ephesians*, 558; cited also in Botner, "The Fragrance of Death," 2.) But see the minority position of Christian A. Eberhart, *Kultmetaphorik und Christologie: Opfer- und Sühneterminologie im Neuen Testament*, WUNT 306 (Tübingen: Mohr Siebeck, 2013), 25-77;

God through the exalted Lord, using a noun that occurs in the New Testament only in Rom 5:2 and Eph 2:18 and 3:12, may also evoke an image of the life-giving blood of the risen Christ as a cultic sacrifice that allows Jews and gentiles into the divine presence.[39]

Eberhart views Jesus' offering to God in terms of Jesus' entire life rather than his death: "Das Opfermotiv in Eph 5,2 bezieht sich damit auf Jesu Proexistenz zugunsten anderer und umfasst auch sonstige positive Aspekte des Lebens Jesus, so etaw seine Taten und seine Verkündigung, welche das Wagnis seiner sich selbst aufs Spiel setzenden Liebe vermitteln" (76). Yet in light of the emphasis on the soteriological significance of Jesus' resurrection and heavenly session in Ephesians, we find Max Botner's reading of Eph 5:2 persuasive:

> Eph 5:2 is situated in a letter whose structure and paraenesis depends entirely upon the moment of Christ's ascension/enthronement (cf. 1:20-22; 2:4-6; 3:12; 4:7-13). This event actualizes the ancient promises (1:4), brings gentiles into God's people (2:11-13; 3:5-6), holds together Jews and gentiles in Christ's body (1:22-23; 2:14-16; 4:4-11) and leads them into the divine presence in the heavenly realms (1:20-22; 2:4-6; 2:18; 3:12); moreover, Christ's blood has the power to consecrate gentiles because it makes available his life (2:13). While the crucifixion is a necessary element of this process—for instance, it puts to death ethnic hostility and makes it possible for the writer to speak metaphorically about Christ's blood—it does not, by itself, achieve any of the effects associated with cultic sacrifice.
>
> It makes good sense, then, to read Eph 5:2 in terms of Christ's ascension and enthronement. As a sacrifice would be burned upon the altar and thus transformed into a substance that could travel to the deity, so the fragrance of Christ's indestructible life ascends to the heavens and is received by God the Father. Or, we might borrow from the writer's language in [the] previous chapter: "He who descended is the same one who ascended far above all the heavens, so that he might be received holy and blameless on our behalf before the divine throne" (cf. 4:10). This interpretation not only has the advantage of cohering with the tenor and theology of the letter, but it also traces a point of correlation between the final element of the ritual complex and Christ's ascension, which I am suggesting the writer envisages as the moment when Christ's sacrifice is "accepted" before the heavenly throne. ("The Fragrance of Death," 11)

[39] The cognate προσάγω is so commonly used in the LXX in contexts that refer to the presentation of sacrifices that BDAG calls the verb a "*terminus technicus* of sacrificial procedure" (e.g., Exod 29:10; Lev 1:2-3, 10; Num 6:12, 14; 2 Chron 29:31; 1 Macc 5:54; 2 Macc 3:32). That Eph 2:13-16 is followed by one of the most-detailed images of the church as the eschatological heavenly temple in all of the New Testament in 2:19-22 is intriguing.

CONCLUSION

The referent for the phrase διὰ τῆς πίστεως αὐτοῦ in Eph 3:12 is the same as that found in variations of the πίστις Χριστοῦ construction in the undisputed Pauline epistles—namely, the faithfulness of the risen Christ toward those who are united to him. Yet the context of the reference to Christ's πίστις in Ephesians is in some ways distinct. In Ephesians 3, the affirmation that Christ's faithfulness enables Paul and his readers to have access to God comes at the conclusion of the apostle's reflection on his own participation in the mission and mysterious plan of God (3:2-12). God's design to reveal his wisdom to the rulers and authorities in the heavenly realm through the church has happened "in accordance with the eternal purpose that he has carried out in Christ Jesus our Lord" (3:10-11). It is this Christ, the agent of God's eternal purpose, whose πίστις toward humanity allows the boldness of confident access to God. And this confession has profoundly pastoral implications for Paul, since the apostle concludes his discussion with an encouragement for his readers not to despair over his imprisonment: "I ask, therefore, that you do not lose heart over my sufferings for you; they are your glory" (3:13).[40]

Paul's conviction that he suffers for the sake of others, including Christ, is a key feature of his reflection upon his own apostolic vocation (2 Cor 1:6; 4:7-15; Col 1:24-25; Eph 3:1-13; 2 Tim 2:10; cf. Phil 1:29-30).[41] Interestingly, in three texts in the Pauline corpus in which Paul (or someone writing in his name) discusses his vicarious apostolic suffering, he also speaks of the faithfulness of the risen Christ:

> **2 Tim 2:8-13**: Remember Jesus Christ, raised from the dead, from the seed of David—that is my gospel, *in which sphere I am suffering*

It appears that some of the pieces of the atonement theology of Hebrews are present in Ephesians 2 (the atoning power of the living Christ's blood; cultic access to God; temple imagery), but they are not put together in the same way (e.g., in Ephesians 2, Christ is not imaged in priestly terms and the temple is the church, with Christ Jesus himself as the cornerstone).

[40] We follow most commentators in viewing διό at the beginning of 3:13 as referring back to all of 3:2-12 and not merely the final clause of 3:12 (so Barth, *Ephesians*, 348).

[41] See L. Ann Jervis, *At the Heart of the Gospel: Suffering in the Earliest Christian Message* (Grand Rapids: Eerdmans, 2007).

hardship even to the point of being chained like a criminal. But the word of God is not chained. *Therefore, I endure everything for the sake of elect, so that they too might obtain the salvation that is in Christ Jesus, with eternal glory.* The word is faithful! For if we have died together, then we will also live together. If we endure, we will also reign together. If we deny him, he will deny us. *If we are faithless, he remains faithful—for he cannot deny himself.*

2 Cor 4:7-14: But we have this treasure in clay vessels, so that the excess of power might be of God and not from us; being afflicted in every way, but not crushed, perplexed, but not despairing, persecuted, but not forsaken, struck down, but not destroyed, always carrying the death of Jesus in the body, so that the life of Jesus in our bodies may also be made visible. For we the living are always being delivered to death for the sake of Jesus, that also the life of Jesus may be made visible in our mortal flesh. *So death is at work in us, but life in you. But having the same Spirit of faithfulness that is in accordance with scripture—"I believed, and so I spoke"—we also believe,* therefore we also speak, knowing that the one who raised the Lord Jesus will raise us also with Jesus, and will bring us with you into his presence.

Eph 3:11-13: This was in accordance with the eternal purpose that [God] has carried out in Christ Jesus our Lord, in whom we have boldness and access with confidence *through his faithfulness. I ask, therefore, that you do not lose heart over my sufferings for you; they are your glory.*[42]

These connections between Paul's vicarious suffering and the faithfulness of the risen Christ are unlikely to be accidental. Paul frames his suffering as beneficial for others in part because he perceives his own

---

[42] We might add Phil 3:8-11, which does not frame Paul's suffering as vicarious, yet nevertheless connects the faithfulness of the risen Christ with Paul's experience of suffering: "More than that, I even regard everything as a loss because of the supreme value of knowing Christ Jesus my Lord. For his sake I have forfeited all things, and I regard them as trash, in order that I might gain Christ and be found in him, not having a righteousness of my own that comes from law but *a righteousness that comes through the faithfulness of Christ, the righteousness from God depending on faithfulness* to know Christ and the power of his resurrection *and the partnership of his sufferings by being conformed to his death,* if somehow I might attain the resurrection from the dead."

afflictions and ultimate vindication as a partaking in the narrative of Christ's death and burial, resurrection, and glorification. In living out the story of Christ through his own suffering and apostolic ministry, Paul embodies the very gospel upon which his mission is centered. In Eph 3:12-13 in particular, the boldness and access that allow believers to approach God in confidence are enabled by the faithfulness of the risen Christ. For the apostle, union with the risen Lord allows Paul's own sufferings on behalf of his readers to be seen as afflictions that lead not to the shame of the Ephesians but to their eschatological glorification (3:13). If, as in Rom 5:2, "glory" (δόξα) in Eph 3:13 has to do with incorruptible life, then Paul is saying that his vicarious sufferings are resurrection for the Ephesians. The conclusion of this section of Ephesians, then, might be paraphrased by slightly amending another Pauline statement of vicarious suffering, "So death is at work in [me], but life is at work among you" (2 Cor 4:12).

CONCLUSION
"In His Faithfulness and Love,
in His Suffering and Resurrection"

The anonymous guerrilla artist Banksy has been the subject of vigorous debates about whether graffiti is art and, more broadly, how and whether the boundaries of what constitutes art can be determined. Visitors to Bethlehem can place their hands on (and even spray paint nearby) a number of famous Banksy stencils situated on the wall separating the West Bank from Israel, a wall that for many symbolizes conflict and injustice. These visitors (and locals, too) may be surprised to learn that in 2013 a Banksy mural painted on the wall of a store in Wood Green, London was removed and fetched $1.2 million at auction.[1] What makes Banksy's work so valuable? Can it possibly have that value once it is removed from the setting that made it so poignant? Similar questions have been raised about biblical texts. Like graffiti art, is the transgressive potential of Paul's words lost, muted,

---

[1] See, for example, Matilda Battersby, "Anger as Banksy's Poundland Mural Ripped from Wall and Set for Auction in Miami for £450,000," *Independent*, February 18, 2013, http://www.independent.co.uk/arts-entertainment/art/news/anger-as-banksys-poundland-mural-ripped-from-wall-and-set-for-auction-in-miami-for-450000-8499802.html. The mural was later returned to the U.K. In October 2018, Banksy activated a shredder that destroyed a painting of his immediately after it was sold at auction for $1.4 million (Scott Reyburn, "Banksy Painting Self-Destructs after Fetching $1.4 Million at Sotheby's," *New York Times*, October 6, 2018, https://www.nytimes.com/2018/10/06/arts/design/uk-banksy-painting-sothebys.html).

or perhaps even enhanced as the ideas are lifted from their original contexts?

Closer to our concerns in this book is another piece of graffiti, this time not a stencil commenting on child labor or political oppression, but a set of words and numbers incised on the wall of the basilica in the agora of Smyrna, possibly as early as the first quarter of the second century.[2] The inscription (pictured on the cover of this book) reads as follows:

ισοψηφα
κυριος   ω
πιστις   ω

A clear example of isopsephy, where Greek letters are assigned a fixed number and specific words are given a number based on adding up the value of the letters,[3] the graffiti can be translated as "equal in value: Lord, 800; faithfulness, 800."[4] It appears that one Christian in the second or third century had concluded, at least on the basis of a numerical correlation, that "the Lord is faithful" (cf. 2 Thess 3:3).[5] It is impossible to know whether the "artist" behind this early Christian graffito intended this statement as a confession, a protest, a prayer, or something else altogether. Yet the idea that *Christ the Lord is faithful*, captured on this piece of graffiti in Smyrna, became so important

[2] Roger Bagnall originally dated this graffiti to before 125 C.E. (*Everyday Writing in the Graeco-Roman East* [Berkeley: University of California Press, 2012], 22–23) but recently has shifted his dating of it to the end of the second century or the early third century (Roger S. Bagnall et al., eds., *Graffiti from the Basilica in the Agora of Smyrna* [New York: New York University Press, 2016], 40).

[3] See Franz Dornseiff, *Das Alphabet in Mystik und Magie*, 2nd ed., Stoicheia 7 (Leipzig: B. G. Teubner, 1925), 91–118, and, more recently, Rodney Ast and Julia Lougovaya, "The Art of the Isopsephism in the Greco-Roman World," in *Ägyptische Magie und ihre Umwelt*, ed. A. Jördens (Wiesbaden: Harrassowitz, 2015), 82–98.

[4] κυριος would be 20+400+100+10+70+200=800 (ω), and πιστις works out to 80+10+200+300+10+200=800 (ω).

[5] The inscription may not be anonymous. Bagnall notes the presence of a second inscription on the same wall, ostensibly scrawled in the same hand, that records the name Artemidoros the Smyrnean (*Graffiti from the Basilica*, 423).

that eventually the Christian cult would be known by the name "the faith."[6]

Though not quite as elemental as an isopsephism, the central claim of this book is a relatively simple one: the story of Christ's faithfulness in Paul's letters, which is evoked in the phrase πίστις Χριστοῦ, does not end with Jesus' death. Instead, we have attempted to show that Christ's πίστις in the Pauline epistles refers also, and in some cases primarily, to the continuing faithfulness of the risen and exalted Christ toward those who are united to him by πίστις. In the Pauline epistles, as in wider cultural discourse of which these writings are a part, πίστις is relational language, "centering on trust, trustworthiness, faithfulness, and good faith."[7] The phrase πίστις Χριστοῦ evokes the story of Christ's own πίστις, but it does so in a way that also highlights human participation in Christ's πίστις.[8] It is Christ's faithfulness toward humanity—the abiding, justifying, mission-empowering trustworthiness of the risen and exalted Lord for those united to him—that allows humans to place their trust in him.

Since the Protestant Reformation, the apostle Paul has often been framed as a theologian of the cross *par excellence*.[9] Luther himself draws upon several Pauline proofs in the sections of the Heidelberg Catechism in which he defines a theologian of the cross in opposition to a theologian of glory (§19–24).[10] We do not intend to

[6] See further Teresa Morgan, *Roman Faith and Christian Faith:* Pistis *and* Fides *in the Early Roman Empire and Early Churches* (Oxford: Oxford University Press, 2015), 265, 305. Morgan's book shows that the modern understanding of "faith" as "religion" is not present in the first century.

[7] Morgan, *Roman Faith,* 503.

[8] As Morna Hooker writes, "Believing faith depends on the faith/faithfulness of Christ: it is the response to Christ's faith, and claims it as one's own" ("ΠΙΣΤΙΣ ΧΡΙΣΤΟΥ," *NTS* 35 [1989]: 340).

[9] In the twentieth century, this view was advocated most forcefully by Ernst Käsemann, whose shadow still looms large over the field of Pauline studies. See, for example, the opening line of Käsemann's essay, "The Pauline Theology of the Cross" (*Int* 24 [1970]: 151–77): "The Reformation quite correctly based its understanding of evangelical theology as a theology of the cross upon Paul" (151).

[10] Pauline texts cited by Luther in these sections include Rom 1:20, 22; 2:12, 23; 4:15; 7:10, 12; 1 Cor 1:21, 25; Gal 3:10, 13; Phil 2:7; 3:18; 1 Tim 4:4. It is in his *Operationes in Psalmos* in which Luther famously declares *crux sola est nostra theologia*, "the cross

minimize or diminish the importance of the crucifixion of Jesus for Paul's soteriology, or for his theology in general. There is no doubt that Paul understood the cross as an apocalyptic, epistemologically revolutionary, and world-creating event (e.g., 2 Cor 5:14-17; Gal 6:14-15).[11] And the Christ-narrative conjured by the phrase πίστις Χριστοῦ includes the crucifixion. In 2 Cor 4:13, the risen Christ looks back upon his time of suffering and declares, using the words of the Psalmist, "I believed, and so I spoke." Yet to the extent that references to Christ's πίστις in the Pauline letters evoke the story of Jesus, that story is truncated if the narrative sequence concludes with the crucifixion. For Paul, Jesus' own πίστις is seen primarily in the faithfulness of the risen Christ to those united to him by πίστις. This is the point articulated explicitly in 2 Tim 2:13: "if we are faithless, [Christ] remains faithful—for he cannot deny himself." Yet we have endeavored to demonstrate the presence of this same conviction regarding the risen Christ's continued faithfulness toward those joined to him in each instance of the πίστις Χριστοῦ construction and related variants in the Pauline epistles (Gal 2:16, 20; 3:22, 26; Rom 3:22, 25, 26; Phil 3:9; Eph 3:12). And even though Christ's trust in 2 Cor 4:13 is located at the moment of his earthly suffering, it is the risen and exalted Lord who says, "I believed, and so I spoke."

RESURRECTION AND EXALTATION IN PAUL'S NARRATIVE SOTERIOLOGY AND ETHICS

No recent interpreter has done more to underscore the importance of narrative for Paul's soteriology than Richard Hays. The genius of Hays' groundbreaking study *The Faith of Jesus Christ* is not found in any particular exegetical argument that Hays develops to support a subjective interpretation of the πίστις Χριστοῦ construction in Paul's

---

alone is our theology" (WA5.176,32–33). On Luther's *theologia crucis*, the foundational English-language work remains Gerhard Forde, *On Being a Theologian of the Cross: Reflections on Luther's Heidelberg Disputation, 1518* (Grand Rapids: Eerdmans, 1997); cf. Robert Cady Saler, *Theologia Crucis: A Companion to the Theology of the Cross* (Eugene, Ore.: Cascade, 2016).

[11] Still worth revisiting is the seminal collection of J. Louis Martyn's essays, *Theological Issues in the Letters of Paul* (Edinburgh: T&T Clark, 1997).

letters. Indeed, Hays' original discussion of "the grammatical issue" of "πίστις followed by a name or a pronoun," which is focused in Gal 3:22 but covers other texts from the Pauline corpus (Gal 2:20; 3:26; Rom 3:21-26), takes up a relatively minor portion of the monograph and does not offer any decisively new syntactical argumentation.[12] Instead, Hays' central and enduring claim in *The Faith of Jesus Christ* is that Paul's theology rests upon a narrative substructure. In a later reflection upon his dissertation, Hays summarizes his argument in this way:

> I remain unrepentant concerning the central thesis of my earlier work: Paul's theology must be understood as the explication and defense of a *story*. The narrative structure of the gospel story depicts Jesus as the divinely commissioned protagonist who gives himself up to death on a cross in order to liberate humanity from bondage (Gal 1:4; 2:20; 3:13-14; 4:4-7). His death, in obedience to the will of God, is simultaneously a loving act of faithfulness (πίστις) to God and the decisive manifestation of God's faithfulness to his covenant promise to Abraham. Paul's uses of πίστις Ἰησοῦ Χριστοῦ and similar phrases should be understood as summary allusions to this story, referring to Jesus' fidelity in carrying out this mission. Consequently, the emphasis in Paul's theology lies less on the question of how we should dispose ourselves toward God than on the question of how God has acted in Christ to effect our deliverance.[13]

---

[12] Hays, *Faith of Jesus Christ: The Narrative Substructure of Galatians 3:1–4:11*, 2nd ed. (Grand Rapids: Eerdmans, 2002), 141–62. As Hays himself writes in a later reflection on the πίστις Χριστοῦ debate, "The objective genitive is a possible construal, and there are at least two passages where Paul does use the verb πιστεύειν with χριστὸν Ἰησοῦν (or the equivalent) as its object (Gal 2:16; Phil 1:29; cf. also Rom 10:12 and Col 2:5). . . . Our interpretive decision about the meaning of Paul's phrase, therefore, must be governed by larger judgments about the shape and logic of Paul's thought concerning faith, Christ, and salvation" (*Faith of Jesus Christ*, 276–77).

[13] Hays, *Faith of Jesus Christ*, 274–75. Notably absent from Hays' summary of the gospel story in this quotation is any reference to the resurrection of Jesus. This illustrates a tendency in Hays' work, reflected also in his analysis of the πίστις Χριστοῦ and its variants, subtly to minimize the plot point of Jesus' resurrection in Paul's gospel narrative. Hays' emphasis on the cross in *The Faith of Jesus Christ* may, of course, reflect the volume's focus on Galatians, although we have attempted to show the importance of Christ's resurrection for Paul's language of πίστις in that letter.

We agree that the theologizing reflected in Paul's letters is grounded in the story of Jesus Christ and that variations of the πίστις Χριστοῦ construction function as "summary allusions to this story." Yet—and this point should hardly be controversial—the narrative about Jesus Christ that undergirds Paul's letters is not halted at the cross. Hays himself elsewhere succinctly summarizes this very point: "Paul's gospel story hinges on the death and resurrection of Jesus."[14]

Our claim that Christ's πίστις refers to the continuing faithfulness of the risen and exalted Christ toward those joined to him by πίστις brings a greater level of coherence to the narrative soteriology reflected in the Pauline letters. It has often been suggested that viewing πίστις Χριστοῦ as a reference to Christ's own faithfulness highlights the participatory dimensions of Paul's soteriology, particularly by showing the close connection between "participation in Christ" and "justification." David Stubbs, for example, describes the relationship in this way: "The 'faith of Christ' reading makes Paul's participatory language cohere quite well with his 'righteousness' language; we are 'made righteous' through our participation in Christ and his 'faithfulness' to God and

---

[14] Hays, "Is Paul's Gospel Narratable?" JSNT 27 (2004): 235. Similarly, in an appreciative summary of Douglas Campbell's contribution to the volume *Narrative Dynamics in Paul* (Douglas A. Campbell, "The Story of Jesus in Romans and Galatians," in *Narrative Dynamics in Paul: A Critical Assessment*, ed. Bruce W. Longenecker [Louisville: Westminster John Knox, 2002]), Hays writes the following:

> Campbell calls attention to the fact that in Rom 8 Paul's narration of the career of Jesus presents him as the "firstborn among many brothers" who are to be conformed to his image (Rom 8.29). Thus, "this story contains an important incorporative aspect as the Spirit of life conforms people to the template" of Christ (Campbell, p. 112). This not only explains how believers can experience the Spirit's life-giving power, but it also suggests a homology between Christ and believers—a homology signaled in the compact expression *pistis Christou* ("faith of Christ"), which is "simply an alternative locution—technically a synecdoche—for the whole event of the cross" (Campbell, p. 121). Those who are in Christ find the pattern of his faithful suffering and death re-enacted in their own lives (cf. Gal 2:19b-20; 2 Cor 4:7-12) and share the same expectation of resurrection. In other words, "the story of Jesus" is not the story of Jesus alone; rather, it is the story of all who are in Christ and therefore share his sufferings and the power of his resurrection. (Hays, "Is Paul's Gospel Narratable?" 229)

God's purposes. Because of this, Paul's theology of justification can be seen to lead naturally into and be one piece with his ethics."[15]

In shifting the focus from Christ's faithfulness to God on the cross to the risen Lord's faithfulness to humanity, our interpretation offers an even more integrated account of justification and participation.[16] The people of God are made righteous through participation in Christ and his faithfulness to them. A number of recent interpreters, frustrated with the dichotomy between union with Christ and the concept of imputed righteousness in traditional treatments of Paul's theology, have begun to speak of "incorporated righteousness" as a way to emphasize that righteousness from God is always "in Christ" righteousness.[17] According to Matthew Bates, "incorporated righteousness" (or "in-the-Messiah righteousness") is "the saving perfect righteousness of Jesus the Christ that is counted entirely ours when we join the Spirit-filled body that is already united to the righteous one, Christ the kingly head."[18] Being united to the righteous one, to put the matter bluntly, assumes that Christ has been raised from the dead. For Paul, that is, followers of Jesus are joined to one who is alive and seated at the right hand of God. In this sense, the justifying πίστις of Christ was not merely staged on a Roman cross; it is given for and to

---

[15] David L. Stubbs, "The Shape of Soteriology and the Pistis Christou Debate," *SJT* 61 (2008):155; cf. Sam Williams: "Christians are justified precisely because they participate in the crucified and justified Messiah, whose destiny embodies theirs" ("Again *Pistis Christou*," CBQ 49 [1987]: 444).

[16] As we discussed in chapter 5, this emphasis on Christ's faithfulness to humanity was already anticipated in several perceptive essays by Shuji Ota, although Ota continues to understand the phrase πίστις Χριστοῦ as a reference to Jesus' death; see esp. Ota, "ΠΙΣΤΙΣ ΧΡΙΣΤΟΥ: Christ's Faithfulness to Whom?" *HJAS* 55 (2014), 15–26.

[17] The phrasing here is adapted from Garwood P. Anderson, *Paul's New Perspective: Charting a Soteriological Journey* (Downers Grove, Ill.: IVP Academic, 2016), 139: "Put simply, the *ek theou* ('from God') righteousness is always an *en Christō* ('in Christ') righteousness. 'Being found *in him*' is the preface to and condition for possessing the righteousness that comes from God (Phil 3:9)" (emphasis original). Cf. Michael F. Bird, "Incorporated Righteousness: A Response to Recent Evangelical Discussion concerning the Imputation of Christ's Righteousness in Justification," *JETS* 47 (2004): 253–75; Constantine R. Campbell, *Paul and Union with Christ: An Exegetical and Theological Study* (Grand Rapids: Zondervan, 2012), 399–404.

[18] Bates, *Salvation by Allegiance Alone: Rethinking Faith, Works, and the Gospel of Jesus the King* (Grand Rapids: Baker Academic, 2017),190.

those who are joined to their risen Lord.[19] Or, as we have stated already, Christ crucified is Christ resurrected is Christ exalted.[20]

For this reason, too, Christ's faithfulness toward humanity holds important implications for Paul's ethics. To the extent that πίστις is a "relational [concept] and [practice], centering on trust, trustworthiness, faithfulness, and good faith," πίστις creates and demands a certain way of life among those who share in the gospel of Christ.[21] Peter Oakes gestures toward this reality in his study of πίστις in Galatians:

> For Paul, πίστις Χριστοῦ is the new way of living that has appeared in the world with the arrival of Christ (cf. Oakes 2015: 126). It is characterized by people's trust in and loyalty to Christ. *Paul may also be thinking of it as characterized by continuing acts of Christ done in loyalty to people: providing strength and inspiration, working miracles (Gal. 3.5), interceding with God on their behalf* (cf. Rom. 8.34). Paul may also draw the picture wider and see God providing these things through Christ and the action of the Spirit.[22]

We hope to have shown that this is precisely how the term πίστις Χριστοῦ functions in the Pauline epistles. It is because Christ is faithful toward those joined to him by πίστις that those who share in Christ's

---

[19] This insight is crucial for the structure of Calvin's *Institutes*, for in Book III Calvin makes union with Christ logically prior to and the grounds for all the benefits humans receive from God the Father, including justification; see Michael S. Horton, "Calvin's Theology of Union with Christ and the Double Grace: Modern Reception and Contemporary Possibilities," in *Calvin's Theology and Its Reception: Disputes, Developments, and New Possibilities*, ed. J. Todd Billings and I. John Hesselink (Louisville: Westminster John Knox, 2012), 49–71.

[20] In this context, one thinks of James D. G. Dunn's insistence that the "unifying strand" amidst the theological diversity of the New Testament is "the unity between the historical Jesus and the exalted Christ, that is to say, the conviction that the wandering charismatic preacher from Nazareth had ministered, died and been raised from the dead to bring God and man finally together, the recognition that the divine power through which they now worshipped and were encountered and accepted by God as one and the same person, Jesus, the man, the Christ, the Son of God, the Lord, the life-giving Spirit" (*Unity and Diversity in the New Testament: An Inquiry into the Character of Earliest Christianity*, 2nd ed. [London: SCM, 1990], 370).

[21] Morgan, *Roman Faith*, 503.

[22] Oakes, "*Pistis* as a Relational Way of Life in Galatians," JSNT 40 (2018): 265, emphasis added.

πίστις are empowered to live faithfully. Perhaps nowhere are the relational and ethical dynamics of πίστις captured more clearly than in 2 Thess 3:1-5:

> Finally, pray for us, brothers and sisters, so that the word of the Lord may advance and be glorified, just as also among you, and that we may be delivered from inappropriate and evil people; for not all have faith (πίστις). But the Lord is faithful (πιστός); he will go on strengthening you and guarding you from the evil one. And we trust (πεποίθαμεν) in the Lord concerning you, that you are doing and will continue to do the things that we command. May the Lord direct your hearts to the love of God and to the endurance of Christ.

The risen Lord Jesus Christ is faithful, and he will strengthen the Thessalonians and guard them from the evil one. At the same time, those who have faith will be delivered from wicked and evil people and can be trusted to follow godly commands. The πίστις of the risen Christ allows those "in him" to become people of faith and faithfulness, trust and trustworthiness.

The Risen Christ's Faith(fulness) in Early Christian Reception of Paul

Just as the meaning of the phrase πίστις Χριστοῦ in the Pauline epistles has been much debated in modern scholarship, so too has the question whether the church fathers speak of the faithfulness of Christ. Consideration of the patristic evidence has yielded conflicting results. It is well beyond the scope of the present study to wade into this debate.[23]

---

[23] An early contribution is Roy A. Harrisville, "ΠΙΣΤΙΣ ΧΡΙΣΤΟΥ: Witness of the Fathers," *NovT* 36 (1994): 233–41. Harrisville's study is limited, however, because the only evidence he considers are direct citations of Pauline letters. For more detailed analyses, see Ian G. Wallis, *The Faith of Jesus Christ in Early Christian Traditions*, SNTMS 84 (Cambridge: Cambridge University Press, 1995), 175–212; Michael R. Whitenton, "After ΠΙΣΤΙΣ ΧΡΙΣΤΟΥ: Neglected Evidence from the Church Fathers," *JTS* 61 (2010): 82–109; Mark W. Elliott, "Πίστις Χριστοῦ in the Church Fathers and Beyond," in *The Faith of Jesus Christ: Exegetical, Biblical, and Theological Studies*, ed. Michael F. Bird and Preston M. Sprinkle (Carlisle, U.K.: Paternoster: 2009), 277–89; Michael F. Bird and Michael R. Whitenton, "The

Several early Christian authors outside of the New Testament do refer to Christ as the object of human πίστις (Acts Pet. 3; Origen, Sel. Ps. 701), as does Paul (Rom 9:33; 10:11; Gal 2:16; Phil 1:29). In light of our thesis regarding πίστις Χριστοῦ and the risen and exalted Christ in the Pauline epistles, a reconsideration of patristic evidence that has been counted in favor of the "subjective" interpretation may be a useful exercise. We conclude our study, however, by reflecting briefly on two passages from the letters of Ignatius that appear to offer intriguing confirmation of our reading of the Pauline evidence from one of the earliest interpreters of Paul. Ignatius also speaks of the faithfulness of the risen Christ, and in contexts in which echoes of Paul linger in his discourse.

In the central section of his letter to the Philadelphians (5.1–9.2), Ignatius provides a defense of "the gospel" (τὸ εὐαγγέλιον, 5.1, 2; 8.2; 9.2) in view of his concern that the gospel is being threatened by advocates of "Judaism" ('Ιουδαϊσμός, 6.1) in Philadelphia. For Ignatius, "the gospel" is not a written account of Jesus' life (i.e., the gospels later deemed canonical); instead, "the gospel" is the story of the Christ event, with a particular emphasis on Jesus' incarnation, death, and resurrection.[24] As the Bishop of Antioch states at the conclusion of his polemical defense of the gospel, contrasting the gospel with the prophets, "But the gospel possesses something distinct, namely, the coming of the savior, our Lord Jesus Christ, his suffering, and the resurrection. For the beloved prophets made their proclamation in anticipation of him, but the gospel is the consummation of immortality" (9.2). According to this summary statement, then, the decisive events of "the gospel" for Ignatius include Jesus' coming to earth, his crucifixion, and his resurrection from the dead.

Faithfulness of Jesus Christ in Hippolytus' *De Christo et Antichristo*: Overlooked Evidence in the Πίστις Χριστοῦ Debate," *NTS* 55 (2009): 552–62.

[24] So William R. Schoedel, *Ignatius of Antioch*, Hermeneia (Philadelphia: Fortress, 1985), 201; see also Charles Thomas Brown, *The Gospel and Ignatius of Antioch*, SBL 12 (New York: Peter Lang, 2000), 15–41; *pace* Charles E. Hill, "Ignatius, 'the Gospel,' and the Gospels," in *Trajectories through the New Testament and Apostolic Fathers*, ed. Andrew F. Gregory and Christopher M. Tuckett (Oxford: Oxford University Press, 2005), 267–85.

In the context of *Phld.* 5.1–9.2, this summary of "the gospel" is important because it follows Ignatius' account of an earlier debate that had ostensibly taken place in Philadelphia concerning the relationship between the gospel and "the ancient records" (ἀρχεῖά), the latter of which is presumably a reference to writings that came to be known as the "Old Testament." Ignatius frames the dispute in this way:

> And I exhort you to do nothing according to contentiousness but in accordance with discipleship to Christ. For I heard some saying, "If I do not find it in the ancient records, I do not have faith in the gospel (Ἐὰν μὴ ἐν τοῖς ἀρχείοις εὕρω, ἐν τῷ εὐαγγελίῳ οὐ πιστεύω)." And when I said to them, "It is written," they answered me, "That is the question at issue." But to me the "ancient records" are Jesus Christ, the inviolable ancient records are his cross and death and his resurrection and the faith that is through him (ἡ πίστις ἡ δι᾽ αὐτοῦ). By these things I want, through your prayers, to be justified (δικαιωθῆναι). (*Phld.* 8.2)[25]

Ignatius suggests that his interlocutors in Philadelphia had indicated that they do not trust the message of good news about Christ if they do not find reference to the gospel in the scriptures.[26] Ignatius appears to have responded much like the informed parent who knows the ketchup is in the refrigerator when she hears a child yelling "I can't find it!" from three rooms away: "It's in there!" Ignatius' opponents then answer by reiterating that this is the very point up for debate, a retort that leads the Bishop of Antioch to redefine the "ancient records" in christological terms: no longer are the ἀρχεῖά written prophetic

---

[25] The Greek text from Michael W. Holmes' edition is as follows: Παρακαλῶ δὲ ὑμᾶς μηδὲν κατ᾽ ἐριθείαν πράσσειν, ἀλλὰ κατὰ χριστομαθίαν. ἐπεὶ ἤκουσά τινων λεγόντων ὅτι Ἐὰν μὴ ἐν τοῖς ἀρχείοις εὕρω, ἐν τῷ εὐαγγελίῳ οὐ πιστεύω· καὶ λέγοντός μου αὐτοῖς ὅτι Γέγραπται, ἀπεκρίθησάν μοι ὅτι Πρόκειται. ἐμοὶ δὲ ἀρχεῖά ἐστιν Ἰησοῦς Χριστός, τὰ ἄθικτα ἀρχεῖα ὁ σταυρὸς αὐτοῦ καὶ ὁ θάνατος καὶ ἡ ἀνάστασις αὐτοῦ καὶ ἡ πίστις ἡ δι᾽ αὐτοῦ ἐν οἷς θέλω ἐν τῇ προσευχῇ ὑμῶν δικαιωθῆναι (*The Apostolic Fathers: Greek Texts and English Translations*, 3rd ed. [Grand Rapids: Baker, 2007], 242).

[26] Many English translations supply the object "it" for the verb πιστεύω in the clause ἐν τῷ εὐαγγελίῳ οὐ πιστεύω (e.g., Holmes, *Apostolic Fathers*; Schoedel, *Ignatius of Antioch*).

accounts; the ἀρχεῖά are the gospel—that is, the story of Jesus' crucifixion, death, resurrection, and the πίστις through him.

The key for our purposes is the phrase "the faith that is through him" (ἡ πίστις ἡ δι᾽ αὐτοῦ). At the very least, Ignatius affirms with this construction that human πίστις is "sourced in Jesus Christ."[27] And if πίστις comes from Christ it would appear to be, at least on some level, a property or characteristic of his to give: the one who mediates πίστις is πιστός.[28] Moreover, the narrative sequence of Ignatius' "gospel," which moves from cross to death to resurrection to πίστις, makes it clear that ἡ πίστις ἡ δι᾽ αὐτοῦ comes from the *risen* Christ. There is no sense in *Phld.* 8.2—or elsewhere in Ignatius' letters, for that matter—that πίστις was demonstrated by Jesus in his death.

Additionally, Ignatius connects ἡ πίστις ἡ δι᾽ αὐτοῦ—along with Jesus' cross, death, and resurrection—with the bishop's own hope for justification. It is by "these things" (ἐν οἷς), by the story of the gospel, that Ignatius hopes to be justified. There is no doubt that Ignatius was influenced by the Pauline tradition and was familiar with at least some letters from Paul, including both 1 Corinthians and Ephesians (Ign. *Eph* 12.2; Ign. *Rom* 4.3).[29] It is not possible definitively to know whether

---

[27] Bird and Whitenton, "The Faithfulness of Jesus Christ," 555. Whitenton describes this phrase as portraying "faith as something that is enigmatically mediated through Jesus" ("After ΠΙΣΤΙΣ ΧΡΙΣΤΟΥ," 108; cf. Herm. Vis. 4.1.8; Herm. Mand. 11.4; Herm. Sim. 6.1.2; 6.3.6). The phrase ἡ πίστις ἡ δι᾽ αὐτοῦ also occurs in Acts 3:16: "And by faith in his name (καὶ ἐπὶ τῇ πίστει τοῦ ὀνόματος αὐτοῦ), his name has made this man strong, whom you see and know; and the faith that is through Jesus (ἡ πίστις ἡ δι᾽ αὐτοῦ) has given him this perfect health in the presence of all of you." Although most commentators take Jesus to be the object of both instances of πίστις in Acts 3:16, Campbell is unpersuaded: "I am, incidentally, not convinced that Acts 3:16 does supply an objective genitive construction, but suggest rendering its two instances of πίστις in terms of 'proof,' and the genitive consequently more as one of content—the proof of God's saving activity in Christ that is supplied by the miraculously healed cripple" (*Deliverance of God: An Apocalyptic Rereading of Justification in Paul* [Grand Rapids: Eerdmans, 2009], 1101–2n14).

[28] Ignatius does write that the God the Father is "faithful in Jesus Christ" (Ign. *Trall.* 13.3: πιστὸς ὁ πατὴρ ἐν Ἰησοῦ Χριστῷ).

[29] For a brief summary of the debated question of Pauline influence on Ignatius, see David J. Downs, "The Pauline Concept of Union with Christ in Ignatius of Antioch," in *The Apostolic Fathers and Paul*, ed. Todd D. Still and David Wilhite, PPSD 2 (Edinburgh: T&T Clark, 2016), 143–61. For a careful discussion of Ignatius' use of the

or to what extent Ignatius' concept of justification might have been developed from his reading of Paul's letters or his knowledge of Paul's teaching.[30] Yet it is certainly intriguing that Ignatius connects his hope for justification with an affirmation of πίστις that comes from the risen Christ, for that is precisely the relationship between justification, πίστις, and the risen Christ that we have traced in Gal 2:16-21, Rom 3:21-26, and Phil 3:9.[31]

Elsewhere Ignatius also connects Christ's faithfulness with elements of the gospel narrative of death and resurrection, possibly even with an allusion to Gal 2:20. At the end of his letter to the Ephesians, Ignatius writes of his plan to compose a follow-up missive to explain to the Ephesians the subject about which he has begun to speak—namely, "the divine plan with respect to the new man Jesus Christ, in his faithfulness and love, in his suffering and resurrection (ἐν τῇ αὐτοῦ πίστει καὶ ἐν τῇ αὐτοῦ ἀγάπῃ, ἐν πάθει αὐτοῦ καὶ ἀναστάσει), especially if the Lord reveals anything to me" (20.1-2a). The syntactical parallels between the prepositional phrases ἐν τῇ αὐτοῦ πίστει, ἐν τῇ αὐτοῦ ἀγάπῃ, and ἐν πάθει αὐτοῦ indicate that Ignatius is referring to Jesus' own faithfulness and love instead of Jesus as the object of human πίστις and ἀγάπη.[32]

Pauline epistles, see Paul Foster, "The Epistles of Ignatius of Antioch and the Writings that Later Formed the New Testament," in *The Reception of the New Testament in the Apostolic Fathers*, ed. Andrew Gregory and Christopher Tuckett (Oxford: Oxford University Press, 2005), 160–86. The strongest textual parallels are Ign. *Eph.* 16.1// 1 Cor 6:9-10; Ign. *Eph.* 18.1//1 Cor 1:18, 20; Ign. *Magn.* 10.2//1 Cor 5:7-8; Ign. *Rom.* 5.1//1 Cor 4:4; Ign. *Rom.* 9.2//1 Cor 15:8-10; cf. Ign. *Eph.* Inscr.//Eph 1:3-4; *Pol.* 5.1// Eph 5:25.

[30] A recent argument for Paul's influence on Ignatius' concept of justification is advanced in Brian J. Arnold, *Justification in the Second Century*, SBR 9 (Berlin: de Gruyter, 2017), 36–76.

[31] Brown writes, "[In] *Phld.* 8.2 as in *Phld.* 5.1, Ignatius connects his own ultimate goal (in 8.2 to be justified, and in 5.1 the 'lot in which I attain mercy') with the εὐαγγέλιον (as well as the prayer of the Philadelphian church). It is the present faith in the past events of Jesus' life, death and resurrection that is the locus of justification for Ignatius" (*The Gospel and Ignatius of Antioch*, 18).

[32] So Whitenton, "After ΠΙΣΤΙΣ ΧΡΙΣΤΟΥ," 94. The subjective use of the pronoun in the clause ἐν πάθει αὐτοῦ καὶ ἀναστάσει clarifies that both instances of αὐτοῦ in the phrase ἐν τῇ αὐτοῦ πίστει καὶ ἐν τῇ αὐτοῦ ἀγάπῃ are subjective as well. Whitenton also points out that "elsewhere in *Ephesians*, every other time that a verbal

Moreover, that Jesus is called "the new man" (τὸν καινὸν ἄνθρωπον) is likely a reference to the perfect humanity that Jesus obtained through his resurrection from the dead (cf. Ign, *Rom*. 6.2; Ign. *Smyrn*. 4.2). Thus, the proposed subject of Ignatius' treatise is the living Christ, his faithfulness, his love, his suffering, and his resurrection. It is quite suggestive that Paul in Gal 2:20 also refers to Jesus' living presence, his faithfulness, his love, and his death: "no longer do I live, but Christ lives in me; and that [life] I now live in the flesh I live in the faithfulness of the Son of God, who loved me and gave himself for me." Moreover, Ignatius' following statement also parallels Paul's language in Gal 2:20 of dying to the self and living in Christ, for Ignatius goes on to describe the Eucharistic bread as "the medicine of immortality, the antidote that allows us not to die but to live in Christ Jesus forever" (20.2). As Whitenton concludes on the basis of these parallels, "At a minimum we may have here evidence that Ignatius connected the faithfulness of Christ with his death and resurrection; at the most we could have evidence of a subjective construal of Gal. 2:20."[33]

The evidence is more suggestive than definitive. Yet at least twice in the letters of Ignatius we find that one of Paul's earliest interpreters identifies πίστις as a property of or a gift from the risen Lord Jesus Christ—and in both instances echoes of Paul's own language reverberate in Ignatius' words. Perhaps, then, our thesis is not as novel as we suggested at the outset of this volume.

---

noun is used with a personal pronoun the force is clearly subjective (Ign. *Eph*. 1.2; 2.1 [*bis*]; 8.1; 9.1; 10.2 [*ter*]; 11.2; 13.1; 15.1; 20.1 [*ter*]; 21.2)" (94).

33 Whitenton, "After ΠΙΣΤΙΣ ΧΡΙΣΤΟΥ," 96.

BIBLIOGRAPHY

Alexander, Loveday. "Hellenistic Letter-Forms and the Structure of Philippians." *JSNT* 37 (1989): 87–101.

Allen, R. Michael. *The Christ's Faith: A Dogmatic Account.* T&T Clark Studies in Systematic Theology. Edinburgh: T&T Clark, 2009.

Anderson, Garwood P. *Paul's New Perspective: Charting a Soteriological Journey.* Downers Grove, Ill.: IVP Academic, 2016.

Arnold, Bradley. *Christ as the Telos of Life: Moral Philosophy, Athletic Imagery, and the Aim of Philippians.* WUNT 2/371. Tübingen: Mohr Siebeck, 2014.

Arnold, Brian. *Justification in the Second Century.* SBR 9. Berlin: de Gruyter, 2017.

Ast, Rodney, and Julia Lougovaya. "The Art of the Isopsephism in the Greco-Roman World." In *Ägyptische Magie und ihre Umwelt,* edited by Andrea Jördens, 82–98. Wiesbaden: Harrassowitz, 2015.

Bagnall, Roger. *Everyday Writing in the Graeco-Roman East.* Berkeley: University of California Press, 2012.

Bagnall, Roger S., R. Casagrande-Kim, A. Ersoy, and C. Tanriver, eds. *Graffiti from the Basilica in the Agora of Smyrna.* New York: New York University Press, 2016.

Bailey, Daniel P. "Jesus as the Mercy Seat: The Semantics and Theology of Paul's Use of *Hilasterion* in Romans 3:25." *TynBul* 51 (2000): 155–58.

Barclay, John M. G. *Paul and the Gift.* Grand Rapids: Eerdmans, 2015.

Barkley, Gary Wayne. *Origen: Homilies on Leviticus 1–16.* FC 83. Washington, D.C.: Catholic University of America Press, 1990.

Barr, James. *The Semantics of Biblical Language.* Oxford: Oxford University Press, 1961.

Barrett, C. K. *The Holy Spirit and the Gospel Tradition.* London: SPCK, 1977.

Barth, Karl. *The Epistle to the Romans,* translated by Edwyn C. Hoskyns. Oxford: Oxford University Press, 1968.

Barth, Markus. *Ephesians.* AB 34A. Garden City, N.Y.: Doubleday, 1974.

———. "Faith of the Messiah," *HeyJ* 10 (1969): 363–70.

Bates, Matthew W. *The Hermeneutics of the Apostolic Proclamation: The Center of Paul's Method of Scriptural Interpretation.* Waco, Tex.: Baylor University Press, 2012.

———. *Salvation by Allegiance Alone: Rethinking Faith, Works, and the Gospel of Jesus the King.* Grand Rapids: Baker Academic, 2017.

Bean, G. E. "Inscriptions of Elaea and Lebedus." *Türk Tarih Kurumu* 29 (1965): 585–97.

Bell, Richard H. "Faith in Christ: Some Exegetical and Theological Reflections on Philippians 3:9 and Ephesians 3:12." In *The Faith of Jesus Christ: Exegetical, Biblical, and Theological Studies,* edited by Michael F. Bird and Preston M. Sprinkle, 111–25. Carlisle, U.K.: Paternoster; Peabody, Mass.: Hendrickson, 2009.

Best, Ernest. *A Critical and Exegetical Commentary on Ephesians.* ICC. Edinburgh: T&T Clark, 1998.

Betz, Hans Dieter. *Galatians: A Commentary on Paul's Letter to the Churches in Galatia.* Hermeneia. Philadelphia: Fortress, 1979.

———. "In Defense of the Spirit: Paul's Letter to the Galatians as a Document of Early Christian Apologetics." *Aspects of Religious Propaganda in Judaism and Early Christianity* (1976): 99–114.

Bird, Michael F. "Justified by Christ's Resurrection: A Neglected Aspect of Paul's Doctrine of Justification." *SBET* 22 (2004): 72–91.

———. "Incorporated Righteousness: A Response to Recent Evangelical Discussion concerning the Imputation of Christ's Righteousness in Justification." *JETS* 47 (2004): 253–75.

Bird, Michael F., and Preston M. Sprinkle, eds. *The Faith of Jesus Christ: Exegetical, Biblical, and Theological Studies.* Carlisle, U.K.: Paternoster; Peabody, Mass.: Hendrickson, 2009.

Bird, Michael F., and Michael R. Whitenton. "The Faithfulness of Jesus Christ in Hippolytus' *De Christo et Antichristo*: Overlooked Evidence in the Πίστις Χριστοῦ Debate." *NTS* 55 (2009): 552–62.

Blass, Friedrich, Albert Debrunner, and Robert W. Funk (BDF). *A Greek Grammar of the New Testament and Other Early Christian Literature.* Chicago: University of Chicago Press, 1961.

Blass, Regina. "Are There Logical Relations in a Text?" *Lingua* 90 (1993): 91–110.

Blutner, Reinhard. "Lexical Pragmatics." *Journal of Semantics* 15 (1998): 115–62.

Bockmuehl, Markus. *The Epistle to the Philippians.* BNTC. London: A&C Black, 1998.

Bontley, Thomas D. "Modified Occam's Razor: Parsimony, Pragmatics, and the Acquisition of Word Meaning." *Mind and Language* 20 (2005): 288–312.

Botner, Max. "The Fragrance of Death—or of Life? Reconsidering the Sacrificial Logic of Ephesians 5:2." Paper presented at the Annual Meeting of the SBL. Denver. November 18, 2018.

Brannon, M. Jeff. *The Heavenlies in Ephesians: A Lexical, Exegetical, and Conceptual Analysis.* LNTS 447. Edinburgh: T&T Clark, 2011.

Brown, Charles Thomas. *The Gospel and Ignatius of Antioch.* SBL 12. New York: Peter Lang, 2000.

Bruce, F. F. *1 & 2 Thessalonians.* WBC 45. Waco, Tex.: Word, 1982.

———. *The Epistle to the Galatians: A Commentary on the Greek Text.* NIGTC. Grand Rapids: Eerdmans, 1982.

Bultmann, Rudolf. *Theology of the New Testament.* Translated by Kendrick Grobel. 2 vols. 1951 and 1955. Reprint, Waco, Tex.: Baylor University Press, 2007.

Calhoun, Robert Matthew. *Paul's Definitions of the Gospel in Romans 1.* WUNT 2/316. Tübingen: Mohr Siebeck, 2011.

Campbell, Constantine R. "Metaphor, Reality, and Union with Christ." In *"In Christ" in Paul: Explorations in Paul's Theology of Union and Participation,* edited by Michael J. Thate, Kevin J. Vanhoozer, Constantine R. Campbell, and T. Robert Baylor, 61–86. WUNT 2/384. Tübingen: Mohr Siebeck, 2014.

————. *Paul and Union with Christ: An Exegetical and Theological Study.* Grand Rapids: Zondervan, 2012.

Campbell, Douglas A. "2 Corinthians 4:13: Evidence in Paul That Christ Believes." *JBL* 128 (2009): 337–56.

————. *The Deliverance of God: An Apocalyptic Rereading of Justification in Paul.* Grand Rapids: Eerdmans, 2009.

————. "The Faithfulness of Jesus Christ in Romans 3:22." In *The Faith of Jesus Christ: Exegetical, Biblical, and Theological Studies,* edited by Michael F. Bird and Preston M. Sprinkle, 57–71. Carlisle, U.K.: Paternoster; Peabody, Mass.: Hendrickson, 2009.

————. *Framing Paul: An Epistolary Biography.* Grand Rapids: Eerdmans, 2014.

————. "The Story of Jesus in Romans and Galatians." In *Narrative Dynamics in Paul: A Critical Assessment,* edited by Bruce W. Longenecker, 97–124. Louisville: Westminster John Knox, 2002.

Carston, Robyn. *Thoughts and Utterances: The Pragmatics of Explicit Communication.* Malden, Mass.: Wiley-Blackwell, 2002.

————. "Word Meaning and Concept Expressed." *The Linguistic Review* 29 (2012): 607–23.

Ciampa, Roy E. "Habakkuk 2:4 in Paul: Echoes, Allusions, and Rewritings." Paper presented at the Annual Meeting of the SBL. Boston. November 28, 2017.

————. *The Presence and Function of Scripture in Galatians 1–2.* WUNT 2/102. Tübingen: Mohr Siebeck, 1998.

Collange, Jean-François. *L'épître de Saint Paul aux Philippiens.* CNT 10A. Neuchâtel: Delachaux & Niestlé, 1973.

Comrie, B., and S. Thompson. "Lexical Nominalization." In *Grammatical Categories and the Lexicon,* 2nd ed., edited by T. Shopen, 334–76. Vol. 3 of *Language Typology and Syntactic Description.* Cambridge: Cambridge University Press, 2007.

Congdon, David W. "The Trinitarian Shape of πίστις: A Theological Exegesis of Galatians." *JTI* 2 (2008): 231–58.

Cotterell, Peter, and Max Turner. *Linguistics and Biblical Interpretation.* Downers Grove, Ill.: InterVarsity Press, 1989.

Croy, N. Clayton. "'To Die Is Gain' (Philippians 1:19-26): Does Paul Contemplate Suicide?" *JBL* 122 (2003): 517–31.

Cruse, David A. *Lexical Semantics*. Cambridge Textbooks in Linguistics. Cambridge: Cambridge University, 1986.

Danker, Frederick W., Walter Bauer, William F. Arndt, and F. Wilbur Gingrich (BDAG). *Greek-English Lexicon of the New Testament and Other Early Christian Literature*. 3rd ed. Chicago: University of Chicago Press, 2000.

Davies, Paul E. Review of *Le Christ et la foi: Étude de théologie biblique*, by Pierre Vallotton. *JBL* 80 (1961): 194.

Dawson, Gerrit Scott. *Jesus Ascended: The Meaning of Christ's Continuing Incarnation*. Edinburgh: T&T Clark, 2004.

De Boer, Martinus C. *Galatians: A Commentary*. NTL. Louisville: Westminster John Knox, 2011.

Deissmann, Adolf. *Bible Studies: Contributions, Chiefly from Papyri and Inscriptions, to the History of the Language, the Literature, and the Religion of Hellenistic Judaism and Primitive Christianity*. Translated by A. Grieve. Edinburgh: T&T Clark, 1901.

———. *St. Paul: A Study in Social and Religious History*. Translated by Lionel R. M. Strachan. London: Hodder & Stoughton, 1912. Translation of *Paulus: eine kultur- und religionsgeschichtliche Skizze: mit je einer Tafel in Lichtdruck und Autotypie sowie einer Karte: die Welt des Apostels Paulus*. Tübingen: J. C. B. Mohr, 1911.

DeSilva, David A. *Galatians: A Handbook on the Greek Text*. Waco, Tex.: Baylor University Press, 2014.

———. "No Confidence in the Flesh: The Meaning and Function of Philippians 3:2-21." *TJ* 15 (1994): 27–54.

Doble, Peter. "'Vile Bodies' or Transformed Persons? Philippians 3.21 in Context." *JSNT* 86 (2002): 3–27.

Dodd, C. H. "ΙΛΑΣΚΕΣΘΑΙ, Its Cognates, Derivatives, and Synonyms, in the Septuagint." *JTS* 32 (1931): 352–60.

Dornseiff, Franz. *Das Alphabet in Mystik und Magie*. 2nd ed. Stoicheia 7. Leipzig: B. G. Teubner, 1925.

Downing, F. Gerald. "Ambiguity, Ancient Semantics, and Faith." *NTS* 56 (2010): 139–62.

Downs, David J. "Faith(fulness) in Christ Jesus in 2 Timothy 3:15." *JBL* 131 (2012): 143–60.

———. "The Pauline Concept of Union with Christ in Ignatius of Antioch." In *The Apostolic Fathers and Paul*, edited by Todd D. Still and David E. Wilhite, 143–61. Vol. 2 of Pauline and Patristic Scholars in Debate. Edinburgh: T&T Clark, 2017.

Drane, John W. *Paul, Libertine or Legalist? A Study in the Theology of the Major Pauline Epistles.* London: SPCK, 1975.

Dunn, James D. G. "ΕΚ ΠΙΣΤΕΩΣ: A Key to the Meaning of ΠΙΣΤΙΣ ΧΡΙΣΤΟΥ." In *The Word Leaps the Gap: Essays on Scripture and Theology in Honor of Richard B. Hays,* edited by J. Ross Wagner, A. Katherine Grieb, and C. Kavin Rowe, 351–66. Grand Rapids: Eerdmans, 2008.

———. "Once More, ΠΙΣΤΙΣ ΧΡΙΣΤΟΥ." In Richard B. Hays, *The Faith of Jesus Christ: The Narrative Substructure of Galatians 3:1–4:11.* 2nd ed. Grand Rapids: Eerdmans, 2002.

———. *Romans 1–8.* WBC 38A. Dallas: Word, 1988.

———. *Romans 9–16.* WBC 38B. Dallas: Word, 1988.

———. *The Theology of Paul the Apostle.* Grand Rapids: Eerdmans, 1998.

———. *Unity and Diversity in the New Testament: An Inquiry into the Character of Earliest Christianity.* 2nd. ed. London: SCM, 1990.

Eastman, Susan Grove. *Paul and the Person: Reframing Paul's Anthropology.* Grand Rapids: Eerdmans, 2017.

Eberhart, C. A. *Kultmetaphorik und Christologie: Opfer- und Sühneterminologie im Neuen Testament.* WUNT 306. Tübingen: Mohr Siebeck, 2013.

———. *The Sacrifice of Jesus: Understanding Atonement Biblically.* Minneapolis: Fortress, 2011.

———. *Studien zur Bedeutung der Opfer im Alten Testament: Die Signifikanz von Blut- und Verbrennungsriten im kultischen Rahmen.* WMANT 94. Neukirchen-Vluyn: Neukirchener, 2002.

Eco, Umberto. *The Role of the Reader: Explorations in the Semiotics of Texts.* Bloomington: Indiana University Press, 1979.

Elliott, Mark W. "Πίστις Χριστοῦ in the Church Fathers and Beyond." In *The Faith of Jesus Christ: Exegetical, Biblical, and Theological Studies,* edited by Michael F. Bird and Preston M. Sprinkle, 277–89. Carlisle, U.K.: Paternoster; Peabody, Mass.: Hendrickson, 2009.

Farrow, Douglas. *Ascension and Ecclesia: On the Significance of the Doctrine of the Ascension for Ecclesiology and Christian Cosmology.* Grand Rapids: Eerdmans, 1999.

———. *Ascension Theology.* Edinburgh: T&T Clark, 2011.

Fee, Gordon D. *The First and Second Letters to the Thessalonians*. NICNT. Grand Rapids: Eerdmans, 2009.

———. *Paul's Letter to the Philippians*. NICNT. Grand Rapids: Eerdmans, 1995.

Fitzmyer, Joseph A. *First Corinthians: A New Translation with Introduction and Commentary*. AB 32. New Haven: Yale University Press, 2008.

———. *Romans: A New Translation with Introduction and Commentary*. AB 33. New York: Doubleday, 1993.

Fodor, Jerry A. *LOT 2: The Language of Thought Revisited*. Oxford: Oxford University Press, 2008.

Forde, Gerhard. *On Being a Theologian of the Cross: Reflections on Luther's Heidelberg Disputation, 1518*. Grand Rapids: Eerdmans, 1997.

Foster, Paul. "The First Contribution to the πίστις Χριστοῦ Debate: A Study of Ephesians 3.12." *JSNT* 85 (2002): 75–96.

———. "The Epistles of Ignatius of Antioch and the Writings That Later Formed the New Testament." In *The Reception of the New Testament in the Apostolic Fathers*, edited by Andrew Gregory and Christopher Tuckett, 160–86. Oxford: Oxford University Press, 2005.

———. "Πίστις Χριστοῦ Terminology in Philippians and Ephesians." In *The Faith of Jesus Christ: Exegetical, Biblical, and Theological Studies*, edited by Michael F. Bird and Preston M. Sprinkle, 91–109. Carlisle, U.K.: Paternoster; Peabody, Mass.: Hendrickson, 2009.

Fowl, Stephen E. *Ephesians: A Commentary*. NTL. Louisville Westminster John Knox, 2012.

Frame, James E. *A Critical and Exegetical Commentary on the Epistles of St. Paul to the Thessalonians*. ICC. New York: Scribner's Sons, 1912.

Frederick, John. "The Perpetual Sacrifice of the Ecclesial Christ: Atonement as Moral Transformation in Ephesians and Second Temple Judaism." In *Spiritual Formation in the Global Context*, edited by John Frederick and Ryan Brandt, forthcoming. Downers Grove, Ill.: IVP Academic, 2019.

Fretheim, Thorstein. "In Defense of Monosemy." In *Pragmatics and the Flexibility of Word Meaning*, edited by Enikö Németh T. and Károly Bibok, 79–115. Amsterdam: Elsevier Science, 2001.

Gane, R. E. *Cult and Character: Purification Offerings, Day of Atonement, and Theodicy*. Winona Lake, Ind.: Eisenbrauns, 2005.

Garlington, Don B. *Faith, Obedience, and Perseverance: Aspects of Paul's Letter to the Romans*. WUNT 79. Tübingen: Mohr Siebeck, 1994.

Gaston, Lloyd. *Paul and the Torah*. Vancouver: University of British Columbia Press, 1987.

Gaventa, Beverly Roberts. "The Singularity of the Gospel Revisited." In *Galatians and Christian Theology: Justification, the Gospel, and Ethics in Paul's Letter*, edited by Mark W. Elliott, Scott J. Hafemann, N. T. Wright, and John Frederick, 187–99. Grand Rapids: Baker Academic, 2014.

Geeraerts, D. "Polysemization and Humboldt's Principle." In *La Polysémie: Lexicographie et Cognition*, edited by R. Jongen. Louvain-la-Neuve: Cabay, 1985.

Gese, Michael. *Das Vermächtnis des Apostels: Die Rezeption der paulinischen Theologie im Epheserbrief.* WUNT 2/99. Tübingen: Mohr Siebeck, 1997.

Gombis, Timothy G. *The Drama of Ephesians: Participating in the Triumph of God*. Downers Grove, Ill.: IVP Academic, 2010.

———. "Ephesians 2 as a Narrative of Divine Warfare." *JSNT* 26 (2004): 403–18.

———. "Ephesians 3:2-13: Pointless Digression, or Epitome of the Triumph of God in Christ?" *WTJ* 66 (2004): 313–23.

Gorman, Michael J. *Becoming the Gospel: Paul, Participation, and Mission*. The Gospel and Our Culture Series. Grand Rapids: Eerdmans, 2015.

Green, Gene L. "Lexical Pragmatics and the Lexicon." *BBR* 22 (2012): 315–33.

———. "Relevance Theory and Biblical Interpretation." In *The Linguist as Pedagogue: Trends in the Teaching and Linguistic Analysis of the Greek New Testament*, edited by Stanley E. Porter and Matthew Brook O'Donnell, 217–40. Sheffield, U.K.: Sheffield Phoenix Press, 2009.

Green, Joel B. "Discourse Analysis and New Testament Interpretation." In *Hearing the New Testament: Strategies for Interpretation*, edited by Joel B. Green, 218–39. 2nd ed. Grand Rapids: Eerdmans, 2010.

Grice, Paul. *Studies in the Way of Words*. Cambridge: Harvard University Press, 1991.

Grieb, A. Katherine. *The Story of Romans: A Narrative Defense of God's Righteousness*. Louisville: Westminster John Knox, 2002.

Gupta, Nijay. "An Apocalyptic Reading of Psalm 78 in 2 Thessalonians 3." *JSNT* 31 (2008): 179–94.

Gutt, Ernst-August. *Translation and Relevance: Cognition and Context.* 2nd ed. Manchester, U.K.: St. Jerome, 2000.

Hansen, G. Walter. *The Letter to the Philippians.* PNTC. Grand Rapids: Eerdmans, 2009.

Harink, Douglas K. *Paul among the Postliberals: Pauline Theology beyond Christendom and Modernity.* Grand Rapids: Brazos, 2003.

Harrisville, Roy A. "ΠΙΣΤΙΣ ΧΡΙΣΤΟΥ: Witness of the Fathers." *NovT* 36 (1994): 233–41.

Haussleiter, Johannes B. "Der Glaube Jesu Christi und der christliche Glaube." *NKZ* 2 (1891): 109–45.

Hawthorne, Gerald F. *Philippians.* WBC 43. Rev. ed. Grand Rapids: Zondervan, 2004.

Hays, Richard B. *Echoes of Scripture in the Letters of Paul.* New Haven: Yale University Press, 1989.

———. *The Faith of Jesus Christ: The Narrative Substructure of Galatians 3:1–4:11.* 2nd ed. Grand Rapids: Eerdmans, 2002.

———. "Is Paul's Gospel Narratable?" *JSNT* 27 (2004): 217–39.

———. "The Letter to the Galatians: Introduction, Commentary, and Reflections." In *The New Interpreter's Bible,* edited by Leander E. Keck, 181–348. Vol. 11. Nashville: Abingdon, 2000.

———. "ΠΙΣΤΙΣ and Pauline Theology: What Is at Stake?" In *Pauline Theology, Vol. 4: Looking Back, Pressing On,* edited by E. Elizabeth Johnson and David M. Hay, 35–60. SymS 4. Atlanta: Scholars, 1997.

Hill, Charles E. "Ignatius, 'the Gospel,' and the Gospels." In *Trajectories Through the New Testament and the Apostolic Fathers,* edited by Andrew F. Gregory and Christopher M. Tuckett, 267–85. Oxford: Oxford University Press, 2005.

Hoehner, Harold W. *Ephesians: An Exegetical Commentary.* Grand Rapids: Baker Academic, 2002.

Holmes, Michael W. *The Apostolic Fathers: Greek Texts and English Translations.* 3rd ed. Grand Rapids: Baker Academic, 2007.

Hooker, Morna. "Another Look at πίστις Χριστοῦ." *SJT* 69 (2016): 46–62.

———. "From God's Faithfulness to Ours: Another Look at 2 Corinthians 1:17-24." In *Paul and the Corinthians: Studies on a Community in Conflict: Essays in Honour of Margaret Thrall,* edited by Trevor J. Burke and J. Keith Elliott, 233–39. NovTSup 109. Leiden: Brill, 2003.

———. "ΠΙΣΤΙΣ ΧΡΙΣΤΟΥ." *NTS* 35 (1989): 321–42.

————. "Raised for Our Acquittal." In *Resurrection in the New Testament: Festschrift J. Lambrecht*, edited by R. Bieringer, V. Koperski, and B. Lataire, 323–41. BETL 165. Leuven, Bel.: Leuven University Press, 2002.

————. "'Who Died for Our Sins, and Was Raised for Our Acquittal': Paul's Understanding of the Death of Christ." *SEÅ* 68 (2003): 59–71.

Horton, Michael S. "Calvin's Theology of Union with Christ and the Double Grace: Modern Reception and Contemporary Possibilities." In *Calvin's Theology and Its Reception: Disputes, Developments, and New Possibilities*, edited by J. Todd Billings and I. John Hesselink, 49–71. Louisville: Westminster John Knox, 2012.

Howard, George. "On the 'Faith of Christ.'" *HTR* 60 (1997): 459–65.

Hultgren, Arland. "The *Pistis Christou* Formulation in Paul." *NovT* 22 (1980): 248–63.

Irons, Charles Lee. *The Righteousness of God: A Lexical Examination of the Convenant-Faithfulness Interpretation*. WUNT 2/386. Tübingen: Mohr Siebeck, 2015.

Jennings, Mark A. *The Price of Partnership in the Letter of Paul to the Philippians: "Make My Joy Complete."* LNTS 578. London: Bloomsbury, 2018.

Jervis, L. Ann. *At the Heart of the Gospel: Suffering in the Earliest Christian Message*. Grand Rapids: Eerdmans, 2007.

Jipp, Joshua W. *Christ Is King: Paul's Royal Ideology*. Minneapolis: Fortress Press, 2015.

————. "Sharing in the Heavenly Rule of Christ the King: Paul's Royal Participatory Language in Ephesians." In *"In Christ" in Paul: Explorations in Paul's Theology of Union and Participation*, edited by Michael J. Thate, Kevin J. Vanhoozer, and Constantine R. Campbell, 251–69. WUNT 2/384. Tübingen: Mohr Siebeck, 2014. Reprint, Grand Rapids: Eerdmans, 2018.

Johnson, Luke Timothy. *The First and Second Letters to Timothy: A New Translation with Introduction and Commentary*. AB 35A. New York: Doubleday, 2001.

————. "Rom 3:21-26 and the Faith of Jesus." *CBQ* 44 (1982): 77–90.

Käsemann, Ernst. "The Beginnings of Christian Theology." In *New Testament Questions of Today*, translated by W. J. Montague, 82–107. Philadelphia: Fortress, 1969.

————. *Commentary on Romans.* Translated by Geoffrey W. Bromiley. Grand Rapids: Eerdmans, 1980.

————. "The Pauline Theology of the Cross." *Int* 24 (1970): 151–77.

Kibbe, Michael. "'The Obedience of Christ': A Reassessment of τὴν ὑπακοὴν τοῦ Χριστοῦ in 2 Corinthians 10:5." *JSPL* 2 (2012): 41–56.

King, Jeffrey C., and Jason Stanley. "Semantics, Pragmatics, and the Role of Semantic Content." In *Semantics versus Pragmatics,* edited by Zoltán Gendler Szabó, 111–64. Oxford: Oxford University Press, 2005.

Kirk, Alexander N. *The Departure of an Apostle: Paul's Death Anticipated and Remembered.* WUNT 2/406. Tübingen: Mohr Siebeck, 2015.

Kirk, J. R. Daniel. *Unlocking Romans: Resurrection and the Justification of God.* Grand Rapids: Eerdmans, 2008.

Kittel, Gerhard, and Gerhard Friedrich, eds. *Theological Dictionary of the New Testament.* Translated by Geoffrey W. Bromiley. 10 vols. Grand Rapids: Eerdmans, 1964–1976.

Kittredge, Cynthia Briggs. "Rethinking Authorship in the Letters of Paul: Elisabeth Schüssler Fiorenza's Model of Pauline Theology." In *Walk in the Ways of Wisdom: Essays in Honor of Elisabeth Schüssler Fiorenza,* edited by Shelly Matthews, Cynthia Briggs Kittredge, and Melanie Johnson-Debaufre, 318–33. Harrisburg, Pa.: Trinity Press International, 2003.

Konradt, Matthias. *Gericht und Gemeinde: Eine Studie zur Bedeutung und Funktion von Gerichtsaussagen im Rahmen der paulinische Ekklesiologie und Ethik im 1 Thess und 1 Kor.* BZNW 117. Berlin: de Gruyter, 2003.

Koperski, Veronica. *The Knowledge of Jesus Christ My Lord: The High Christology of Philippians 3:7–11.* CBET 16. Kampen, Neth.: Kok Pharos, 1996.

————. "The Meaning of δικαιοσύνη in Philippians 3:9." *LS* 20 (1995): 147–69.

Kurek-Chomycz, Dominika. "Fellow Athletes or Fellow Solders? συναθλέω in Philippians 1.27 and 4.3." *JSNT* 39 (2017): 279–303.

Lambrecht, Jan. "Loving God and Steadfastly Awaiting Christ (2 Thessalonians 3,5)." *ETL* 76 (2000): 435–41.

Lambros, Spyridon. *Excerptorum Constantini de natura animalium libri duo. Aristophanis historiae animalium epitome subjunctis Aeliani Timothei aliorumque eclogis.* Berlin: Reimer, 1885.

Landmesser, Christof. "Der paulinische Imperativ als christologisches Performativ: Eine begründete These zur Einhelt von Glaube und Leben im Anschluß an Phil 1,27–2,18." In *Jesus Christ als die Mitte der Schrift: Studien zur Hermeneutik des Evangiums*, edited by C. Landmesser, H. J. Eckstein, and H. Lichtenberger, 543–77. BZNW 86. Berlin: de Gruyter, 1997.

Lang, T. J. *Mystery and the Making of a Christian Historical Consciousness: From Paul to the Second Century.* BZNW 219. Berlin: de Gruyter, 2015.

———. "Spectres of the Real Paul and the Prospect of Pauline Scholarship." *Marginalia Review of Books.* Review of *Remembering Paul* by Benjamin L. White. May 26, 2015. https://marginalia.lareviewof books.org/spectres-of-the-real-paul-and-the-prospect-of-pauline -scholarship-by-t-j-lang/.

———. "Trouble with Insiders: The Social Profile of the Ἄπιστοι in Paul's Corinthian Correspondence." *JBL* 137 (2018): 981–1001.

Lappenga, Benjamin J. *Paul's Language of Ζῆλος: Monosemy and the Rhetoric of Identity and Practice.* BibInt 137. Leiden: Brill, 2016.

Liddell, Henry George, Robert Scott, and Henry Stuart Jones (LSJ). *A Greek-English Lexicon.* 9th ed. Oxford: Clarendon, 1996.

Lightfoot, J. B. *Saint Paul's Epistle to the Galatians: A Revised Text with Introduction, Notes, and Dissertations.* London: Macmillan, 1892.

Lincoln, Andrew T. *Ephesians.* WBC 42. Dallas: Word, 1990.

Longenecker, Bruce W. "Πίστις in Romans 3.25: Neglected Evidence for the 'Faithfulness of Christ'?" *NTS* 39 (1993): 478–80.

Longenecker, Richard N. *The Epistle to the Romans: A Commentary on the Greek Text.* NIGTC. Grand Rapids: Eerdmans, 2016.

———. *Galatians.* WBC 41. Dallas: Word, 1990.

———. *Introducing Romans: Critical Issues in Paul's Most Famous Letter.* Grand Rapids: Eerdmans, 2011.

Louw, Johannes P. *Semantics of New Testament Greek.* Philadelphia: Fortress, 1982.

Louw, Johannes P., and Eugene A. Nida, eds. *Greek-English Lexicon of the New Testament: Based on Semantic Domains.* 2nd ed. New York: United Bible Societies, 1989.

Lyons, John. *Semantics.* 2 vols. Cambridge: Cambridge University Press, 1977.

Macaskill, Grant. *Union with Christ in the New Testament.* Oxford: Oxford University Press, 2013.

Malherbe, Abraham J. *The Letters to the Thessalonians: A New Translation with Introduction and Commentary.* AB 32B. New York: Doubleday, 2000.

Marossy, Michael David. "The Rule of the Resurrected Messiah: Kingship Discourse in 2 Timothy 2:8-13." *CBQ*: forthcoming.

Marshall, I. Howard. *Aspects of the Atonement: Cross and Resurrection in the Reconciling of God and Humanity.* Carlisle, U.K.: Paternoster, 2007.

————. *The Pastoral Epistles.* ICC. Edinburgh: T&T Clark, 1999.

————. "Salvation, Grace and Works in the Later Writings in the Pauline Corpus." *NTS* 42 (1996): 339–58.

Martyn, J. Louis. "The Apocalyptic Gospel in Galatians." *Int* 54 (2000): 246–66.

————. *Galatians: A New Translation with Introduction and Commentary.* AB 33A. New York: Doubleday, 1997.

————. *Theological Issues in the Letters of Paul.* Edinburgh: T&T Clark, 1997.

Matlock, R. Barry. "Detheologizing the ΠΙΣΤΙΣ ΧΡΙΣΤΟΥ Debate: Cautionary Remarks from a Lexical Semantic Perspective." *NovT* 42 (2000): 1–23.

————. "'Even the Demons Believe': Paul and πίστις Χριστοῦ." *CBQ* 64 (2002): 300–318.

————. "ΠΙΣΤΙΣ in Galatians 3.26: Neglected Evidence for 'Faith in Christ'?" *NTS* 49 (2003): 433–39.

————. "The Rhetoric of πίστις in Paul: Galatians 2.16, 3.22, Romans 3.22, and Philippians 3.9." *JSNT* 30 (2007): 173–203.

————. "Saving Faith: The Rhetoric and Semantics of πίστις in Paul." In *The Faith of Jesus Christ: Exegetical, Biblical, and Theological Studies,* edited by Michael F. Bird and Preston M. Sprinkle, 73–89. Carlisle, U.K.: Paternoster; Peabody, Mass.: Hendrickson, 2009.

————. "Sins of the Flesh and Suspicious Minds: Dunn's New Theology of Paul." *JSNT* 72 (1998): 67–90.

McFadden, Kevin W. "Does Πίστις Mean 'Faith(Fulness)' in Paul?" *TynBul* 66 (2015): 251–70.

Milgrom, Jacob. *Leviticus 1–16: A New Translation with Introduction and Commentary.* AB 3. New York: Doubleday, 1991.

Moffitt, David M. *Atonement and the Logic of the Resurrection in the Epistle to the Hebrews.* NovTSup 141. Leiden: Brill, 2011.

———. "Atonement at the Right Hand: The Sacrificial Significance of Jesus' Exaltation in Acts." *NTS* 62 (2016): 549–68.

———. "Jesus' Heavenly Sacrifice in Early Christian Reception of Hebrews: A Survey." *JTS* 68 (2017): 46–71.

Moo, Douglas J. *Galatians*. BECNT. Grand Rapids: Baker, 2013.

Morgan, Teresa. *Roman Faith and Christian Faith: Pistis and Fides in the Early Roman Empire and Early Churches*. Oxford: Oxford University Press, 2015.

Morris, Charles. *Foundations of a Theory of Signs*. Chicago: University of Chicago Press, 1938.

Moule, C. F. D. Review of *Le Christ et la foi: Étude de théologie biblique*, by Pierre Vallotton. *SJT* 14 (1961): 419–22.

Mounce, William D. *Pastoral Epistles*. WBC 46. Nashville: Thomas Nelson, 2000.

Muddiman, John. *A Commentary on the Epistle to the Ephesians*. BNTC. London: Continuum, 2001.

Murphy-O'Connor, Jerome. *The Theology of the Second Letter to the Corinthians*. Cambridge: Cambridge University Press, 1991.

Neale, Stephen. "Paul Grice and the Philosophy of Language." *Linguistics and Philosophy* 15 (1992): 509–59.

Nida, Eugene A. *Exploring Semantic Structures*. Internationale Bibliothek für allgemeine Linguistik 11. Munich: Fink, 1975.

Novenson, Matthew V. *Christ among the Messiahs: Christ Language in Paul and Messiah Language in Ancient Judaism*. Oxford: Oxford University Press, 2012.

Oakes, Peter. *Galatians*. PCNT. Grand Rapids: Baker Academic, 2015.

———. "*Pistis* as Relational Way of Life in Galatians." *JSNT* 40 (2018): 255–75.

O'Brien, Peter. "The Importance of the Gospel in Philippians." In *God Who Is Rich in Mercy*, edited by Peter O'Brien and David G. Peterson, 213–33. Grand Rapids: Baker, 1986.

Ogereau, Julien M. "Paul's Κοινωνία with the Philippians: *Societas* as a Missionary Funding Strategy." *NTS* 60 (2014): 360–78.

Orr, Peter. *Christ Absent and Present: A Study in Pauline Christology*. WUNT 2/354. Tübingen: Mohr Siebeck, 2014.

Ota, Shuji. "*Absolute Use of ΠΙΣΤΙΣ and ΠΙΣΤΙΣ ΧΡΙΣΤΟΥ in Paul*." *AJBI* 23 (1997): 64–82.

———. "The Holistic *Pistis* and Abraham's Faith (Galatians 3)." *HJAS* 57 (2016): 1–12.

———. "*Pistis* in Acts as Background of Paul's Faith Terminology." *HJAS* 56 (2015): 1–12.

———. "ΠΙΣΤΙΣ ΧΡΙΣΤΟΥ: Christ's Faithfulness to Whom?" *HJAS* 55 (2014): 15–26.

Pahl, Michael W. *Discerning the 'Word of the Lord': The 'Word of the Lord' in 1 Thessalonians 4:15.* LNTS 389. Edinburgh: T&T Clark, 2009.

Pelikan, Jaroslav, and Helmut T. Lehman, eds. *Luther's Works.* 55 vols. Philadelphia: Muehlenberg and Fortress; St. Louis: Concordia, 1955–1986.

Peterman, G. W. *Paul's Gift from Philippi: Conventions of Gift Exchange and Christian Giving.* SNTSMS 92. Cambridge: Cambridge University Press, 1997.

Pietersma, Albert, and Benjamin G. Wright. *A New English Translation of the Septuagint.* Oxford: Oxford University Press, 2007.

Plummer, Robert L. *Paul's Understanding of the Church's Mission: Did the Apostle Paul Expect the Early Christian Communities to Evangelize?* Paternoster Biblical Monographs. Eugene, Ore.: Wipf & Stock, 2006.

Poirier, John C. "The Meaning of Πίστις in Philippians 1:27." *ExpTim* 123 (2012): 334–37.

Porter, Stanley E. *Linguistic Analysis of the Greek New Testament: Studies in Tools, Methods, and Practice.* Grand Rapids: Baker Academic, 2015.

Porter, Stanley E., and Andrew W. Pitts. "Πίστις with a Preposition and Genitive Modifier: Lexical, Semantic, and Syntactic Considerations in the πίστις Χριστοῦ Discussion." In *The Faith of Jesus Christ: Exegetical, Biblical, and Theological Studies,* edited by Michael F. Bird and Preston M. Sprinkle, 33–53. Carlisle, U.K.: Paternoster; Peabody, Mass.: Hendrickson, 2009.

Powers, Daniel G. *Salvation through Participation: An Examination of the Notion of the Believers' Corporate Unity with Christ in Early Christian Soteriology.* CBET 29. Leuven, Bel.: Peeters, 2001.

Quarles, C. L. "From Faith to Faith: A Fresh Examination of the Prepositional Series in Romans 1:17." *NovT* 45 (2003): 1–21.

Rayo, Agustín. "A Plea for Semantic Localism." *Noûs* 47 (2013): 647–79.

Robertson, Archibald Thomas. *A Grammar of the Greek New Testament in the Light of Historical Research.* 4th ed. Nashville: Broadman, 1947.

Ruhl, Charles. *On Monosemy: A Study in Linguistic Semantics.* Albany: State University of New York, 1989.

Rüpke, Jörg. *Religion of the Romans.* Cambridge: Polity, 2007.

Saler, Robert Cady. *Theologia Crucis: A Companion to the Theology of the Cross.* Eugene, Ore.: Cascade, 2016.

Scalise, Charles J. "Allegorical Flights of Fancy: The Problem of Origen's Exegesis." *GOTR* 32 (1987): 69–88.

Schliesser, Benjamin. "'Christ-Faith' as an Eschatological Event (Galatians 3.23-26): A 'Third View' on Πίστις Χριστοῦ." *JSNT* 38 (2016): 1–24.

———. "'Exegetical Amnesia' and ΠΙΣΤΙΣ ΧΡΙΣΤΟΥ: The 'Faith *of* Christ' in Nineteenth-Century Pauline Scholarship." *JTS* 66 (2015): 61–89.

———. "Glauben und Denken im Hebräerbrief und bei Paulus: Zwei frühchristliche Perspektiven auf die Rationalität des Glaubens." In *Glaube: Das Verständnis des Glaubens im frühen Christentum und in seiner jüdischen und hellenistisch-römischen Umwelt,* edited by Jörg Frey, Benjamin Schliesser, and Nadine Ueberschaer, 503–60. WUNT 373. Tübingen: Mohr Siebeck, 2017.

Schmitz, Otto. *Die Christus-Gemeinschaft des Paulus im Lichte seines Genetivigebrauchs.* NTF 1/2. Gütersloh: Bertelsmann, 1924.

Schoedel, William R. *Ignatius of Antioch.* Hermeneia. Philadelphia: Fortress, 1985.

Schumacher, Thomas. *Zur Entstehung Christlicher Sprache: Eine Untersuchung der paulinischen Idiomatik und der Verwendung des Begriffes πίστις.* BBB 168. Göttingen: V&R unipress; Bonn: Bonn University Press, 2012.

Segal, Alan F. "Heavenly Ascent in Hellenistic Judaism, Early Christianity, and Their Environment." *ANRW* 23.2:1333–94. Part 2, *Principat,* 23.2. Edited by H. Temporini and W. Haase. Berlin: de Gruyter, 1980.

Seidl, Ernst. *Pistis in der griechischen Literatur bis zur Zeit des Peripatos.* Innsbruck: Verlag, 1952.

Shopen, T., ed. *Categories and the Lexicon.* 2nd ed. Vol. 3 of *Language Typology and Syntactic Description.* Cambridge: Cambridge University Press, 2007.

Silva, Moisés. *Philippians.* 2nd ed. BECNT. Grand Rapids: Baker Academic, 2005.

Smith, Julien. *Christ the Ideal King.* WUNT 2/313. Tübingen: Mohr Siebeck, 2011.

Sperber, Dan, and Dierdre Wilson. *Relevance: Communication and Cognition.* Cambridge: Harvard University Press, 1986.

Sprinkle, Preston M. *Law and Life: The Interpretation of Leviticus 18:5 in Early Judaism and in Paul.* WUNT 2/241. Tübingen: Mohr Siebeck, 2008.

————. "Πίστις Χριστοῦ as an Eschatological Event." In *The Faith of Jesus Christ: Exegetical, Biblical, and Theological Studies,* edited by Michael F. Bird and Preston M. Sprinkle, 164–84. Carlisle, U.K.: Paternoster; Peabody, Mass.: Hendrickson, 2009.

Stanley, David Michael. *Christ's Resurrection in Pauline Soteriology.* AnBib 13. Rome: E Pontificio Instituto Biblico, 1961.

Stegman, Thomas D. *The Character of Jesus: The Linchpin to Paul's Argument in 2 Corinthians.* AnBib 158. Rome: Pontico Istituto Biblico, 2005.

————. "Ἐπίστευσα, διὸ ἐλάλησα (2 Corinthians 4:13): Paul's Christological Reading of Psalm 115:1a LXX." *CBQ* 69 (2007): 725–45.

————. "Paul's Use of *Dikaio-* Terminology: Moving Beyond N. T. Wright's Forensic Interpretation." *TS* 72 (2011): 496–524.

Stenschke, Christoph W. "'Holding Forth the Word of Life' (ΛΟΓΟΝ ΖΩΗΣ ΕΠΕΧΟΝΤΕΣ): Philippians 2:16A and Other References to Paul's Understanding of the Involvement of Early Christian Communities in Spreading the Gospel." *JECH* 3 (2013): 61–82.

Stettler, Hanna. *Die Christologie der Pastoralbriefe.* WUNT 2/105. Tübingen: Mohr Siebeck, 1998.

Stowers, Stanley K. "ΕΚ ΠΙΣΤΕΩΣ and ΔΙΑ ΤΗΣ ΠΙΣΤΕΩΣ in Romans 3:30." *JBL* 108 (1989): 665–74.

————. *A Rereading of Romans: Justice, Jews, and Gentiles.* New Haven: Yale University Press, 1994.

Stubbs, David L. "The Shape of Soteriology and the *Pistis Christou* Debate." *SJT* 61 (2008): 137–57.

Stuhlmacher, Peter. "'Er ist unser Friede (Eph 2,14): Zur Exegese und Bedeutung von Eph 2,14-18." In *Neues Testament und Kirche: Für Rudolf Schnackenburg,* edited by Joachim Gnilka, 337–58. Freiburg: Herder, 1974.

————. *Revisiting Paul's Doctrine of Justification: A Challenge to the New Perspective.* Downers Grove, Ill.: InterVarsity Press, 2002.

Tallon, Jonathan R. R. "Faith in Paul: The View from Late Antiquity." Paper presented at the Annual Meeting of the British New Testament Society. Manchester, U.K. September 5, 2014.

————. "Faith in John Chrysostom's Preaching: A Contextual Reading." Ph.D. diss., University of Manchester, 2015.

Thielman, Frank. *Ephesians*. BECNT. Grand Rapids: Baker Academic, 2010.

Thiselton, Anthony C. *The First Epistle to the Corinthians: A Commentary on the Greek Text*. NIGTC. Grand Rapids: Eerdmans, 2000.

Thrall, Margaret. *A Critical and Exegetical Commentary on the Second Epistle to the Corinthians*. 2 vols. ICC 47. Edinburgh: T&T Clark, 2000.

Trebilco, Paul R. *Self-Designations and Group Identity in the New Testament*. Cambridge: Cambridge University Press, 2012.

Ulrichs, Karl F. *Christusglaube: Studien zum Syntagma pistis Christou und zum paulischen Verständnis von Glaube und Rechtfertigung*. WUNT 2/227. Tübingen: Mohr Siebeck, 2007.

Vallotton, Pierre. *Le Christ et la foi: Étude de théologie biblique*. Nouvelle série théologique 10. Geneva: Labor et Fides, 1960.

Viagulamuthu, Xavier Paul B. *Offering Our Bodies as a Living Sacrifice to God: A Study in Pauline Spirituality Based on Romans 12,1*. Tesi Gregorians Serie Spiritualita 7. Rome: Editrice Pontificia Universita Gregoriana, 2002.

Wagner, J. Ross. *Heralds of the Good News: Isaiah and Paul in Concert in the Letter to the Romans*. NovTSup 51. Leiden: Brill, 2002.

Wallace, Daniel B. *Greek Grammar beyond the Basics: An Exegetical Syntax of the New Testament*. Grand Rapids: Zondervan, 1996.

Wallis, Ian G. *The Faith of Jesus Christ in Early Christian Traditions*. SNTMS 84. Cambridge: Cambridge University Press, 1995.

Wanamaker, Charles A. *The Epistles to the Thessalonians: A Commentary on the Greek Text*. NIGTC. Grand Rapids: Eerdmans, 1990.

Ware, James P. *The Mission of the Church in Paul's Letter to the Philippians in the Context of Ancient Judaism*. NovTSup 120. Leiden: Brill, 2005.

Watson, Francis. *Paul and the Hermeneutics of Faith*. 2nd ed. London: Bloomsbury T&T Clark, 2016.

Wedderburn, A. J. M. "Some Observations on Paul's Use of the Phrases 'in Christ' and 'with Christ'." *JSNT* 25 (1985): 83–97.

Weima, Jeffrey A. D. *1–2 Thessalonians*. BECNT. Grand Rapids: Baker Academic, 2014.

Westfall, David M. "Thine Be the Glory: Christ the Mercy Seat in Romans 3:25." Paper presented at St. Andrews Symposium for Biblical and Early Christian Studies. St. Andrews, U.K. June 5, 2018.

White, Benjamin L. *Remembering Paul: Ancient and Modern Contests over the Image of the Apostle.* Oxford: Oxford University Press, 2014.

Whitenton, Michael R. "After ΠΙΣΤΙΣ ΧΡΙΣΤΟΥ: Neglected Evidence from the Church Fathers." *JTS* 61 (2010): 82–109.

Williams, Sam K. "Again *Pistis Christou.*" *CBQ* 49 (1987): 157–92.

Wilson, Deirdre. "Relevance and Lexical Pragmatics." *Italian Journal of Linguistics* 15 (2003): 273–91.

Wilson, Dierdre, and Dan Sperber. *Meaning and Relevance.* Cambridge: Cambridge University Press, 2012.

———. "Relevance Theory." In *The Handbook of Pragmatics,* edited by Laurence Robert Horn and Gregory Ward, 607–32. Malden, Mass.: Blackwell, 2004.

Wilson, Mark. "*Hilasterion* and Imperial Ideology: A New Reading of Romans 3:25." *HvTSt* 73 (2017): 1–9.

Wishart, Ryder A. "Monosemy in Biblical Studies: A Critical Analysis of Recent Work." *BAGL* 6 (2017): 99–126.

Wright, N. T. *Paul and the Faithfulness of God.* Vol. 4 of Christian Origins and the Question of God. Minneapolis: Fortress, 2013.

Young, Stephen L. "Romans 1.1-5 and Paul's Christological Use of Hab 2.4 in Rom. 1.17: An Underutilized Consideration in the Debate." *JSNT* 34 (2012): 277–85.

Zoccali, Christopher. *Reading Philippians after Supersessionism: Jews, Gentiles, and Covenant Identity.* New Testament after Supersessionism. Eugene, Ore.: Cascade, 2017.

MODERN AUTHOR INDEX

ANCIENT SOURCES INDEX

6:18-20	126n44	2:21	90
8:7	81	3:1	90, 97
8:22	71	3:1-5	95, 96n31
9:13	89n14	3:1–4:11	83, 95
10:2	71, 81	3:2	87n10, 89, 95, 97, 100
10:5	81n37, 89n14	3:2-5	96n31
10:7	71, 81, 86n9	3:3	97, 100
10:15	66n2, 81, 89n14	3:4	97
10:17-18	37n64	3:5	87n10, 89, 95, 96,
13:5	66n2, 82, 113n14		97, 100, 160
Galatians		3:6	100
1:3	86	3:6-9	97
1:3-4	85	3:6-12	97
1:4	89n15, 107, 157	3:7	100
1:10	86, 86n9, 104, 105	3:8	95n25, 100
1:12	87	3:9	100
1:16	87	3:10	155n10
1:22	87	3:11	91n20, 92, 98, 98n37,
1:23	87		100, 112n13
2:7	48n17, 87	3:11-12	84, 91, 95, 97
2:14	91n20	3:12	91n20, 100
2:15-21	90	3:13	85, 90, 99, 155n10
2:16	2, 2n2, 15n35, 17,	3:13-14	98, 107, 157
	52n29, 59, 83, 84n4, 88,	3:14	96, 99, 100, 100n40
	88n13, 90, 92, 92n22,	3:16-17	84
	92n23, 93, 94, 107,	3:19	100n40
	138, 156, 157n12, 162	3:19-22	100
2:16-20	88, 133	3:20	84n5
2:16-21	165	3:21	91, 91n20, 100, 111
2:17	94	3:21-22	84, 95, 100
2:19	90, 91n20	3:22	2, 2n2, 52n29, 83, 100,
2:19-20	88, 94, 97, 158n14		100n40, 107, 133, 156
2:20	2, 14, 15, 84, 85, 88,	3:23	102
	89, 90, 90n17, 91n20,	3:23-24	101
	92, 92n22, 93, 94,	3:23-28	101
	98, 98n38, 103, 107,	3:24	102
	156, 157, 165, 166	3:25	103

2:13-16	148, 149n39	3:19	139n15
2:13-22	148	4:2	139n15
2:14	146, 148	4:4-11	148n38
2:14-16	148, 148n38	4:5	135n5, 137
2:15	148	4:7-13	148n38
2:16	144, 145, 146, 148	4:8	144
2:17	146, 146n33	4:8-10	3n6
2:17-18	145, 146	4:9-10	144
2:17-22	141	4:10	148n38
2:18	143, 145, 146, 147, 148n38, 149	4:13	113n14, 135n5, 137
		4:15-16	139n15
2:19	141	4:30	99
2:19-22	149n39	5:1-2	148n38
3:1	140, 142	5:2	139n15, 148n38
3:1-13	150	5:6	148
3:1-14	140n17	5:25	139n15, 164n29
3:2	140	5:28	139n15
3:2-3	142	5:33	139n15
3:2-12	150, 150n40	6:12	143n26
3:2-13	140, 142	6:15	142
3:5-6	147, 148n38	6:16	135n5, 137
3:6	142, 142n22	6:19	142
3:10	143n26, 144	6:21	113n14
3:10-11	143, 150	6:23	113n14, 135n5, 137, 138
3:11-12	133, 143, 145	6:24	139n15
3:11-13	151	Philippians	
3:12	2, 2n2, 17n38, 48n17, 71, 71n16, 133, 134, 134n2, 135n5, 136, 137, 138, 139, 140, 143, 144, 145, 146, 147, 148n38, 149, 150, 150n40, 156	1:5	47, 51
		1:6	48n18
		1:7	45, 47
		1:12	47
		1:12-26	45n6
		1:13	45, 53
3:12-13	152	1:14	45, 47, 47n13, 47n14
3:13	134, 150, 152	1:15	47n13
3:16-17	139n15	1:15-17	56
3:17	113n14, 135n5, 137, 139n15	1:16	47
		1:17	45, 47n13